Danielle LaForest
Rm. 214
Social 33
pd. 5/6
Mr. Hunt.
2001/2002

Read
chapters
#1-6
for exam
tommorow

Rd chapters #2-6

A CHANGING WORLD

Global Political and Economic Systems

by J.C. Couture, Dennis Nosyk, and Jim Parsons

REIDMORE BOOKS INC., EDMONTON, CANADA

Canadian Cataloguing in Publication Data

Couture, Jean-Claude, 1955-

A changing world

ISBN 1-895073-06-5

1. Political science. 2. Economics. I. Nosyk, Dennis, 1950- II. Parsons, Jim, 1948- III. Title.
JA66. C67 1991 320 C90-091561-7

REIDMORE
BOOKS
INC.

Reidmore Books Inc.
18228 - 102 Avenue
Edmonton, Alberta T5S 1S7
toll-free 1-800-661-2859
ph. (403) 444-0912
fax (403) 444-0933
http://www.reidmore.com
email: reidmore@compusmart.ab.ca

ABOUT THE AUTHORS

Jean-Claude Couture is a teacher and the Social Studies Department Head at Harry Collinge High School in Hinton, Alberta. Mr. Couture received his undergraduate honors degree in history from McGill University, a Provincial Certificate from the University of Alberta, and has completed numerous graduate level courses at the University of Alberta.

Dennis Nosyk is currently a teacher and Department Head of Humanities at Leduc Composite High School in Alberta. Mr. Nosyk received his undergraduate degree and a diploma in Educational Administration from the University of Alberta, and his masters degree in Curriculum and Instructional Leadership from the University of Oregon.

Jim Parsons has been a professor for 14 years at the University of Alberta in the Department of Secondary Education. His specialties include social studies, literature, research, and religious education. When he was a teacher, he taught junior high school social studies and language arts. Jim Parsons has written 20 books, numerous educational articles, and has presented a number of workshops throughout North America.

Reidmore Books wishes to thank the following professors, who reviewed drafts of the manuscript for content and fact, for their helpful suggestions:

Dr. Tom Keating,
Political Science Department,
University of Alberta,
Edmonton, Alberta

Dr. David Pearce,
Western Centre for Economic Research,
University of Alberta,
Edmonton, Alberta

Dr. Ted Chambers,
Faculty of Business,
University of Alberta,
Edmonton, Alberta

Dr. Patrick Malcolmson,
Political Science Department,
University of Alberta,
Edmonton, Alberta

Reidmore Books wishes to thank the following people, who reviewed drafts of the manuscript for instructional design and suitability as a student textbook, for their helpful suggestions:

Dirk Huysman,
John G. Diefenbaker High School,
Calgary, Alberta

Debra Covey,
John G. Diefenbaker High School,
Calgary, Alberta

Rick Theriault,
John G. Diefenbaker High School,
Calgary, Alberta

Bob Guglich,
Holy Trinity High School,
Edmonton, Alberta

Mike Carby,
Archbishop O'Leary High School,
Edmonton, Alberta

CREDITS

Typesetting & Design: Pièce de Résistance Ltée., Edmonton, AB
Editorial: Nancy Mackenzie, Jane Spalding, Carolyn Pogue, Melanie Johnson
Cartoons: Gary Delainey & Gerry Rasmussen

Lithography: The Graphic Edge Inc., Edmonton, AB

Index: Gardner Indexing Service, Edmonton, AB

Excerpts and/or Adaptations:
p. 46 Hossie, Linda. "Ontario 1990 - A Breakthrough for Women in Politics." *Globe and Mail*, November 3, 1990, D6.
Reprinted with permission from the *Globe and Mail*.
p. 75 Bhengu, Ruth. "Black South Africa Speaks on Youth." *New Internationalist*, May 1986, 9.
Reprinted with permission from the *New Internationalist*.
p. 95 Stern, Sydney Ladensohn and Schoenhaus, Ted. *Toyland: The High-Stakes Game of the Toy Industry.* Chicago: Contemporary Books, Inc., 1986.
Reprinted with permission from Contemporary Books, Inc.
p. 177 Douglas, Tommy. *Star Weekly*, June 4, 1960.
Reprinted with permission of the Toronto Star Syndicate/Tommy Douglas.

PHOTOS:
Abbreviations:
   United Nations: UN
   National Archives of Canada: NAC
   Entries are by page number, coded as follows: T = Top B = Bottom L = Left R = Right

8	Courtesy The Ontario Ministry of Tourism and Recreation (Toronto)
11	UN Photo 169325/M. Grant
18	TL-©Bill Tomcich/Focus Stock Photo
20	Miller Comstock Inc./©Zefa UK
21, 56, 60-TR	BL-Reuters/Bettmann Newsphotos
24	TL-©D. Whitely/Focus Stock Photo
30, 47, 117	The Bettmann Archive
34	Sophia Smith Collection, Smith College
42	Courtesy The Office of the Governor General of Canada
46	Courtesy Rosemary Brown/The New Democrat Party
48	Courtesy Department of the Secretary of State of Canada
60-TL, 68, 70, 121, 122, 130, 136, 139	Novosti Information Service
63	NAC/C16812
80	©J. Share/Focus Stock Photo
82	BL-©Chris Bruun/Focus Stock Photo
83, 156	©Roy Ooms/Take Stock Inc.
85	Courtesy Canadian International Development Agency/Pat Morrow
90	©Robert Fried/Focus Stock Photo
92	Courtesy Volvo Canada
96	Courtesy Bill Phipps
98	Courtesy Imperial Oil Ltd.
100	©Angus McNee/Take Stock Inc.
104, 112, 113	Stock Editions
106	Miller Comstock Inc./©O. Bierwagen
109	TL-© M. Coughlan/Focus Stock Photo
131	NAC/C10057
143	Miller Comstock Inc./©Dallas & John Heaton
149	Miller Comstock Inc./©Neil Newton
150	Courtesy VIA Rail Canada Inc./W.H. Coo
155	©Kim Stallknecht/Take Stock Inc.
161, 163, 165, 168, 170	Courtesy Marianne Lindvall-Morse
174	Courtesy The Canadian Wheat Board
176	Courtesy The Department of Culture and Communications, Government of the Northwest Territories
180	Miller Comstock Inc./©J. Pickerell
185	Courtesy Petro-Canada Inc. (Photo by Tagish Communications)

We have made every effort to correctly identify and credit the sources of all photographs, illustrations, and information used in this textbook. Reidmore Books appreciates any further information or corrections; acknowledgment will be given in subsequent editions.

printed in Canada

Throughout all human time, there has been little change in our basic nature or in the problems we face. Those who lived thousands of years before microwave ovens and walkmans still ate and entertained themselves. Making choices about how to live securely was just as real for our ancestors as it is for us. And, deciding what to produce and who should get it is not just a question for economists. It is one that every member of society helps to answer.

All humans have the same basic needs because we develop in the same way physically. We are all born as screamers, crying out to those who gave us life to meet desires we can't even comprehend. Unlike most other beings, when we are young we are incapable of taking care of ourselves and our physical needs. We grow up and learn to meet our physical and other needs. We unify into **kinship** groups for psychological, emotional, and spiritual reasons.

In our kinship groups, we eat, sleep, reproduce, and die, much as other beings do. But, to humans, each of these activities also holds great meaning. We are thinkers. We design patterns and systems to improve the things we have. We dream. We try to change our world because we have visions of how it could be. The first humans who planted corn did so only because they had a sense of both the past and the future.

Humans build and construct. We build shelters, but we also build friendships and families. We enjoy physical activities, but we enjoy them more with some people than with others. We build to survive in a physical environment, but we also build toward a future.

We build belief systems and cultures. We build structures to house our physical bodies, and we build **structures of knowledge** that help us house our mental understandings. We hope and work toward a set of experiences that are more satisfying than painful. We want to remember and be remembered by those we love. We are, in short, civilized.

To be civilized is to get along with each other. We couldn't do that without **political** and **economic systems.** This book describes some different political and economic ideas. It also describes how societies have tried to put those ideas into practice in the face of changing national and international conditions.

In this book you will find special visuals called PEEK boxes that demonstrate how things in our lives influence one another. For example, our different political and economic ideologies are influenced by factors such as the time and place. You will also find *Case Studies* which provide anecdotes and practical examples of ideas described in the text. You will find a complete *Glossary* at the end of this book. You will also find key concept questions (*Getting It Straight*) to help direct your reading. *Getting Organized* and *Reaching Out* at the end of each chapter will help you apply your knowledge to your own life and the lives of those around you.

The editorial cartoons remind us that it is important to laugh and try to accept our differences and our similarities.

A Comment to Students about the Questions in this Book

Just as chapters open with a *Getting It Straight*, each chapter closes with a *Getting Organized* section. These questions have a particular structure, each based on an important social studies skill. The six questions are based on the following format. Questions 1 and 2 always focus on reviewing important concepts from the chapter you have just read. Question 3 asks you to focus critically on and attempt to solve an important problem within society. Question 4 encourages you to do more research into an important area that was only touched briefly in the book. Question 5 is always a question that calls for creative thinking. It is based on a "what if" principle, and asks you if a rather radical idea could work. Question 6 always pushes you to greater skill in inquiry.

Following the *Getting Organized* section comes the *Reaching Out* section, designed to get you involved in your community and with your classmates. Politics and economics can be very personal subjects, and we encourage you to think of them that way. Even if your teacher does not assign all of the questions, we would encourage you to consider them on your own. In short, we place great faith in the abilities of senior high social studies students to consider complex issues, to think, and to act responsibly.

I. Why is Inquiry Important?

Before you read this book, there are two simple questions we'd like to ask you. Do you trust us? Even before you read this book, will you believe what we have to tell you in this book?

You probably believe that we want you to say "Yes;" but, that's not the case. On the other hand, if you said "No, we don't trust anything in this book," we would be disappointed. We've done our homework. We've studied the facts and concepts, and we've tried to deliver the goods in an enjoyable and scholarly way.

What we believe shapes the facts that we present. Does this represent an error in our work? Are there mistakes in our thinking? We think not. What you see when you read our book, or any other, is that the point we make about how beliefs or ideology shape how humans understand what they hear, read, or see is just as true for us as it is for anyone else.

This truth places a strong responsibility on your own ability to judge what's what. Yes, we want you to trust our work—but only up to a point. The most important skill you will develop in social studies is the skill to evaluate the facts you find. You must learn to be a critical inquirer. If you do not, you may never learn how to solve the problems you face in life.

Throughout the text, we will ask you inquiry questions. These questions are found at the end of each chapter, in the captions to cartoons, and in the Case Studies. The questions are based on a model that can be used to analyze and evaluate the issues that are an important part of this social studies curriculum.

The Inquiry Model we will use follows these steps:

1. Identify and focus on the issue or problem.
2. Establish the questions and procedures that will guide your research.
3. Gather and organize data you will use to answer the issue or problem.
4. Analyze and evaluate the data you have gathered.
5. Make a decision about the issue or question you have identified.
6. Evaluate the decision you have made and the process you have used.

Remember, although these steps are important, they are not always followed in an exact sequence. The important point is to realize that it is important to consider important considerations carefully. A quick decision may be alright when you are buying a pair of socks, but not when you are addressing important issues about politics and economics.

II. How to Read a Cartoon

Reading and understanding a political cartoon is an inquiry skill. The cartoons you will find in this book are different than the text you will read. The text tries to consider all the points of view. But a cartoon often focuses on a single issue or aspect. Political cartoonists take stands. Sometimes these stands are simple, sometimes they are complex. Often they are controversial.

When cartoonists create their cartoons, they highlight some points, but ignore others. If you are to understand the cartoon, you must analyze what the cartoonists say. You will also have to understand what they don't say. The following list of questions can help you.

Analyzing a Cartoon

1. What characters did the cartoonists draw in the cartoon?
2. What do these cartoon characters represent?
3. What action is taking place? What does the action mean?
4. When cartoonists place strange things in the cartoons, why do they do it?
5. What point are the cartoonists trying to make?

Evaluation

1. Did the cartoonists make their point well?
2. Is the point consistent with what you know or have learned from other sources?
3. What does the cartoon ignore or leave out?
4. Is the cartoon accurate?

Chapter One:

THE GROWTH OF ORGANIZATION

GETTING IT STRAIGHT

1. What is the fundamental nature of human beings?
2. What is politics?
3. What is economics?
4. What are the basic elements of organization for any society or group?
5. How have human organizations changed over time?
6. How do the political and economic structures of a country evolve?

The First Political and Economic Systems

Classes that run on time, teachers and facilities to help students learn—these are part of the organization of your school. Most people take them for granted. But how did the organization evolve? How do people and societies make rules to which everyone **consents**? Which is more desirable in human affairs, cooperation or **competition**? The answers are both simple and complex.

Working in a group involves understanding the needs of others as well as yourself. Interpreting, evaluating, and acting upon these needs leads to political and economic decision-making. An historical review of systems of organization—families or nations— will help put this in perspective.

An understanding of **reciprocity** will help us grasp the importance of cooperation and organization. Reciprocity means a mutual exchange, or equal giving and taking. As you will read, humans found that by living cooperatively, by giving and taking (or selling and buying) they could manage to live more comfortably with strangers.

To further your understanding of reciprocity and how it works in a global sense, a game is provided in the appendix at the back of this textbook.

By studying the sites where humans lived together in groups, anthropologists can tell us much about human organizations, even those from prehistoric times. Life in **precivilized** times was in many ways just as complex as it is today. For many of our ancestors, it was also more dangerous. But there were a number of differences between the ways that humans organized themselves into groups then, and the organization of society today.

Families

Anthropologists tell us that ancient communities were organized on the principle of kinship. Our ancestors did not define themselves as citizens, members of a community, by their work, or by their adherence to a religion or philosophy. They defined themselves as members of families. In a family, each of our ancestors was part of a group that stayed together for one main purpose—**security**. In groups, humans were more able to protect each other and meet each other's

RECIPROCITY

Robert Axelrod, an American professor of political science, examined the issue of how societies learn to cooperate in *The Evolution of Cooperation*. This book is often regarded as an essential first step in understanding the variables that enter into decision-making. Axelrod writes about *The Prisoner's Dilemma*, an age-old situation of choice. The prisoner's dilemma is deciding whether to cooperate with the authorities without knowing if his partner in crime can be trusted. Here is a variation of the dilemma:

You and your friend are caught cheating on a test. The teacher interviews you individually. The teacher says, "If you tell me now who stole the copy of the test, I'll take it easy on you." Without being able to communicate with your friend, what would you do? Would you squeal on your friend and risk her/his revenge? What if you were both involved? Do you trust your friend not to implicate you as the sole thief? If you don't trust your friend, how would your action be different than if you do?

Axelrod's research indicates that cooperation is not only ethical, but practical. In real life situations, the action that yields the greatest long term mutual benefit is reciprocity.

Reciprocity is important in understanding how people come to interpret and evaluate each other's actions. It serves as a basis for continuing to act with each other even in the face of problems. Reciprocity is one of the basics in understanding how and why people can make political decisions that work, and why people organize.

basic needs. In this way, humans helped each other increase their chances of survival and prosperity. Taking care of the kinship group, or family, was the basis for social order.

Families roved as hunters and food gatherers. When the women of the family unit invented agriculture, the family settled into one specific, geographical area. For a long time, even as these agricultural settlements grew, they were founded on the **organizing principle** of kinship. Families identified and made decisions about their needs. The needs of the families were the needs of the village. Economic exchange between people was like giving gifts on birthdays. They helped each other because they were, after all, family. One family member wouldn't think of making another family member pay for something. Exchange was the way families took care of each other and survived, not a method used to gain material wealth.

These families were together in groups for several reasons. An organization created for the purposes of security is a political system. Structures for distributing **goods** and **services** make up an economic system. So, these family groups, although simple and small, were political and economic groups.

To help you understand why and how these groups functioned, we have put together a model called a PEEK box. To understand it, consider the structures of political and economic systems. These structures are based on the work of Susan Strange, a well-known political economist who wrote *States and Markets*. Strange argues in her book that it is silly to think about **politics** and economics separately. In researching this book, we have studied her work and modified it with our ideas so we can focus on important, high school-level issues. We use the example of the family group to show how the model applies to an actual group structure.

The PEEK Box

These boxes are called PEEK boxes, after the four sides: Politics, Economics, Environment, and Knowledge. As you read and study the text, you will find PEEK boxes that help you define the politics, economics, environment, and knowledge of different societies. This will help you understand the political and economic choices of societies.

PEEK	
AT A FAMILY GROUP IN A HUNTING AND GATHERING SOCIETY	
Politics	**Economics**
- elders make and enforce rules through consensus - security of the group emphasized	- adapted to use natural resources available with a minimum of waste - production and consumption shaped by hunting and gathering technology
Environment	**Knowledge**
- sensitive to natural shifts in environment (e.g. seasons, food supply) so migration needed at times	- survival depends on working together in family units - each member performs a function
Field of Action	
- a life within a self-sufficient group trying to satisfy needs and wants in a traditional economy	

Knowledge

This side of the box represents the acquired and stored knowledge of a society. It also includes new ideas that are being generated. The way a society interprets and evaluates problems contributes to the knowledge structure of a society. For example, in medieval times, the idea that all good Christians would go to heaven made miserable living conditions a bit more tolerable.

For the family group, knowledge included the fact that it is more difficult to survive alone, and that each family member has skills that benefit the group. For a larger organized group, such as a city or a nation, the structure of knowledge is more complicated.

It is important to think of the structure of knowledge as the web of ideas that generate patterns and ways of making decisions. This book focuses on patterns of political and economic ideas. Political and economic ideologies are patterns of ideas that are used to interpret, evaluate, and act on the daily problems of managing a group's affairs.

Economics

This side of the box represents **production** and **consumption**. This includes choices between what is produced and who consumes the goods and services.

In precivilized history, a family's economic needs determined each member's role. For example, children gathered fuel, men hunted, and women built the shelter.

Decisions are made in a group or society according to its level of economic development. The economic systems of today are very different from our ancient history example. As technology becomes more complex, work production and consumption will be different. The walkman you may own was not even dreamed of by your parents when they were young. Compact discs now gobbled up by hungry consumers were not even popular until 1988. Japanese producers had already developed a far superior technology: digital tape players. However, because they needed to recover their costs in developing the compact disc technology, they held back the new technology. As you can see, economics is much more complicated now than it was when we lived in kinship groups.

Politics

The structure of politics forms the pattern of **political relations** in a society. These include the **institutions** that are the sources that provide order and security within a society.

For the family group, politics would be the decision-making structure used to keep peace between family members. Most likely, the parents were the decision-makers: the people who made and enforced the rules.

Today, it's more complex. Nations have political institutions to maintain security against domestic and international threats. There are many ways to maintain safety and security; therefore, there are many different political institutions. For example, the Canadian **government**, through the Department of Health and Welfare, ensures that food is safe. The maximum number of rodent hairs allowed in chocolate is 3 per 100 grams. The maximum number of insect fragments allowed in 25 grams of coffee is 60. Governments in democracies exist to protect the security of the people.

Environment

Other factors affect a family's activities, besides the structures of knowledge, economics, and politics. These are classified as **environmental factors**.

For families this could include a variety of events. For example, if there were a drought, the family might have to move. If one of the family members was sick, it would also change how the family functioned.

Today, both the domestic and international environment play an important role in the development of a society. The need to protect and replenish the environment, and the availability of resources affect a nation's choices about political and economic questions. International instability, trade wars, or oil shortages created by events like the Persian Gulf War can affect consumers and producers alike. People in areas like Eastern Europe understand the importance of environmental factors in economic development because many of the region's rivers are so polluted that even industries cannot use the water.

No economic or political system exists in isolation. The interest rate you pay for your car loan is influenced as much by interest rates in Japan as decisions your own governments make. Other factors that form the structure of the environment can include energy supplies, crop failures, wars, or movements in the stock market. In short, major changes anywhere in the world can affect the environment in which you live. Usually these events are outside your direct control. Think of the structure of the environment as the physical context in which groups or societies make choices.

The Field of Action: Unpredictable, Complex

The four structures—politics, economics, environment, and knowledge—are the major factors that affect the activities of a group or society.

On our box model, you see how these four structures are the four sides connecting to the base of the box, which we call the **field of action**. This represents the activities of a group or society. It is much like a football field, but it represents the scope of possible activities of a society instead of the scope of a playing field.

For the family, the field of action is what they can do with the knowledge, economics, politics, and environment that they have. For example, they likely could not construct an airplane because they do not have the knowledge, economics, politics, or environmental structure to do so. They could, however, make pizza.

The field of action is the scope of activities possible for a group. It changes as the knowledge, economics, politics, and environment change and new possibilities arise.

The model we have presented shows how four facets of a society contribute to its functioning, and to the development and activities of its political and economic systems. In these examples, each facet (or side of the box) is linked to the others. None of the sides operates in isolation from the others. Over time, as a group or society evolves, the field of action and the sides of the box alter to reflect new conditions and changing ideas.

The Creation of Cities

Sociologists remind us that families are still important social organizations. However, families are no longer the main structure of society. The organizing structure, kinship groups, changed with the growth of cities 6000 years ago.

Cities first developed in Mesopotamia (now called Iraq). Here, families settled in the Fertile Crescent, on the plains of the Tigris and Euphrates rivers. As more and more people gathered together, the groups became too large for all the families to meet and discuss their needs. A more complex structure evolved to help strangers live together peacefully. The city was not simply a place for people to live; it transformed the way humans thought and lived with each other.

P E E K	
AT A CITY **(in Mesopotamia, for example)**	
Politics	**Economics**
- increasingly complex levels of decision-makers and enforcers (e.g. civic employees: refuse collectors, an army)	- sharing work, food, and shelter - interdependence and specialization of production (rise of trade)
Environment	**Knowledge**
- living among strangers is a challenge - increased communication and trade with foreigners	- complicated problem of meeting needs and wants of large groups - need for specialized people to administer civic affairs
Field of Action	
- a complex network of economic exchange and political organization to achieve security	

The two central concepts in this book, politics and economics, were among the human activities most drastically changed.

As cities grew, the organizing structure of the kinship group became less important. Families didn't all know each other anymore. Living among strangers changed human behaviour and relationships. Establishing rules and guidelines to achieve some degree of reciprocity became necessary.

To understand why human behaviour and relationships changed when cities were formed, imagine living all your life in a place where everyone knew you. Suddenly you moved to a city where you were surrounded by strangers. You felt uncertain about trusting them. You knew one thing. You cared more for your own family than for other families, and you knew that the same was probably true for others. Other people's concerns were probably not your concerns. Your **mutuality of interests** couldn't be taken for granted. In fact, to assume that you thought just like a stranger was dangerous.

To stress the differences between strangers and families may seem like overstating the obvious. But imagine how these changes affected the ways that people lived together. Survival and security are always the central needs of humans. In precivilized times, people worried about finding food and protecting themselves. In post-industrial times, we worry about food distribution and the destructive capabilities of nuclear warheads. The details may be different, but the need is the same. Our ability to meet our needs comes through our ability to control our circumstances—to create and adjust our political and economic structures to help us survive and protect ourselves.

The cartoonists are making what they feel is an important point about the growth of early cities. What point of view is expressed in this cartoon? Do you agree?

Formal Rules Are Created

For centuries, families survived quite nicely without formal controls. Kinship groups controlled their own activities. They did not need formal controls, or laws. But as cities grew, more formal controls became necessary. To answer this need, the first legal systems came into existence, and the law became a central organizing structure for social groups.

Laws were made to regulate agreements between strangers. Obligations between strangers had to be **enforced**. Rules were recorded so that groups within societies could force others to obey the laws. These enforcing groups became part of political institutions. Police forces, civil servants, and teachers all helped to carry out the wishes of the society.

Cities grew and prospered for economic reasons. It was easier for humans to survive and prosper if they shared work, food, and shelter. Living in cities meant that specialization of economic need-meeting activities was possible. People could exchange goods and services with others who also **specialized**. The structure of production and consumption, or the economy, grew more complex.

Today, the production and sale of bread, a relatively very simple product, involves many people and processes. In 1990, a $1.39 loaf contained just 6 cents worth of wheat.

Because of the new, more complex structure of the economy, a new way of trading evolved. Exchanging goods between strangers created a need for a new system. It is no accident that numbers were changed by ancient Babylonians from simple lines to a more complex system; each numeral became a concept that

Toronto is a good example of a city that has grown. Name some of the advantages and disadvantages of living in a large, growing city.

represented many items. The economic life within a city of exchange between strangers also made it necessary for more specific laws that governed economic activity. Once symbols for goods, rather than the goods themselves, became an accepted way to make exchanges, the world was never the same. Money had arrived.

For every political and economic activity that was taken for granted within the kinship family, a formal and concrete regulation was created within the social structure of the city. Our present-day politics and economics are a direct result of changes that took place as cities grew.

HAMMURABI'S CODE OF LAWS

Political organizations write their rules. They want to outline their expectations of how to achieve and maintain security. The first code of laws is said to have been compiled under King Hammurabi of Babylonia. The first cities started there. The Code of Hammurabi became the structure that determined relationships between strangers in Babylonia. The 3600 lines of cuneiform text outlines the whole Babylonian social structure, including economic conditions, industries, law, and even family life. Hammurabi's Code was the first attempt to record the structure of a society's beliefs and the methods of achieving security and prosperity.

The Growth of Organization

As larger and larger groups of strangers began to live together, they needed more formal controls. They also needed groups of people to administer them. These administrators formed the first governments, and were busy building, compiling, and carrying out the laws. Today all nations maintain some form of **bureaucracy**. Administrators within this bureaucracy are in charge of helping the rest of the population improve its security and prosperity.

One group of administrators was assigned the task of creating, or legislating, laws that were just, easy to understand, and easy to remember. Today, this branch of government is called the **legislative branch**. Another group of administrators enforced, or executed, the laws. Today, this branch of government is called the **executive branch**. Still another group of administrators interpreted the laws, to judge if certain laws had been broken, and to decide the punishment for breaking these laws. Today, this branch of government is called the **judicial branch**. With these specializations of governmental roles, political institutions grew more complex. Security of citizens was achieved by delegating the making, enforcing, and interpreting of laws to hired or elected officials.

Organizing within a Global Community

As organizations grew, they became more complex. Eventually, the result was the organization of individual nation states and an increasingly global economy. Some now argue that a form of world government is just around the corner. As groups develop relationships with other groups, a system of increasingly complex trade develops.

Corporations are becoming as powerful as some countries. Exxon's tanker fleet, for example, is 50 per

CASE STUDY:
WHAT DO CANADIANS BELIEVE?

This Case Study summarizes a *Maclean's* magazine survey about Canadian beliefs. You may want to refer to the January 2, 1989, issue of *Maclean's* yourself.

The *Maclean's* survey seems to indicate that Canadians want to retreat into a lifestyle that is safe and predictable. Sociologists explain this desire by saying that the family is one of the the few constants in an ever-changing world. Of Canadians surveyed, 85 per cent ruled out the possibility that they would run for public office. However, most said that Canada needed someone to take these jobs. Helping neighbours and doing volunteer work in the community ranked high on the list of priorities for Canadians. A big concern mentioned by many respondents was for quality of life and the environment. Canadians said they feel unable to control what is happening, and they feel uninformed. For example, when asked, Will water be safe to drink by the year 2001? no one was sure. Yes responses were as plentiful as negative ones.

Consider what seems to be important to Canadians as you ponder the *Maclean's* survey and read about Canadian concerns in your local daily newspaper.

QUESTIONS:

1. List three things that this survey tells you about Canadians. Compare your list with the lists of your classmates.
2. Compose a survey designed to collect information about what your classmates' concerns are. Survey the class. What are your findings?
3. How much do you think the answers to these questions have changed in the last 50 years? What future event might encourage changes in the way Canadians think?
4. Collect copies of Canadian magazines. Cut out pictures and create a collage that you believe expresses a current trend in Canadian society.

cent larger than the Soviet Union's fleet. According to some experts, in 25 years **transnational** corporations could own over 50 per cent of everything on the planet!

Human organizations—political, economic, cultural, or religious—exist within a larger environment or context. When we talk about national political and economic systems in this book, we are misleading ourselves to some degree. No nation or political jurisdiction is an isolated system. In fact, there are many levels of organization in society. For every group—classroom, workers' union, or city—there are some political, economic, environmental, and knowledge factors that determine its activities, or its field of action.

On any given day, a political or economic system is part of a complex web of relationships, at many levels. Factors that are external to each system influence what political and economic decisions are made by municipal, provincial or territorial, and national politicians.

Think about Canada's political and economic systems. As Canadians, we elect members of **parliament**, sign agreements with other countries, and regulate the economic activities of corporations. But how much control over international crises do we have? As Canadians, we must remember that Canada is part of a global community. Can politicians and bureaucrats, **dissidents** and conformists alike, really determine what happens in their own systems? The global community affects politics and economics within countries.

Political and economic systems are complicated. Each responds to a variety of changing factors, both at home and in the global community. For example, the chart on page 12 shows how different countries react to the political and economic threats they see around them. We need to think of political and economic systems as the way issues are resolved. Over time, the choices societies make become patterns and these patterns become ingrained into the thinking of the society. These patterns become institutions and lifestyles. These lifestyles become ideologies, religious structures, and educational systems. Canada's politics and economics exist within the greater sphere of the global community.

This mosaic by Norman Rockwell, entitled The Golden Rule, *depicts people of many different nationalities standing together. The global community affects politics and economics within countries.*

SECURITY IN THE WORLD

Achieving security for its citizens is an important goal in modern states. The statistics below show that some countries believe the military threat to them is very great. Take a quick look at the history and geography of the countries listed in the statistics. What PEEK factors would help explain the different priorities of these nations?

1. **Largest Military Forces in the World**

Soviet Union	4 258 000
China	3 030 000
United States	2 124 900
India	1 260 000
Vietnam	1 249 000
North Korea	1 040 000
Iraq	1 000 000

2. **Countries with the most soldiers per 1000 citizens in (1986)**

Iraq	49.9
Israel	47.5
Syria	38.8
North Korea	38.5
Cuba	29.5

3. **Military share of Gross National Product (1984)**

Iraq	50.0%
Israel	27.1%
Saudi Arabia	21.7%
Syria	16.6%
Angola	14.2%

4. **Books or Bombs?**

Deciding to prepare youth to kill or to learn is a question that every country faces.

In 1990, the countries with the highest ratio of soldiers to teachers were:

Ethiopia	494 to 1
Iraq	428 to 1
Oman	275 to 1
Chad	233 to 1
Yemen	200 to 1
Pakistan	154 to 1

Can you think of reasons some nations have high ratios of soldiers to teachers? What might these statistics tell us about a state's main reason for existing?

How Do You Fit In?

Your class exists as a group of students gathered to gain knowledge of social studies. Your small group is part of a larger group, the school. The school is part of a larger group, the school board. The school board exists because provincial or territorial legislation gave it the right and responsibility to provide education for citizens. This mandate exists because the British North America Act of 1867 gave provincial governments the right to control education.

Organization in education is even further complicated. Who pays for your school texts? Who pays for your desks? What factors determine the kind of furniture and supplies your school has? There are many factors that influence the organization of any group, community, or society. To understand some of them, here is a PEEK box for your classroom.

PEEK
AT A CLASSROOM

Politics	Economics
- ordered and secure - rules set by outside authorities	- education paid for by the state - students receive educational services
Environment	**Knowledge**
- rising oil prices	- the teacher will pass on knowledge to the students - the course is based on the facts as we know them
Field of Action	
- Crazy Hat Day - more funds for field trips	

Knowledge

In school, your knowledge includes the belief that the teacher can help you learn the content of this course, that the course is based on the truth, and that studying it will better prepare you for living. Your teacher's knowledge includes theories, or ideologies about education and learning.

Economics

Economics describes the pattern of how goods and services are produced and distributed. Most social studies classes are led by a teacher, with students sitting in rows. You arrive at the assigned bell and leave when the bell rings. You receive a grade and credit if you pass. Education is paid for by the state. The educational system you experience uses the same method of producing and distributing educational services found in most industrialized countries. It is based on a factory or assembly line model. This is no accident. You are preparing for what lies ahead in the real world of nine to five life.

Politics

The pattern of politics includes the institutions and sources of security in your school. There is no need to explain to you how school order and security are maintained. Except so-called fun days like Crazy Hat Day or Dress Hawaiian Day, life in most schools is ordered and secure. There are few surprises. You may think that the rules are repressive, but actually most of your society lives by similar rules. They are rules set by outside authorities that apply to more than just life in school. Even if your principal wants to declare your school an independent state, it is unlikely that he or she has the **power** to do so.

Environment

This structure includes the outside factors and situations that affect your classroom and school. The fact that the price of oil rises when there is a conflict in the Middle East, as happened in August 1990, means oil-producing governments can expect greater tax revenues. This possibly means that it can afford to spend more on education. This also might mean that your school will get more money for field trips or to hire more teachers.

The PEEK box illustrates how the field of action in your school or classroom works. Each panel or facet connects to the others. The influences on your political and economic life are not isolated. They come from a variety of sources and, together, they affect your world.

SUMMARY

When people began to live in large groups, they found a greater need to develop a set of regulations that they could all live by. As cities grew, so did the need for more formal written rules. Most of the rules determined how citizens would satisfy the needs of the group. These rules developed into political and economic systems. Different political and economic systems came about due to various factors influencing decision-makers. The development of these systems was influenced by the way people saw the world and responded to various situations. Various ideologies evolved among different groups. In the next chapter you will learn how political systems developed and you will be introduced to several types of political systems.

GETTING ORGANIZED

1. To understand the term security, it is important to know what you believe must be kept secure. What are your most prized possessions? Do a short survey by age level. Ask one person under 10, one under 25, one between 25-50, and one over 50 to name their most prized possessions. Make a list of your findings.

2. What is happening in your environment as you read this book? Make a chart that lists:
   (a) the world scene
   (b) the national scene
   (c) the local/provincial scene
   (d) arts and entertainment, and
   (e) your school
   List the concerns in each area and tell how these concerns are important to you.

3. We owe much of our civilization to Mesopotamia (now Iraq). Research early Mesopotamia. List five observations you find interesting.

4. When people govern you, they assume that you have a mutuality of interests. Are they correct? Are your concerns like the concerns of others in your community? Ask your friends to list their biggest concerns in the following areas:
   (a) the future
   (b) the present
   (c) their dreams
   (d) what would they change if they could?
   (e) what do they lose sleep over?

5. A case is often made that specialization has helped the world progress. If this is true, why aren't schools specialized with students who are good at math doing everyone's math, or those who are good in English writing everyone's essays? Instead, you must know everything. Could specialization by students in schools work? Visualize a system in place. What would it be like? How would it impact you? Make a short case either for or against such a system.

6. Choose an organization that you or your family belong to. What are the characteristics of this organization? Create a chart that expresses the power structure of the organization you have chosen.

REACHING OUT

1. The barriers between countries are being broken down at an increasing rate. Political and economic systems increasingly are being tied together. One important element of this process of globalization is computer technology. While computers have brought many benefits to society, they have costs as well. According to the *New Internationalist*, the average computer crime in the USA involves the loss of $220 000 while average bank robbery involves $6600.

   (a) Invite a business person or someone involved with computers to explain how computers impact the workplace and society in general. You should list the ways computers influence and control individuals' lives and their right to privacy.

2. Surveys of public opinion are common these days. Your class might do some work in this area. Use your library's resources and weekly news magazines that discuss shifting tides in public opinion.

   (a) As a class, poll the students in your school. A good question might be, What are your three most important concerns as you prepare to leave high school?

   (b) After the lists are collected, categorize the responses into groups that correspond to the four elements of the PEEK model.

   For example, a concern about getting a job would fit under Economics, a concern about pollution would fit under Environment. Your class should poll two groups—students and people over 30—comparing their responses to this question: The biggest worries I have about the state of Canada and the world are _____. Categorize their responses within the PEEK model. What accounts for the differences in the two groups? What accounts for similarities?

   (c) Based on your survey, write a paragraph that answers this question: What are the essential concerns of individuals in modern society?

Chapter Two:

IDEAS ABOUT POLITICAL ORGANIZATIONS

GETTING IT STRAIGHT

1. Why do people organize politically?
2. How can people achieve and maintain security?
3. What is ideology?
4. How do our ideologies influence the ways we do things?
5. How do political systems control the lives of individuals?

Who Cares about Politics?

Politics is much like sports in that it has two main groups: participants and spectators. Yet there is a major difference. You can choose to participate in sports, but you are forced to participate in politics. No one can choose to avoid political participation completely. If you decide not to vote, you are giving another person more say in who gets elected. Your deliberate choice is an important political statement.

Many people believe that politics exists somewhere out there. This is not the case. Everyone is a politician, because politics is about our everyday lives. Politics involves even the simplest questions we ask ourselves as we look in the mirror every day—questions like: Why do I have to go to school today? Who decided that we should use this textbook? and, Why is it so difficult for ordinary people to get into universities in Canada?

These questions centre on some fundamental political issues. Who decides how you should live? A multitude of people and groups affect your life. The different levels of organization in society all develop rules and make decisions for the security of society's members. The country has laws about education, as do the provinces and territories. The school board regulates the activities of all the schools. The school also makes decisions that affect the classroom, and in the classroom, all these choices affect you.

Politics involves each one of us. It is more than distant leaders and old buildings. The definition of

CASE STUDY:

GROUP POLITICS

If you want to understand power, one good way is to examine a group to which you belong. Consider the exercise below as a study of group politics. When you have compared your answers in class, you will have basic knowledge of the way political groups work.

GROUP ANALYSIS:

From the list below, select an example of a group or organization with which you are familiar.
- a classroom
- a school team
- your family
- your religious or community group
- your workplace

Prepare an analysis of that group or organization for the class by answering the following:

1. Why is your group organized?
   (a) What goals do the members have? Are they political (to achieve security) or economic (to produce or consume)?
   (b) What is your group's history?
2. How is your group organized?
   (a) Are decisions reached through **consensus**, by vote, or by the executive?
   (b) What roles do members have in decision-making?

3. How do decision-makers in the group:
   (a) regulate behaviour?
   (b) use force or **constraint**?
   (c) limit access to resources?
   (d) treat members of the group (equally or unequally)?
4. In one or two sentences, describe the pattern of your group's organization. This is the operating principle for your group. Remember, when you are describing this pattern, you are making a general statement that reflects a variety of your observations and experiences. Consider your attitude toward the group. Do you feel your interests are being served? To check your summary, ensure you have described how the group interprets, evaluates, and acts in a variety of situations.
5. Construct a PEEK box that identifies some of the political, economic, environmental, and knowledge elements that help shape the field of action of your group.

When you are gathering information, you might find it useful to review the chart of Political Organizations on page 24. This chart will provide questions you can ask yourself about how the group functions as a political unit.

How does an organization such as a Boy Scout troop act as a political group?

politics is broad and sometimes difficult to understand. Political theorists have argued for ages about what, exactly, makes up politics. Some suggest that politics includes only the decision-making and the power possessed by those who hold elected political office. However, recall from chapter 1 that the way a *group* structures its relationships is very important. Politics is often about the use of power to achieve security *between* people.

Power

Studying the balance between power and security helps us to understand some of the reasons people organize into groups. Thomas Hobbes, a sixteenth century philosopher, believed that people organize for group security, and to prevent all-out war in society. John Locke, a seventeenth century philosopher, believed political organizations allow people to better pursue their own interests, especially to enjoy the material wealth they accumulate working independently.

Supporters of **dictatorship** argue that special plans or missions are needed for society. They say that the security and economic interests of individuals are less important than those of the government. On the other extreme, **anarchists** are suspicious of any formal

This cartoon focuses on one aspect of how political campaigns work in North America. What is unusual about the cartoon? How is the cartoon critical of political campaigns?

institutional power being imposed on people. They point to the history of both democratic and dictatorial governments as examples of how power is imposed on people by formal organizations. Anarchists believe that all forms of large government strip people of their security.

Power and decision-making are easier to understand in less formal structures than in those of government or nation states. Teen clubs, students' unions, or church groups might not exist as formal political organizations, but they practise the same elements of decision-making as governments. A motorcycle gang might not look like a political organization, but it acts in political ways. Power and security exist in groups. Individuals become members to accomplish particular goals, and a degree of order and security is maintained by the group for its members.

Any group that sets and distributes power, attempts to accomplish goals, and brings order and security is a political group. In this text, we take the view that all groups, whether their systems of organization are formal or informal, are political in nature.

How to Achieve Security

There is little doubt that to achieve and maintain security, and to produce and distribute resources, people need to organize. However, the ways they should organize remain in dispute.

Anarchists believe that individuals should not consent to having decisions made on their behalf by others. Decisions should be made in small groups with the interests and security of everyone considered. They say governments are unnecessary and cause more problems than they solve. Decision-making that does not heed the day-to-day living of humans is rejected as a threat to human survival.

For **liberals**, democratic decision-making means that the people agree to submit to laws and decisions made by the leaders they have elected to office.

In **authoritarian** and **totalitarian** dictatorial **regimes**, self-government is obliterated. Instead of asking for the consent of the people, leaders take political power and authority. The consent of the people is not required in dictatorships. People must submit, whether they consent or not. In authoritarian regimes, submission, and not consent, is the primary principle.

Marxists explain that because people grow up in one society with one pattern of understanding, they have little chance of reaching a full understanding of human life. The economic activities of their society teach a single interpretation of reality. For example, agricultural societies tend to value tradition, while industrial societies tend to value change. Some Marxists believe that only by managing the economy of a country can people's attitudes and beliefs be properly developed.

Chapter 1 described how human life changed when cities grew. A formal legal system replaced the informal kinship group as the organizing structure for social life. In cities, humans could never again centre their lives on a social structure based on kinship. As the business of the city grew, living and working with strangers became the normal way of life.

Even strangers, when they live together long enough, come to share similar concerns and ways of thinking. Human organizations would never be quite like families again, but living close together encouraged a social similarity. Within cities, and then within countries, people who were once strangers began to develop patterns of thinking that were more similar to each other's. Those patterns can be thought of as structures of knowledge.

Some of these patterns were written formally into laws. Others became the informal patterns that society used to judge appropriate or inappropriate behaviour. Like people married to each other for a long time, people within the same geographical area became used to each other's presence and behaviour. Groups developed what are called norms or mores (pronounced mor-ays) that defined good taste within their society. Most importantly, groups developed patterns of understanding that defined how life and history should be interpreted and understood.

Values are the basis behind different ideologies. Ideology consists of both conscious beliefs and unconscious patterns of thinking. When the term **ideology** was first used, it meant a system of ideas that encouraged political or social action. The French philosopher Destutt de Tracy coined the word in 1796 as the name for the rational study of the science of ideas. Those who have studied ideologies since de Tracy have usually focused on how ideas motivate actions.

Many groups or subcultures, such as the punks illustrated above, have their own standards of what is acceptable or correct in their society. Obvious examples are unique hair and clothing styles.

What Does Ideology Mean to You?

In this book, we define ideology as a *structure of beliefs and a pattern of thinking that motivates human social and political action.* This definition has two parts. First, people may consciously choose a set of beliefs to act as guiding principles for decisions they make. Second, people make decisions based on unconscious, but very powerful, values or ways of thinking that they probably don't even realize they have.

IDEOLOGY HELPS US UNDERSTAND OTHERS, BUT . . .

Sometimes, we fail to recognize genius because our pattern of thinking differs from that of the genius. In an educational journal called the *Phi Delta Kappan*, Dr. Milton E. Larson wrote about creative people unrecognized by the people around them. What generalization might explain why the famous people listed below were sometimes less than successful?

- Einstein was four years old before he could speak and seven before he could read.
- Beethoven's music teacher called him hopeless as a musical composer.
- Thomas Edison was told by his teachers that he was too stupid to learn anything.
- Walt Disney was fired by a newspaper editor who believed that he didn't have any good ideas.
- Leo Tolstoy failed college.
- Louis Pasteur was rated mediocre in chemistry in college.
- Winston Churchill failed the sixth grade.

There are many examples of how ideologies are acted upon in society. On a small scale, schools that stream students into non-academic classes and then treat academic and non-academic students differently are making statements about the potential of their students. Remember Einstein!

On a larger scale, governments that practise **apartheid**, like South Africa, and restrict the freedom of specific racial groups, are making statements about

This photograph is a striking reminder that apartheid has been a very real problem in South Africa. Although the South African government began to change some of its laws in the early 1990s, discrimination remains a harsh reality for many of the country's citizens.

the worth of those racial groups. People within either society, the school, or the country, are expected to believe that unequal treatment is natural and proper. It is a real challenge for both valued members of society, and non-valued members to understand life any differently. When you are treated as if you are inferior for a long time, it is often hard to believe you are equal. Although de Tracy saw ideology as negative because it obstructed the truth, ideology has a practical value. Without ideology, people could not mentally organize their experiences. Ideology helps people give meaning to the actions of others. Without ideology as a tool, people could never work to solve the problems that stand in the way of their progress or survival. Outsiders may never really understand a group's actions, but these actions are full of meaning for people inside that group.

Ideologies: Helping Us Interpret Our World

Humans must interpret what happens to them the best way they can. Ideology helps in this interpretation process. For example, what we know and understand about other people helps shape the ways we choose to understand their actions toward us. Their motives and intentions may be unknown, so we often guess what they might be.

Our ideologies help us label and categorize why others do what they do. These ideologies organize our thoughts and help us understand the actions of others. We must remember, however, that our understandings are not always correct. They are important to us not because they *are* right, but because *we believe* they are right. Although ideologies help us understand others, they can sometimes confuse us if we don't understand another culture.

CASE STUDY:

HOW FAR WOULD YOU GO?

As you read the following Case Study, think about the effects Greenpeace has on the environment.

As David McTaggart says, ''You've got to be prepared to keep the number one thing in mind: you're fighting to get your children into the twenty-first century, and to hell with the rules.'' David McTaggart is an environmentalist, and for the past two decades he has fought to save the environment. McTaggart wages a personal war against polluters.

A native of Vancouver, McTaggart worked as the owner of a construction company. Following a business setback and a divorce, he decided to sail the South Pacific. From 1969 to 1972, he cruised. In 1972, his life changed. He heard that the French government planned nuclear weapon tests on the Moruroa Atoll in French Polynesia. A recently formed group called Greenpeace advertised that it needed a boat to carry protesters into the test zone. McTaggart answered the ad.

What followed proved to McTaggart that people sometimes have to take the law into their own hands. During McTaggart's first protest trip into the test zone, his boat was rammed by the French navy. On a second trip, French commandos attacked McTaggart and the crew. What really bothered McTaggart the most, he said, was that these violent attacks came on international waters, where any boat should be safe.

Moving to England, McTaggart worked to draw attention to the assault on whales by Iceland and other countries. Using McTaggart's boat, the *Rainbow Warrior*, Greenpeace made the plight of whales known to the world.

Greenpeace originated in Vancouver in 1970 as a small group opposed to nuclear testing in the Pacific. It is now a world-wide organization which, through nonviolent confrontation, addresses a wide range of environmental concerns:

June 23, 1975
A Greenpeace vessel intercepts a Soviet whaling ship. Two protesters are nearly hit with a harpoon.

February 28, 1980
A Greenpeace member releases 300 dolphins trapped in a Japanese harbour. He spends three months in jail.

August 16, 1986
Greenpeace activists attempt to intercept the American aircraft carrier *Constellation* in Vancouver Harbour because it is carrying nuclear weapons.

September 23, 1987
Greenpeace releases a major study that shows that many paper products contain dioxin. The organization later criticizes the pulp and paper industry for trying to ignore the problem.

Today, Greenpeace is an organization with more than 3 million members in 22 countries. It spent $32 million in 1990 alone on its environmental campaign.

Working outside the boundaries of traditional politics is the hallmark of Greenpeace. Its influence cannot be denied. A prominent Canadian politician once stated: ''I think much of what Greenpeace has done is superb. They are there because the rest of us were not attending to what our conscience should have made us attend to.'' This comment testifies to the contribution that anti-political, or radical, action can make in public life.

continued

CASE STUDY *continued*

QUESTIONS:

1. Why did David McTaggart join Greenpeace?
2. How effective do you think these activities were? In the long run, do you think that unlawful activities like the ones that Greenpeace participated in can be valuable to humanity? If so, in what ways? If not, why?
3. Greenpeace members often break the laws of different countries to try and effect change. What do you think of this type of action? Are there laws that are more important than the laws of countries? Are countries actually breaking these laws when they pollute or test nuclear weapons? Make a short list of what these laws might be. Working with others in your class who feel the same way, make a longer list to share with your class.
4. Do you think David McTaggart is right? Must people be ready to fight if they are going to have any power to negotiate?
5. What do you think of the activities of Greenpeace? Would you be willing to protest in the same way? If so, for what global issues would you be willing to fight?

The confrontation between the government and the Mohawk people in Oka, Quebec in 1990 pointed out how people act on their ideologies. The government believed it was protecting the interests of the Canadian public. The Mohawk believed they were protecting sacred land.

A Society's Ideology

Groups of humans make decisions and act according to ideologies. When countries work to solve problems and address issues, they direct their resources and the actions of people to deal with particular problems. The very action of working to solve problems shapes the future. Not acting to curb pollution, for example, means that the pollution will increase. It also tells others that we don't care if it does. Choosing to act, even in the face of incredible odds, may get results. It also sets the tone and spirit for our lives.

A society's ideology shapes its government. If humans view the world as an arena of conflict, like Hobbes viewed it, there is only one way to have control. Laws must be created to cover every possible political and economic activity. Rules exist to keep humans in line. Societies that believe humans are uncooperative and naturally in conflict have highly structured laws.

Some societies choose to believe that humans are basically cooperative. They believe that humans can work cooperatively to resolve problems with a minimum of central or external decision-making authority. If humans see the world as cooperative, fewer rules are needed to keep humans in line. Humans will naturally keep themselves in check.

So, there are different ideologies, different ways of interpreting life, different ideas about what goals are important and how goals should be reached.

The knowledge that there is a problem, the positive attitude toward finding a solution, and the willingness to act, are what make us human. This personal ideology helped motivate Rick Hansen to achieve his goals.

The following chart shows how decision-making takes place in both democratic and authoritarian regimes. Although the chart is a simplification, it is based on some important and fundamental guiding principles.

Political Organization in the 1990s

The Political Organizations chart illustrates some of the differences between democratic and authoritarian regimes. It outlines these two systems in more specific terms by comparing the range of political decision-making discussed so far in this text.

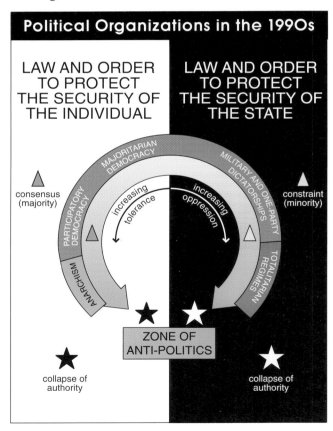

On the sides of the loop in the chart on the previous page, you will notice basic differences between two extremes. On the left, we have listed "law and order to protect the security of the individual." On the right, we have listed "law and order to protect the security of the state." As you scan the chart, notice that *consensus* and *constraint* increase in importance as you move toward the ends of the loop on either side. The different types of political organizations are placed on the outer ring of the loop. Don't worry if you might not understand their relative placement yet. As you read this book, you will understand the reason for their location.

Look carefully at the area between the two ends of the loop. This is the *Zone of **Anti-Politics***. This zone is particularly interesting because it is where formal political action, interpretation, and evaluation break down. Depending on the end of the loop, political action may rupture into an abandonment of authority and citizenship.

In regimes where total obligation is demanded and freedoms are meaningless, the individual may choose to act in an anti-political way. Acting anti-politically means taking non-conventional political action, such as joining the Nobody for President movement in the USA to protest a political structure. In repressive regimes, anti-politics can become very important. Through anti-political actions, individual citizens may discover, or rediscover, methods of practical, personal, or political action that were stopped by the regime in power. Likewise, in liberal democracies, if groups or individuals feel that traditional mechanisms of law and order have failed them, they may choose direct action.

There are constraints on your freedom to express your political views. In both a dictatorship and a **democracy**, power is exercised. The difference between the two is the source of the constraint. In a dictatorship, it is by a few. In a democracy, it is by many.

Governments of countries can and do change, but their need to maintain security for their citizens remains. Groups are smaller and less complex than governments. They can change more rapidly and dramatically. You probably belong to some groups—a school team, a work community, or a club. If you do, you likely know how quickly these groups can change from consensus or constraint, depending on the situations they face.

Political systems can be compared by how they interpret human nature and society. Should you want to compare democracy to dictatorship it will be helpful to ask questions: Do you believe that conflict is a natural part of human history? Do you believe that all people are equal? Supporters of dictatorship see both conflict and inequality as natural occurrences throughout history. Those who support democracies, generally liberal thinkers, usually have a greater faith in human nature to overcome conflict. While they may not believe that people are equal, they believe they should be.

The Political Organization chart focuses on what leaders and regimes do when they come to power. When comparing one political system to another, we should consider how systems direct resources and people. Questions about how political systems regulate lifestyles, exercise physical force, limit access to resources, or manipulate public opinion are all worth looking at.

SUMMARY

In this chapter you read about how ideology shapes the structure of a society's knowledge. Understanding a society's ideology is important to understanding that society, but there are limitations. Our ideologies are important because they help us understand others and ourselves. *Ideologies help us compare the different interpretations, ideas, and actions of others.*

In the study of politics and political power, to understand our truth means to understand how we are a part of our political system, our economic system, and the international environment. We also must realize that the political and economic choices societies make are based on complex factors. Knowing how we understand life and how we come to know what we believe will help us understand ourselves. In turn, we can never really understand others until we know something about their ideologies.

As you read the rest of this book, you will see how a person's or a society's ideology affects political and economic decisions. To understand a particular economic or political organization within a country, try to understand how that country views the nature of humans and the nature of history. Do countries see humans as basically cooperative or uncooperative? Is history a story of conflict or cooperation? How a society answers these two simple questions will tell you a lot about how that society will organize life for its citizens.

Our *truth* consists of more than what we believe. It is also made up of what we don't believe and of what we have chosen not to believe. Because we cannot be all things, there are limits to our understanding of the field of action in which we, and others, live. A communist is both a communist and a non-capitalist. A fascist is both a fascist and a non-democrat. It is important to know both the truth of what we believe and the truth of what other people believe.

Our knowledge and what we believe is often limited by other factors. Some of these include: Who has the power to express their interests in a society? and Who controls the access to economic resources? No choice is based on complete knowledge or complete political and economic freedom. Limits to choices are constantly imposed upon us in our changing world.

GETTING ORGANIZED

1. One of the main points of the chapter is that the word *politics* is broader than most people think. You have personal political relationships with many people. Choose two people you know very well (parent, friend, coach) and list three ways you influence them to do what you want.

2. Power takes many forms: money, influence, physical strength, age, and so on. Here is our challenge: see if your class can list 100 different and legitimate kinds of power.

3. What is the difference between a hero and a villain? Partly, it's perspective. In the news, there are almost always heroes and villains. What is currently happening in your world? Who are the heroes of the day? Who are the villains? Is there another perspective on these people? What is it?

4. What is the ideology of the society where you live? If you are like other North Americans, you watch television. In the ads, more than products are being sold. There is a *lifestyle* being sold, too. What is it the ads want you to buy?

5. Anarchists are against government. Do you think we could exist if there were no governments? What do you think Canada would be like if it were in a state of anarchy? Could it work? What would be the impact on you? Make a short case either for or against the anarchist's point of view.

6. Write an essay that answers the following question: To what extent should a society control the lives of individuals within that society?

REACHING OUT

1. Invite one or more community activists to your class. Ask them to outline their concerns or issues, and to outline the steps they have taken to tackle their problems.

   Your class might form groups and rate the activities and goals of the speakers. On a scale of 1 to 5 (with 5 being *very strong support*, 3 being *moderate support*, and 1 being *limited support*), rate the speakers based on their presentation and your support for them. Think about the importance of the issue or social cause, practicality of the steps taken to achieve the goal, and society's support now, and what you believe will be society's support 10 years from now.

   Prepare a written defence of your group's rating. Have one member of the group present it to the class.

2. Consider the photograph of Rick Hansen on page 24 and the statement under the photo.

   (a) Invite a variety of community activists or volunteers into your class and have them sit on a panel. Ask them to respond to this statement: The reason I work to support the cause I do is because _____.

   (b) Prepare a newspaper article on the results of your panel discussion. Headline your newspaper article, "Why do people work for change?"

   In your article, focus on this question: In what ways can individuals influence decisions and life in their communities? or, What characteristics distinguish active citizen from people who are not involved in their community?

Chapter Three:

THE DEVELOPMENT OF DEMOCRACIES

GETTING IT STRAIGHT

1. Why have political and economic systems changed over time?
2. What is a democracy?
3. How did the ideas of democracy evolve?
4. What is a direct democracy?
5. How do the early political thinkers influence politics today?
6. What are checks and balances?
7. What are the three branches of government?

Chapter 2 briefly described the organizing principles of democracies. This chapter will explore how democratic decision-making can be used to organize groups and governments. The chapter will also highlight the ideas of people who have contributed to democratic thought, and explore some of the issues that modern democratic governments face. As you read, think about how democratic thinkers have described human nature and the nature of social organizations. Then, decide for yourself how successful democracy is as a form of political organization.

The thinkers included in this chapter were major contributors to liberal democratic ideology, especially in modern Western democracies. You will read about the roots of democracy in Greece. You will be asked to evaluate the beliefs of Socrates, Thomas Hobbes, and John Locke. Modern democracy continues to be influenced by great thinkers. You will read about the relationship between the spirit of a people and the way society organized.

How do you see the evolution of humans through history? One French philosopher, Michel Foucault, made a study of society and had some definite ideas about the use of power in society. Think about the power of ideologies as you read. Each of the thinkers you read about in this chapter might not agree with all the actions of modern democracies, yet each has made a unique contribution to the structure of modern democratic thought.

Evaluating Political and Economic Systems

Ideologies are never cast in concrete. They are refined as individuals and societies re-interpret and re-evaluate them. As you review the ideas presented in this chapter, remember how these ideas were developed—people relied on their knowledge and beliefs to respond to situations they faced. In this chapter, the Case Studies represent current challenges and issues that democracies face. Each time a democracy meets a challenging issue, both its ideology and structure of knowledge are tested. The test may seem small; but as problems are solved, the structure of democratic thought takes shape.

After you read about the ideas of each thinker presented, answer the questions listed under *Issues* on page 30 as if you were that person. Then you will be on your way to understanding their interpretations and ideas. The ideas presented here are only summaries of the work of these people. You may want to read more about their ideas by consulting the bibliography at the end of this book.

WHOSE TRUTH?

How do you see the evolution of humans throughout history? If you are like most historians, you believe that humans have progressed. Not everyone agrees. French philosopher Michel Foucault (1926-1984) saw human history as a series of increased human understandings, followed by severe setbacks.

Foucault argued that human nature is not naturally good and that humans must work hard to avoid using power to manipulate others. Foucault's study of prisons gave modern social science a good definition of how power works. Each society (like a prison) constructs its own definition of truth. The real power of any society is that it can limit and construct reality: it only allows people to know and experience one kind of truth.

Foucault pointed out that there is no global understanding of social deviance or of psychological disorders like mental illness. What is bad in one society could be good in another. Madness in one society is sanity in another. The same political activity can be seen as an example of terrorism or an act of liberation. *Truth is defined by the social group that holds the power in society.* It depends on who is looking at it and what those people believe.

Consider this: in Western societies, men have held the power. This includes control of language. It is only in the last two decades that this has been successfully brought to the attention of society. *Mankind, workmanship, manmade* are words that were acceptable once, but no longer. To most people, these words and hundreds like them, are not acceptable as generic terms. In addition, they are inaccurate.

ISSUES:

1. In history, is conflict or harmony more important?
2. Do people want or need order imposed on them?
3. Are there inequalities among people (based on race, class, intelligence, or physical characteristics) that limit their full participation in society or societal groups?
4. Should groups or governments pursue a specific plan or direction for society?
5. How are decisions made?
6. Whose rights are protected?

While reviewing the knowledge that helped shape **democratic systems**, remember the PEEK box model. Ideas evolve in relation to political, economic, environmental, and knowledge factors. Ideas evolve in relation to the field of action as well. At the conclusion of the chapter, a PEEK box model for democratic governments is provided.

Ancient Roots of Democracy

It is said that democracy is not a system, but a process. Democracy is an old idea. Its roots go to ancient Athens. Five centuries before Christ was born, the Athenians of Greece coined the term *demokratia*. *Demos* means "the people." *Kratia* means "authority." Democracy means rule by the people, for the people.

The first democracy evolved slowly, out of the government that existed in ancient Greece. The Athenians practised two important activities in their city-state. First, they believed that citizens should be able to express their ideas at general meetings. Second, when laws were passed by the Assembly, all citizens were equally subject to them. Athens operated as a **direct democracy**. A direct democracy allows all citizens a vote on all issues. Would a direct democracy work in Canadian society?

The democracy of Athens was not the kind of democracy we know. Of the total population of Athens in 430 BCE, only 20 per cent of the people were citizens. Women, slaves, and anyone born outside the state could not become citizens. Women had responsibility for children, clothing, food and supplies, the care and control of servants, and the training of girls. Slaves were responsible to their masters. These people were not allowed to vote.

Although only a small percentage of the people of Athens could take part in a democratic meeting, the meetings were difficult to conduct. There were about 22 000 citizens of Athens. To pass a law, a quorum of 6000 citizens was needed.

The Assembly met about 40 times each year. Its agenda included items such as roads, water supply, and trading partners. Because every decision affected all the citizens, most citizens came. Perhaps the most difficult decisions the Athenian democracy made were about war.

Socrates was obligated by the laws of his society. He was tried and executed for his beliefs.

CASE STUDY:

ATHENIAN DEMOCRACY IN ACTION

Television has made good use of courtroom drama. *Street Legal* and *LA Law* are two of many shows that highlight the actions of courts and juries. Where did the ideas about courts, trials, and juries come from? Like many other democratic ideas, this one was adopted from the political activities of ancient Greece.

One intriguing contribution of Athenian democracy was the idea of trial by a jury of other citizens. Athenians used groups of either 501 or 1001 citizens for their juries. Juries were picked by lottery. Coloured balls determined who had jury duty. One colour meant you served, another colour meant you did not. The Athenian example of trial by jury continues as a basic principle of present-day democracies.

The most famous trial in Athenian history was the trial of Socrates. Socrates' life and trial help us understand both the nature of Athenian democracy and the general limitations of democracy.

In 399 BCE, Socrates was charged:

This indictment and affidavit is sworn by Meletus son of Meletus of Pitthos against Socrates son of Sophroniscus from Alopece; Socrates does wrong in not recognizing the gods which the city recognizes, and in introducing other new divinities. He also does wrong in corrupting the young men. The penalty demanded is death.

Socrates' criticism of democracy meant he was both loved and hated. Most trials in Athens ran very smoothly, but the trial of Socrates did not. In Athens, a water clock that took six minutes to drain was used to limit the length of time that any witness or speaker could talk. Still, Socrates' trial dragged on.

Finally, Socrates was found guilty by a narrow vote of the 501 jurors. The penalty was execution. Few Athenians really wanted Socrates dead. The trial and the charges troubled almost everyone. Yet, the citizens of the jury agreed. Socrates had to be silenced. His criticisms of the state had frightened many Athenians.

Socrates was encouraged to escape. He was given a chance to leave Athens, but he refused. He would not violate the will of Athens. He submitted himself to Athens as a citizen. He had fought as a soldier to defend Athens in his youth. And he would not destroy her now. Socrates ''readily and cheerily'' drank the poison brought to him by his executioner.

The story of Socrates' trial and execution helps us understand democratic societies. To supporters of democracies, Socrates represents the will of the people. Socrates disagreed with the decision made by the jury. Yet he would not escape. This shows that, although Socrates did not believe in the form of government Athens chose to use, he was obligated as a citizen to obey it. The choice was his to be a citizen. He made the choice, and obeyed the laws—even at the cost of his life. For Socrates, the law of the state was supreme. He agreed with the democratic principle that, to maintain order and security, it was the citizen's duty, role, and obligation to obey the law no matter how unjust.

continued

CASE STUDY *continued*

QUESTIONS:

1. Why was Socrates put on trial? What reason did the citizens of Athens give? Do you think that was the real reason?

2. What did Socrates believe about citizenship? Do you agree or disagree? In what ways?

3. How does the trial of Socrates help us understand the limitations of democracy?

4. Are there people like Socrates in your society today? If so, who? What makes these people like Socrates?

5. Divide your class into two groups. One group will support Socrates. The other group will work against Socrates. Piece together your "evidence." Hold the "Trial of Socrates" in your classroom. After the trial write a closing argument to the jury to support your points.

Unlike modern societies, the people who sent Athens to war were the same people who did the fighting. Every Athenian citizen was also a soldier. The citizen of Athens had a strong sense of commitment to the polis or city-state.

For citizens of Athens, order and security were primary responsibilities. The citizen of Athens looked out his window and saw enemies everywhere. Because Athens was rich, it faced constant threats of invasion. Ironically, although war itself was considered an enemy, military conquests, and the internal division wars created, eventually led to the downfall of this early democracy. However, in one form or another, the Athenian democracy existed for almost 200 years.

The Origins of Modern Democracy

Democracy did not vanish from the Earth when the Athenian democracy fell. Other Greek city-states also experimented with democracy. Rich variations of democratic decision-making have existed in tribal societies around the world, from pre-contact North America to Africa. In Europe, democratic ideals were adopted by groups long before states used democracy as a way to govern. Democratic beliefs have functioned in trade unions and religious groups for hundreds of years. This movement was called worker democracy, or decentralized decision-making. These small, but important, participatory democracies have all influenced the growth of democratic thinking. It would be a mistake to think of democracy as an invention of Western society.

Thomas Hobbes

English philosopher Thomas Hobbes (1588-1679) did not believe in a democracy in which everyone voted. However, Hobbes was the first Western thinker to argue that social organizations grew because people needed and wanted them. He rejected the idea that kings had a divine right to rule. Instead, he argued that individuals were intelligent. They understood that without government "life would be solitary, poor, nasty, brutish, and short." To avoid a constant state of war, individuals should surrender their rights to a higher authority. In Hobbes' system, this authority was named a Leviathan.

The Leviathan's job was to protect the governed from harm. Peace, order, and security were possible only under the rule of a capable, strong leader, Hobbes believed. This Leviathan must have the resources and ability to repel foreign invasions. Hobbes' ideas seem almost common sense today. People organize to prevent conflict between individuals and groups both from within and from outside the state.

Although Hobbes was considered an important contributor to democratic thought, there is an anti-democratic element in Hobbes' ideas. Many proponents of democracy believe that Hobbes placed too much faith and power in a strong leader. Leaders who claim to know what is best for the society are always potentially dangerous. History is filled with examples of power gone wrong.

Anyone who has seen a house party get out of hand knows what Hobbes was talking about. Without strong and decisive leadership, groups can become mobs. Hobbes' attitude toward order was practical. It was better to step on a few rights in order to avoid chaos. Hobbes even defended the right of the Leviathan to prevent conflict by regulating religious beliefs.

THOMAS HOBBES REFINES HIS IDEOLOGY.

Here the cartoonists show Thomas Hobbes struggling with how he wants to be addressed. Why would the way people are addressed be such an important consideration, especially in terms of power and respect?

John Locke

English philosopher John Locke (1632-1704) believed that human progress was shaped by competition for property. People were forced to resist tyrants or mobs who would rob them of their property. Locke said that people organize because organizations answer two important needs. First, they prevent conflict. More important, they help people preserve their property.

Locke emphasized the rights of property owners to have a say in affairs. In the 1600s, only English property owners could vote. In Locke's writings, he never mentions whether or not he felt this was a good idea. However, Locke did believe that all humans were created equal and had **natural rights** that could not be taken away. However, the abilities of people to reap benefits from the Earth were not equal. Differences in skill and ability naturally meant that power, wealth, and status were unequally distributed in society.

It is important to remember that Locke was a liberal. He believed that governments were created through the consent of the governed. But he thought that government should be limited to helping property owners protect and secure their property. Because not all people were property owners, he felt that not all people should be protected by the right to vote.

Hobbes and Locke held similar beliefs about how to deal with political questions that England faced in the seventeenth century. Both agreed that government should exist by the consent of the governed. However, they disagreed about why laws should be made. Hobbes believed that humans needed protection from their own conflict-oriented nature. Law existed to protect the state so it, in turn, could protect citizens. Locke believed that law existed to protect the individual from the government.

The Right to Vote

The idea that all adults should vote is very recent. It emerged only after World War I. The need for mass armies helped justify mass democracy. After all, how could the state ask people to die for the nation if they did not have a say in the daily affairs of the nation?

It may surprise you that not everyone in Canada has always enjoyed the benefits of a democracy. Some groups have only gained the right to vote quite recently. For example, until 1988, federal judges could not vote. In 1989, prisoners and patients in psychiatric hospitals challenged their exclusion from the right to vote.

One organizing principle of modern democracies is a belief that all adult citizens should have the right to vote. This is called **universal suffrage**. But, universal suffrage didn't come in one single action. Most democratic countries have extended the right to vote gradually.

Looking back, it seems curious that women were not given the right to vote in provincial elections until 1918. Quebec did not allow women to vote until 1940. In the studies below you will read the reasons given for not allowing women and Asians the right to vote. These reasons reflect different interpretations of human nature. They also reflect the goals of those in power.

The women featured above were an integral part of the war effort during World War I. Their efforts forced society to realize the value of women in the work force.

CASE STUDY:
VOTING IN CANADA

In this Case Study, you will read about the power inherent in the right to vote. As you read, think about how World War I changed what members of society thought about women.

For years, women were traditionally workers in the home. During the war, women were quick to meet the challenge of working in war-time factories. For the first time, they joined the work force in significant numbers.

After the war, there was a widespread feeling that some women had earned the right to vote. They had proved themselves "worthy." During World War I, Prime Minister Borden responded by granting female nurses serving overseas the right to vote. However, his move had a political motive. He secretly hoped that they would help balance the vote as a block to groups that were against **conscription**. In 1917, the Military Voters Act extended the right to vote to wives, mothers, and sisters of men who served in the military. For women, the key to getting the vote was to get involved in the affairs of the state.

THE JAPANESE AND THE CHINESE

Because few Canadians would do the work needed to build railways, promoters of the Canadian Pacific Railway lobbied the government to increase immigration of Chinese labourers. But even after they had lived in Canada for many years, Chinese Canadians were excluded from voting.

Racial differences were used to justify excluding Chinese Canadians and other Asiatic Canadians from voting until 1947. Japanese Canadians were not given the right to vote until 1949.

An editorial in the *Lethbridge Herald* in 1907 summed up the mood of many of the country's citizens at that time:

The Alberta government would be well advised if it passed legislation making it impossible for Japanese and Chinese to vote in this province. Make these yellow men realize they are not going to have any influence on our affairs. They have no right to compete with White voters.

QUESTIONS:

1. Conduct an outside research project of your own about the history of voting in Canada. In this research study, pay particular attention to those who have been denied the right to vote. Answer these questions: What groups have been excluded? Why? Have these groups since been given the right to vote? Why?

2. Elections take place at all levels of government and influence many aspects of our lives. School board elections, provincial, territorial, and federal elections are only a few examples of Canadian elections. Your own school might elect a student council. List as many Canadian elections as you can. How many did you list?

3. What do you think? Should involvement in the community or the nation's affairs be a condition of voting? Should any individual or group be excluded from voting? If so, who? Why would you make this exclusion?

4. Voting for government **representatives** is an important right in any democracy. If you were in charge of setting criteria for voting, what would you think were important? Briefly list these criteria. How do these criteria compare with those already established in Canada?

Echoes from the Past

To Hobbes, society was under a constant threat of being torn apart by enemies of the people. These enemies could be either internal or external. Hobbes justified whatever actions leaders thought necessary to maintain order and security. Locke believed leaders were bound by strict rules of conduct which he called natural laws. Violating these laws violated the rights of individuals. He felt that these natural laws should be listed in a contract, or constitution, between the government and the people. He called this **constitutionalism.**

The impact of Locke's ideas can be seen clearly in both the Canadian Charter of Rights (1982) and the American Declaration of Independence (1776). Both documents speak of the equality and worth of the individual. They also state that the government rules by the consent of the citizens. The American Declaration of Independence reads:

> *We hold these truths to be self-evident, that all Men are created equal, that they are endowed by their Creator with certain inalienable rights, that among these are Life, Liberty, and the Pursuit of Happiness— That to secure these Rights, Governments are instituted among Men, deriving their just Powers from the Consent of the Governed, that whenever any Form of Government becomes destructive of these Ends, it is the Right of the People to alter or abolish it, and to institute new Government.*

The Canadian Charter of Rights provided a clearer definition of the general principles that define the rights and freedoms of Canadians. The ''fundamental freedoms'' outlined in section 2 for example, include ''freedom of conscience and religion and freedom of thought, belief, opinion, and expression.'' Sections 7 to 14 outline legal rights such as the ''right to be secure against unreasonable search or seizure.'' Section 15 guarantees equality before the law based on ''race, national or ethnic origin, colour, sex, age or mental or physical disability.'' These rights are protected in order to provide for the security of the individual. Also, these rights are protected within ''reasonable limits, prescribed by law as can be demonstrably justified in a free and democratic society.'' This was an important statement to include; rights are guaranteed but within limits. The courts decide these limits.

Government: The Spirit of a People

Charles Louis de Secondat Montesquieu (1689-1755) was a French jurist and political philosopher. He was one of the first to recognize that human organizations reflect particular cultures. Organization depends on religion, wealth, and even the physical environment and climate. Montesquieu believed that the structure of governments reflects the spirit of a people. For example, monarchies developed in countries where family ties and loyalties were considered important. Dictatorships or tyrants ruled in countries dominated by fear. To Montesquieu, governments were logical extensions of the activities already going on in societies.

Because Athens was a democracy with limited citizenship and was dedicated to military service, Montesquieu theorized that human freedom was constrained in that city-state. He felt that the belief that the citizen should be the soldier and defend the polis led to a loyalty based on fear. Montesquieu believed that such small group loyalties were dangerous. They led to distinctions between groups, ethnic conflicts, religious wars, and final conquest. Montesquieu was accurate. These conflicts eventually dismembered Greece.

As we are doing with the PEEK box model in this text, Montesquieu studied how the environment shaped people. He came to believe that trade and commerce were important aspects of a stable society.

CASE STUDY:

THE CHARTER OF RIGHTS AND LAWFUL DETENTION

To everyone who has gone through junior high school, *detention* has a clear meaning. To a police officer it is an important and complex issue. When can an officer lawfully detain you? What are the limits to lawful detention?

Section 10 of the Charter states that "Everyone has the right on arrest or detention...to retain and instruct counsel without delay and to be informed of that right..." In 1985 the Supreme Court of Canada was asked to rule on the Therens case. Therens was asked to give a breath sample after he was involved in a traffic accident. Although he agreed, Therens' lawyer moved to have the charge dismissed. He argued that his client had not been informed of his right to obtain counsel.

Section 24(c) of the Charter says that "evidence shall be excluded" if the administration of justice was not followed or was brought into "disrepute." Simply, if the police do not follow proper procedures, the evidence will be thrown out of court. The court ruled in favour of Therens.

You may agree with this decision. What of the June 1990 court decision that random checks are legal under the Charter?

Gerald Ladouceur was stopped while driving in Ottawa in April 1982 (10 days after the Charter had been passed into law). The police testified that the only reason they stopped him was to check that his license and insurance were in order.

They discovered that Ladouceur's license had been suspended. He was fined $2000. He later challenged the conviction, arguing that the Ontario Highway Traffic Act that permits random stops is a violation of section 9 of the Charter, "freedom from arbitrary detention."

The court narrowly ruled against the appeal. In a five to four decision, the judges ruled that random checks are an "effective deterrent" to stop "the carnage on the highways." The four judges who disagreed with the decision warned that the police were being given far too much power. They argued that the established check stops were sufficient to deter traffic violators. They argued that more power could make police "much more intrusive and occasioning a greater invasion of privacy."

QUESTIONS:

1. Did parliament intend to allow random checks of drivers?
2. What do you think should limit police powers?
3. It would not be practical to go back to the public trials of ancient Greece. That system was cumbersome and time-consuming. On the other hand, the system represented the will of the people. Does the Supreme Court of Canada reflect the will of Canadians?
4. Create and conduct a class survey that answers the question: What limits should there be to the power of the law?

Trade helped people to be tolerant and to **compromise**. Commercial trade forced people to get along with others. Montesquieu believed England was an example of a state where this positive citizenship had grown. The English, Montesquieu argued, believed that political power must be carefully controlled. Through trade, England developed a tradition that gave individuals the right to pursue their private interests, specifically the accumulation of property.

According to Montesquieu, the English government was a successful democracy because it had developed **checks and balances** that limited the power of leaders. These checks and balances came about because England had a **separation of powers**. Western countries have since refined the idea of separation of powers.

Separation of powers is a simple idea, at least in theory. The idea is that all governments have three basic functions, and that these should be separate. As you learned in chapter 1, these three functions are to legislate, execute, and interpret and judge the laws. In modern democracies, these functions are executed by the legislative, the executive, and the judicial branches of government.

SUMMARY

Over thousands of years, a variety of thinkers contributed to the organizing principles that led to the formation of democratic states. As democratic nations grew and developed, the ideas that provided the basis for their organization also grew and developed.

The next chapter will show how Canada and the United States have developed similar, but different, political systems based on the same organizing principles. As you have seen with the PEEK box model, each democratic system develops differently depending on the different economic, environmental, and knowledge factors existing in each country.

PEEK
AT A DEMOCRACY

Politics	Economics
- security of the people ensured by checks and balances on leaders - use of consensus to achieve goals	- individual political freedom is linked quite often to economic freedom to produce and consume what one wishes (within limits)

Environment	Knowledge
- ongoing struggle to protect people's democracy from opponents on the outside (e.g. Athens; Allies against Hitler in World War II)	- belief that citizens have rights and dignity - accept the need for exchange of ideas and open goals for society

Field of Action
- democracies have risen up in a variety of areas, from Africa to North America - a number of these are discussed in subsequent chapters

GETTING ORGANIZED

1. *Democracy* is probably the most important word in social studies.

   (a) What is it? Without looking in a book, write your own definition of democracy. Share your definition with others. What are the key elements in the definition you wrote?

(b) After you have constructed your definition, write it in your notebook. Later, at the end of this unit, look back at your definition. Is it still the best definition of democracy? Compare what you have learned about democracy to what you now know.

2. Locke wrote about natural rights. Do you believe humans have natural rights? Should these rights apply to everyone in the world? Should they apply equally? Review or research briefly Locke's writings. Do you agree with him?

3. Before answering this question, make sure you understand the separation of powers in the three branches of government.

   Think about how school governments operate. Is there a separation of powers at work similar to the federal or local governments? Who has the different powers? If schools are not like governments, how are they different?

4. Read the constitution of Canada, the United States, or another country. Are there any points with which you personally disagree?

5. Many people insist that any form of censorship is a violation of human rights. What would life be like if there were no censorship? What impact would that have on you? Write a short case either for or against censorship.

6. In a short essay, take a side on the following question: To what extent should a democracy control the lives of its citizens in the area of censorship?

REACHING OUT

1. All democracies have to deal with the problem of checks and balances. After people are elected to office, their activities and decisions are monitored. Over the next two weeks, clip newspaper articles about investigations or allegations surrounding public officials.
   (a) List possible alternative steps the Canadian people or government could take to deal with these allegations.
   (b) Select one story and write a paragraph outlining a possible course of action for the individual involved.

2. Your school probably has a dress code or general policies regarding student behaviour. Invite the school's administration into your class to explain how these policies were developed and who has approved them (usually school boards have been involved as well as teachers and administrators). Their talk might be titled: Student Discipline—Who Decides and Why?
   (a) Prepare a 300 to 500 word essay that includes the following:
   - the sources of the principal's power to make and enforce decisions
   - the assumptions and beliefs of those in authority (e.g. trustees, school administrators)
   - your own view on the extent to which school authorities control the lives of students.

   Your teacher will be able to suggest strategies for organizing an essay that builds an argument or takes a position.

Chapter Four:

DEMOCRATIC GOVERNMENTS:
CANADA AND THE UNITED STATES

GETTING IT STRAIGHT

1. What is a parliamentary democracy?
2. What is a representative democracy?
3. What is meant by accountability in a democratic government?
4. How does the Canadian political system work to make decisions?
5. How does the US political system work to make decisions?

As you saw in chapter 3, democracy has been shaped by great thinkers over several centuries. This chapter looks at the practice of democracy in two countries.

Many people believe that Canada and the United States are so similar that they could be one country. While it is true they are similar and have developed friendly trade and security relationships, they are quite different. During the time that these two countries developed as nations, different politics, economics, environment, and knowledge resulted in different political and economic structures. This chapter looks first at Canadian democracy and then at American democracy. Democracy is shaped by the way people think and the way their ideas of democracy are used in each country's field of action.

TO VOTE OR NOT TO VOTE

In the November 8, 1988, presidential election, only one out of every two American voters voted. Some people call the non-voting group the Stay-at-Home Party or the Nobody-for-President Party. There are 86 million US voters in this group.

Young people vote less often than other eligible voters. Only one person in four between the ages of 18 and 25 voted in the November 1990 elections for governor in California.

Why don't all Americans vote? The reasons have to do with patterns noticed in all democracies, but there are some unique American reasons.

- Reason 1: In the United States, voters must register themselves to vote. In Canada, people called enumerators come to your door and register you.
- Reason 2: In the United States, the president is elected by an electoral college. Each state, based on its population, has a certain number of seats in this college. The presidential candidate who wins a majority of votes in any given state gets all the electoral college seats for that state. As a result, voters for one party will not bother to vote if they think their party

will lose. In the 1988 election, the Republican presidential candidate George Bush got 1 965 486 votes in Michigan. Democratic presidential candidate Michael Dukakis was close behind with 1 675 783 votes. But, in the winner-take-all system, Bush got all 20 of Michigan's electoral college votes.

- Reason 3: Many voters believe that the system is controlled by the majority "white middle class." In California, for example, 20 per cent of the population speaks Spanish. Language and culture are barriers to voter participation.
- Reason 4: Many avoid voting so that they will not be called for jury duty. One out of five citizens gave this reason for not voting in 1988. Most counties in the US use voter registration lists as their selection pool for jurists. Other countries use tax lists or other means.

The low turnout in US elections is an issue that challenges the American political system. Changing the registration system and encouraging voter turnout by assisting minority candidates are just two possible changes proposed. But the system will not change unless there is pressure. Do you think it should change?

Political Parties in Canada

Political parties are groups of people with similar political goals and views who try to change or influence the politics of their country. The three main political parties in Canada are the Progressive Conservatives, the Liberals, and the New Democrats.

Progressive Conservatives
(the PCs, the Conservatives, the Tories)

Major Policies (past and present):
- generally pro-business with emphasis on federal debt reduction
- generally favour a less centralized party structure than the Liberals

Ramon John Hnatyshyn, as Canada's 24th governor general (since Confederation), presents rock star Bryan Adams with an Order of Canada.

Liberals
(the Grits)

Major Policies (past and present):
- generally pro-business, with traditional leanings toward ethnic voters (strong immigrant support in the past)
- supported spending on expanded social welfare programs in the 1970s and 1980s
- centralized party structure

Sources of Support:
- more likely to be urban and central Canadian
- eastern Canadian support at some times
- lost Quebec support in the late 1980s
- historically the dominant party in Canada

New Democratic Party
(the NDP, the New Democrats)

Major Policies (past and present):
- generally pro-union and supportive of labour groups, small businesses
- emphasize social welfare state
- moving toward policies that will assist business development
- a more relaxed organizational structure, but centralized at the national level

Sources of Support:
- cuts across income and occupation lines
- stronger in the prairies (Manitoba and Saskatchewan)
- recently have gained support in Ontario and British Columbia

Sources of Support:
- more likely middle aged and older citizens, especially in rural areas
- since 1984 have dug into broader base of former Liberal supporters
- strong in western Canada in the 1980s

Policies or party platforms continually change. The Liberals lost the 1911 federal election to the Conservatives. At that time, the Liberals supported **free trade** with the United States. The Conservatives opposed it. In 1988 the Conservatives supported free trade while the Liberals opposed it.

Canada's Parliamentary Democracy

The Structure of Government

Canada's government is a **parliamentary democracy**. The ten provincial and two territorial governments take care of matters such as municipal affairs, education, and the organization of law enforcement and courts. Federal government responsibilities include foreign affairs, defence, postal service, and the maintenance of "peace, order, and good government." When this structure was created in 1867, the idea was to limit the power of provincial governments. Today, with new inventions and advances in technology, there are disagreements about which level of government should control issues of common concern, like telecommunications, air travel, and the environment. Pick up any newspaper today and you will read about governments in conflict.

On the diagram on page 44, you can see the different parts of the Canadian government at the federal, provincial, territorial, and municipal levels. Let us look carefully at the federal government and how it works.

House of Commons

Imagine a car full of your friends out for a night's entertainment. There are seven of you in the car: two want to go to a movie, two want to check out a friend's house, and the other three are not too sure. How do you decide? Debate, some compromise, a few threaten—"I'm going home"—but eventually you agree. Canada's federal government works something like this. The difference is that each person in the government represents tens of thousands of Canadians and their decisions affect millions.

The legislative (law-making) branch of the government consists of the House of Commons (295 members) and the **Senate** (traditionally 104 members). The real law-making authority is the House of Commons because this group is elected. Each member of parliament (MP) in the House of Commons is a representative of constituents in a province or territory.

The Cabinet

When a party wins more than half the seats in the House of Commons, it has a **majority government**. (If no party has a majority, two parties will try to join forces—this is called a **minority government**). The leader of the party is asked by the **governor general** to form the government. The government includes the prime minister (party leader), and a **cabinet** of ministers who are in charge of executing the laws and policies set up by parliament. Each minister directs a government sector, such as agriculture. The governing party is accountable, or answerable, to parliament for its actions. **Accountability** is limited if the party has a majority of the seats in the House of Commons. This is why, with three-quarters of the seats, Brian Mulroney's government could continue to push through the GST, a very unpopular sales tax, in 1990.

The Senate

The Senate's role is to check the power of the House of Commons. Senators study and review legislation on controversial issues such as the media, poverty, and the goods and services tax (GST). Many Canadians

The Structure of Government in Canada

	Federal Government	Provincial Government (10 in Canada)	Territorial Government (2 in Canada)	Municipal Government (5000 in Canada)
LEGISLATIVE BRANCH	**Governor General** **House of Commons** (members elected in 295 constituencies) **Senate** (appointed)	**Lieutenant Governor** ***Legislative Assembly** (elected in provincial ridings) *(called National Assembly in Quebec)	**Commissioner** **Legislative Assembly** (elected in territorial ridings)	**Village, Town, or City Council**
EXECUTIVE BRANCH	**Prime Minister** (leader of the party with most seats) **Cabinet** (selected by the prime minister) **Civil Servants** (execute parliamentary decisions)	**Premier** (leader of the party with most seats) **Cabinet** (selected by the premier) **Civil Servants** (execute legislative decisions)	**Government Leader** (leader of the party with most seats in Yukon; selected by majority of MLAs in NWT) **Executive Council** (selected by the government leader) **Civil Servants** (execute legislative decisions)	**Mayor** (elected in municipal ridings) **Council Committees** **Public Service** (execute council decisions)
JUDICIAL BRANCH	**Supreme Court** (Appeal Court) (judges appointed by governor general on advice from prime minister) **Federal Court** (Trial Court)	**Provincial Supreme Court** (Appeal Court) **Superior Trial Court** (judges appointed by the federal government) **Provincial Courts** (judges appointed by the premier; small claims, criminal, youth and family courts) **Quebec uses a combination of English Common Law and the Civil Code. The rest of Canada uses English Common Law.	**Territorial Supreme Court** (judges appointed by the federal government) **Territorial Court** (judges appointed by by the commissioner; equivalent to provincial courts and to Court of Sessions of the Peace in Quebec)	**Municipal Bylaws applied by Provincial Courts**

believe that the Senate could be more effective if it was elected, because it would be more representative of the regions of Canada. In 1989 an Albertan, Stan Waters, made history by becoming the first person elected to the Senate. The Senate will continue to be an issue in the 1990s.

The Supreme Court

It is the job of the judicial branch to interpret the law. There are many judicial bodies at various levels of government. Even your local school board will hear appeals on administrative decisions. Since the civil and criminal law is a provincial or territorial responsibility, these courts are most often reported in the media.

The highest court in Canada is the Supreme Court. Since 1982, when the Charter of Rights and Freedoms was introduced, the Supreme Court has made many rulings on cases which set precedents for securing the rights of citizens. In 1985 a charge of impaired driving was thrown out of court because the individual charged was not read his "right on arrest or detention . . . to retain and instruct counsel." The 1990s will see the growing importance of the Supreme Court in interpreting the rights of citizens.

In Canada's parliamentary system, when a cabinet minister gets into trouble, opposition parties often try to win public support by embarrassing the minister and the government. Why might this be damaging to the party in power? Why might it be damaging to the work of a democratic government?

Power

At one time, British monarchs had total power to make and enforce laws. As parliaments claimed their own power, the monarchy became more symbolic. Today in Canada, the governor general approves legislation on behalf of the queen. At all times, parliament is supreme in practice. The governor general is an important symbol in Canada, but has little power.

Power ebbs and flows even within a stable environment. Although the British monarchs and their representatives have lost power in Canada, another group has gained power—women.

A BREAKTHROUGH FOR WOMEN IN POLITICS?

Adapted from an article by Linda Hossie which appeared in The Globe and Mail.

As you read, think about this question: What changes might occur as women gain more power and status within all levels of Canadian governments?

Never in Canadian history have women served in so many ministerial positions as they have in the Ontario legislature in the 1990s. Eleven women were appointed to the cabinet—making up 42.3 per cent of the cabinet. Quebec, typical of most provinces, has 6 women out of a 30 member cabinet. The Ontario appointments include important portfolios like health care. Pollster Michael Adams sees the Ontario situation as part of a growing trend toward egalitarianism in the 1990s. Adams claims that Canadians "are no longer deferring to elites or our members of parliament. We want to see our leadership reflect us."

Women will bring a new face to politics in Canada, says Anne Swarbick, minister responsible for women's issues: "One of the things that we talked about was that when the public watches Question Period, a lot of people become more cynical about government because of the sandbox mentality they see."

An NDP advisor claims that women's values and skills are "more collective, more humanly supportive." Perhaps she is right. Certainly the last word should go to former British Columbia Cabinet Minister Rosemary Brown: "In the 50s and 60s, nobody took the time to talk about child care. It was never mentioned. Violence against women was just not discussed—ever. Issues like incest, child abuse, human issues were never discussed. These issues were brought into the public arena by women."

Is this a fair assessment? Certainly precedents in other countries suggest that women in government tend to alter priorities. For example, in Norway, where for the last two government terms women have comprised at least 40 per cent of the cabinet, government spending priorities have shifted. Spending on child care, care for the elderly, and environmental programs has increased, while spending in defence has not kept pace. Faced with declining oil revenues from North Sea oil, the Norwegian cabinet even thought of cutting defence spending to pay for more day care centres. Such an approach to setting priorities would be difficult to imagine in a male dominated cabinet like Brian Mulroney's today.

Straight to the top! More and more women now hold ministerial positions in legislature and cabinet, and in the future Canada may have a female prime minister. Rosemary Brown, pictured here, has been involved with Canadian politics since the 1970s. Investigate what role she has played in the Canadian political scene.

The United States

The US system of separation of powers is based on the **presidential system**. Contrary to popular opinion, the founders of the American system of government were not supporters of mass democracy. One warned against "moderates and democrats and other rats!" Still, the founding fathers of the American Constitution did not want a dictatorship either. As they worked to shape the government they desired, a unique blend of institutions emerged that would not allow one group of elected officials to become too powerful. The job was basic: give the elected officials enough power to protect the security of the people, but not enough to make decisions without the support of the people.

This famous historical painting shows the signing of the American Declaration of Independence on July 4, 1776. The American system of government developed as the country grew.

The United States was first governed by an elected **House of Representatives** and an appointed Senate. The idea of an elected Senate came later. Today the House of Representatives includes a different number of representatives from each state, based on population. The Senate has equal representation from each state. These two groups make up the legislative branch, called the Congress. The main duty of Congress was to pass laws.

The House of Representatives had the right to supervise and monitor the activities of the other government departments, especially how money was spent. Departments were created by Congress over the years as they were needed. The Senate had the right to approve the president's appointments to cabinet. People appointed to head cabinet positions are called secretaries. The president's cabinet is appointed by the president. It is not made up of elected officers, and people in the cabinet cannot hold any other office in the legislative branch. They are accountable only to the president. The president also makes appointments to the Supreme Court, subject to Senate approval.

Because the United States has such a powerful military, the office of the president has been called the most important political position in the world. But the president's power is both great and weak. He can veto any law passed by Congress simply by refusing to sign the bill. His veto, however, can be over-ridden by a two-thirds vote in the two Houses of Congress.

The president is the chief of the armed forces and the chief executive officer of the US government. His main job is to oversee the daily operation of the government. To complete this difficult job, the president has many advisors to assist him. In practice, congressional committees set the broad direction of the various departments, like Defense, Health, Education, or Welfare. The president then works to ensure that these jobs are carried out. There is no question, however, that the president's job is first and foremost to protect the security of the country.

The writers of the United States Constitution had no clear plan for the way government would work as the nation grew. Instead of a structure carved in stone,

The Structure of the Government in the United States

LEGISLATIVE BRANCH	EXECUTIVE BRANCH	JUDICIAL BRANCH
The Congress House of Representatives *(directly elected, two-year terms)* **Senate** *(directly elected, six-year terms)*	**The President** *(indirectly elected for four-year term)* **Cabinet** *(appointed by president and confirmed by Senate)*	**The Supreme Court** *(members appointed for life)*

they established principles to limit the powers of each group in government. As a result, the American system of separation of powers developed as the country grew, and as everyday problems arose.

US courts function under the same principles as Canadian courts. Courts act independently to settle disputes between citizens, and between citizens and the government. Courts in both countries are concerned with the equal and just application of the law. One difference between the US and Canada is that in the US each state controls its own criminal law. In Canada, the federal government makes criminal law for all of Canada.

The courts have influenced liberal democracies by helping to shape how societies think. For example, Canadian courts have made a number of important decisions since the introduction of the Charter of Rights in 1982. Today, the courts continue to set standards on such important issues as parental rights and the freedom of speech. The work of the courts shows that all parts of society can work together to influence the natural and legitimate freedoms citizens hold within the society.

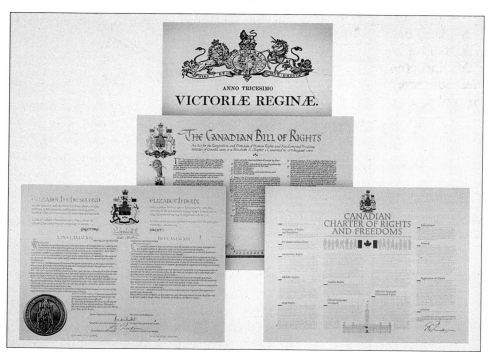

One object of the Canadian Charter of Rights and Freedoms is to protect the democratic rights of Canada's citizens.

CASE STUDY:

SEGREGATION OVER-RULED

As you read this Case Study, think about how changing circumstances can affect the law.

Perhaps the most important and famous US Supreme Court Case occurred in 1954 in Brown vs. the Board of Education. This decision overturned the *separate but equal* doctrine of public education that had existed for more than 50 years. Until this decision, states could segregate students by racial origin. Blacks went to one school and whites to another. The Supreme Court ruled that no form of segregation was legal. Chief Justice Earl Warren declared that racial segregation "deprived the children of the minority group of equal educational opportunities." He also found that separate facilities were "inherently unequal" and in violation of the Constitution's "equal protection under the law" clause. This Supreme Court decision gave Black Americans a legal basis for their civil rights movements of the 1960s.

This decision was important in a practical way. Although there were protests, states which had violated these laws were forced to obey the courts. The legislative system designed the law. The judicial system interpreted it. And the executive made sure it was obeyed.

Chief Justice Warren's interpretation of the Constitution showed how important the environment and changing circumstances are to ideology and laws. There are as many legal interpretations as there are people who interpret. Each interpretation is based on a unique history, environment, ideology, or time. Supreme Court justices in another country or political situation might have interpreted the law differently, based on what they know. Because people hold various ideological positions, political appoint-

ments to the Supreme Court in both the United States and Canada shape how laws are interpreted.

QUESTIONS:

1. In Brown vs. the Board of Education, the Supreme Court of the United States overturned the *separate but equal* doctrine of public education. What was this doctrine?

2. Why did Chief Justice Warren overturn this doctrine? In writing his decision, what points did he make?

3. Why was this 1954 Supreme Court decision important in the history of the United States?

4. In essence, the US Supreme Court and Chief Justice Warren stated that separate facilities could never be equal. But was he right? In a small group, recreate several different possibilities that could outline the relationship between minority and majority groups:

   (a) minority and majority separate, majority has more status

   (b) minority and majority separate, minority has more status

   (c) minority and majority separate, both have same status

   (d) minority and majority together, majority has more status

   (e) minority and majority together, minority has more status

   (f) minority and majority together, both have same status

Consider each of these cases individually. The US Supreme Court chose (e) as the best. Can a case be made for *each* of these political arrangements? If so, what? If not, why not?

SUMMARY

Democracy is shaped both by ideas and practicalities of solving problems in a field of action. Although democratic governments differ, they are based on certain accepted organizing principles, like the accountability of representatives to the constituencies that elect them. Democracy is a way of doing things, not a particular kind of institution. Democracy expresses the human desire to have a say in what happens in the world. Democracy offers the hope that personal ideas and interests will be made known to a decision-making body.

As you have read, there are different types of democratic government. Canada has a **constitutional monarchy** and the United States has a system based on separation of powers. In Canada, bills are initiated by the cabinet and passed into law by the House of Commons. In the US, the House of Representatives and the Senate pass laws.

In the next chapter, you will read about another type of government: dictatorship. Later in *A Changing World: Global Political and Economic Systems*, you will read more about democratic governments, especially as they relate to economics.

GETTING ORGANIZED

1. In Canada, many people do not vote for any level of government. Ask five people of voting age whether they voted in the last election. If they did not, ask why.
2. Things change in politics. In this chapter, the major political parties of Canada were reviewed as they existed in early 1991. Reread these reviews. Have there been changes since this book was written? What are they?
3. Think about the issues of prejudice and stereotyping. What current stereotypes and prejudices exist in your society? Do these keep some people outside the functioning political life of the society? If so, how?

4. Who is the prime minister now? What major issue does he or she face today? Is this person popular? Why or why not? What are the main leadership problems this person faces? What is your opinion of the prime minister?
5. Ronald Reagan was an actor before he became president of the United States. Could others do it too? In a small group, pick a possible political candidate from among the most popular movie actors or musicians. Design a short election campaign for him or her. What do you want in a representative? Could it work? How would it impact you?
6. Draw a vertical line down the centre of a piece of paper. On one side, write Voting Should Be Compulsory. On the other, write Voting Should Not Be Compulsory. List 10 good reasons to support each statement. Work together if you like.

REACHING OUT

1. You have read about a variety of democratic ideas and practices in different countries. Listed below are political practices that all democracies share to some degree. For each of these practices, identify one or two examples from the text or current events.
   (a) free and open elections
   (b) a balance of influence from interest groups
   (c) use of compromise and persuasion
   (d) open access to the media
   (e) respect for minority views
   Create a chart with your information and give it a title. Of these practices, which is the most important for the preservation of democracy? Justify your answer in a paragraph.
2. The newspapers are full of court cases involving points of law and challenges to the Charter of Rights and Freedoms. Start a personal file of clippings on these cases, summarizing the issues involved and identifying which sections of the Charter are being used to defend rights cases. File each case, using the relevant section of the Charter (e.g. a case about mobility rights would be numbered #6).

3. Invite a lawyer or police officer to speak to the class on the issue of the security of the individual in the Canadian democracy. Use ''how has the Charter changed the rights of the individual?'' as a focus question. Prepare a summary of these changes that ranks the three most important changes.

4. Consider the practices of democratic government listed in question 1. Create a mural that depicts these practices in action. You might try to have at least two photos displaying each practice. Use magazines or newspapers. Select an appropriate title for your mural.

Chapter Five:

DICTATORSHIPS: THE RULE BY ELITES

GETTING IT STRAIGHT

1. What is a dictatorship?
2. What are the three questions you should ask when studying any government?
3. How did early thinkers influence the rise of dictatorship?
4. What is elitism?
5. What is the difference between reactionaries and revolutionaries?
6. What structure of knowledge is common to all dictatorships?
7. What is a one-party dictatorship?

Three basic questions must be asked when studying any government:

1. Who rules?
2. What organizing principles do rulers use to legitimize their power?
3. How did the leaders get their power?

Although democracies and dictatorships are very different, they both exist to protect the security and economic interests of a society. The difference lies in the answer to this question: Whose interests are protected, a broad cross-section of individuals or a select group?

On paper, dictatorships can look much like democracies. Dictatorships and democracies may even have the same political institutions. Both may have parliaments with elected representatives, courts, and a police force that enforces the laws of the land. Also, like democratic governments, dictatorships usually build sewers, schools, roads, and hospitals.

The cartoonists are inviting us to compare and contrast democracies and dictatorships. What simple point are they trying to make? In what ways is this point accurate?

Students of politics are sometimes confused by the fact that, throughout the world, dictatorships are more numerous than democracies. How could this be? Do people choose to live under a dictatorship? The answer is yes and no. Sometimes there is no choice. Sometimes people will not desert their homeland when a dictator assumes power. Sometimes dictatorships are not as harsh as those of us in the West believe they must be.

In dictatorships and democracies, the daily activities of the government may not seem to differ. What differs are the organizing principles. In one way or another, all societies restrict and constrain behaviour by passing laws. These laws name some activities *undesirable* and organize a group of people whose job it is to control those illegal activities. In a democracy, laws protect the freedoms and security of the people

CASE STUDY:
LOOKING AT OTHERS

In this Case Study you will read how the writing of journalists can be affected by their ideologies. As you read, think of your own beliefs about dictatorships. Think about how your ideas have been affected by newspaper articles.

One journalist visits the Soviet Union and writes about the lack of food. Another visits and notes that even manual labourers can take a vacation at a resort every weekend. The first gives an impression that the Soviet Union is in a rapid state of economic and social decline. The second suggests that the people of the Soviet Union are living quite well. Why the difference? Reporters are no different than the rest of us. We see what we want to see.

A journalist has the power to create a positive, negative, or balanced view. Which one will the journalist choose? Sometimes it is difficult, if not impossible, to see past personal beliefs. The case of American journalists who visit the Soviet Union is particularly striking.

George F. Will was a popular columnist who wrote for *Newsweek* magazine. He was also a **right-wing** confidant of former president Ronald Reagan. He chose to write about a Soviet society in a constant state of economic and social decline. In a series of articles in 1986, Will wrote that the Soviet society was "suffocating in antiquated double-talk." He called the leaders "brain-dead." He called the Soviet Union a "conspicuous invalid," and said that the country was being driven toward collapse which was its "deserved destination." He wrote that Soviet society was backward because neon lights did not light up the night streets of Moscow. In short, Will exposed the Soviet Union for not having the same things that the US had, and being the worse for the difference.

Was Will right? Was the Soviet society in a state of decline and near collapse? In the past there have been many important Soviet advances. The Soviet Union moved from a weak military power defeated in a war with Japan to a world military superpower. They put the first man in space. They built a full-employment society from the economic wreckage that the tsars left in 1917. And, although living standards are below those of the United States, there are not 30 million people living below the poverty line as there are in the US.

Perhaps George F. Will was no different from Soviet journalists. They also filled their reports with negative points of view about American life. The result was that many, in both countries, were blind to any perspective but their own. They saw with their ideologies, and they saw just what they wanted to see.

QUESTIONS:

1. What does the Case Study say about some American and Soviet journalists? What are the implications for communication if we all "see with our ideology"?

continued

CASE STUDY *continued*

2. Do you have an ideological viewpoint about the Soviet Union? What is it? Can you imagine changing it? If so, what would change your perception?

3. From a practical point of view, why do you think many Americans view the Soviet Union the way they do? Write a generalization that expresses how North Americans view the Soviets. Make a "bumper sticker" with a political slogan that expresses this generalization.

4. According to an October 1990 *Report on Business* magazine article, 73.6 per cent of Moscow residents were dissatisfied with the way their government handled the economy. Eighty per cent of Canadians felt dissatisfied, too. What might be some differences and similarities about these complaints?

who consent to them. Except some benevolent dictators who pass laws for the good of the people, most dictatorship laws protect the security of the powerful elite.

Dictatorships obtain and hold power in ways that are unacceptable in a democracy. For example, dictatorships may use threats or direct force, indoctrination and control of the media, controlled participation, or the elimination of the expression of public discontent. The organizing principle of a dictatorship is that people need limits and they need guidance to get along. In the context of this belief, a one-party state that limits or controls individual political activity, by force if necessary, is quite acceptable.

Ancient Roots of Dictatorships

Plato

When the Greek philosopher Plato (427-347 BCE) wrote about democracy, he presented many ideas sarcastically. "Democracy is a charming form of government for variety and disorder, dispensing a sort of equality to equals and unequals alike," he wrote. To Plato, democracy was foolish because it allowed disorder in society. The job of government was to ensure order, and a government that produced disorder was, in his opinion, worse than no government at all.

Plato viewed humans as unequal in both skills and talents. His theory was simple. People should only do what they were good at doing. Trade and commerce were for those successful in business. Manual labour was for those with speed, strength, and dexterity. Teaching was for those good at explaining. Plato believed that the average person had neither the ability nor interest to forget daily worries and become involved in politics. Government should be left to those who were good at it. His view went against the democratic ideal of a government by and for the people.

According to Plato, the best society would work like a machine. Each part of the machine would work together to provide what citizens needed and wanted most—justice. Political organization was necessary because society would crumble without a strong government to ensure justice for the people. For Plato, the best way to guarantee justice was to guarantee order and security.

Plato's structure of political power was based on his beliefs about the nature of humans and about the way social organization should best be accomplished. Plato was a thinker who lived in a world of ideas. He did not get involved in practical, day-to-day politics. Because he had little practical knowledge, many have criticized his belief that elite groups should be trusted with the authority to make decisions for all people. But Plato was authoritarian. He believed that an elite group knew best how to make decisions and what decisions to make. What do you think of Plato's ideas?

Plato's ideas contribute to the structure of knowledge that helps to explain the totalitarian socialist regimes of Lenin and Stalin, and the dictatorships of many Eastern bloc countries.

The Idea of Elitism

Elitism suggests that influence, authority, and the power to make decisions should be in the hands of a few people or in a distinct group. Elitism is not new. It exists and has existed in many areas of human activity. In sports, some people have more talent than others. Gretzky and Lemieux in the National Hockey League are perfect examples. They lead their teams because they are considered more creative, more innovative, and more talented than most of their team mates.

Sylvester Stallone is a member of an elite group, too. Between 1989 and 1993, he is expected to make $120 million from his movies. Plato, and others, believed that any area of activity had similar elites.

People with leadership abilities usually rise to the top in any group, formal or informal. Both countries and social groups need leaders. Within their groups they have more influence than other group members.

An understanding of elitism helps us understand why dictators rise to take power. There are many ways an elite can come to political power. As a result, there are many kinds of dictatorships. In theory, dictatorships can be broken into three basic groups: one-party states, military regimes, and totalitarian dictatorships. In practice, dictatorships are difficult to categorize.

Benazir Bhutto became the first woman to lead Pakistan. She emerged from an elite segment of Pakistani society.

ELITES IN PAKISTAN

Pakistan is an example of a country where elites are fighting for power. In June 1989, Benazir Bhutto's leadership was challenged by Islamic fundamentalists. Fundamentalists stated that because Bhutto is a woman she had no right to hold power. Bhutto retaliated by saying she was elected and is the daughter of former leader Zulfiqar Ali Bhutto.

After becoming prime minister, Bhutto tried to calm the fears of male fundamentalists by wearing plain clothing and little jewelry. Bhutto was challenged by rival fundamentalists who saw her as a threat to their traditional power. In 1990 Bhutto was replaced.

Vilfredo Pareto

Vilfredo Pareto (1848-1923) is not a well-known political thinker, but he had some important observations about how elites worked. He was an Italian economist and sociologist. He believed that every society has two kinds of elites. One group of elites is conservative and wants to keep things the way they are. These people work to protect the power they have by controlling privileges, institutions, and resources. They have privileges that provide them with the wealth of the society. Because this group enjoys material wealth and status, they are reluctant to change the way society works. The second elite group desires change. Specifically, they want the power, influence, and authority to make decisions.

As Pareto studied history, he saw a constant battle between those who had power and those who did not.

History bears out Pareto's analysis. Except those few countries with a stable democracy, most countries have a history of conflict between elite groups fighting for power.

Pareto's idea of two elites fighting for power helps explain political life in many countries. **Reactionaries** resist change. **Revolutionaries** support change. In some societies, where democratic organizing principles do not exist, elites in power will do almost anything to keep power. They often take serious measures to restrict those who want to take away their power. The elite that wants power will do almost anything to achieve that power. This is why revolutions occur so often around the world. There is almost constant conflict, or the threat of conflict. Elites in power may resort to **repression** and force to ensure that their authority is absolute.

Here the cartoonists make a statement about the balance of power in a country ruled by a political elite. What point are they making?

Theories of Dictatorship

In chapter 3 you answered the following questions as if you were Socrates, Hobbes, Locke, and Montesquieu. In this chapter, answer them twice: once as if you were Plato, and once as if you were Pareto. If you can do this, you are well on your way to understanding their interpretations and ideas. Remember that the ideas presented here are very brief summaries of their work. You may want to read more about their ideas.

ISSUES:

1. In history, is conflict or harmony more important?
2. Do people want or need order imposed on them?
3. Are there inequalities among people (based on race, class, intelligence, or physical characteristics) that limit their full participation in society?
4. Should groups or governments pursue a specific plan or direction for society?
5. How are decisions made?
6. Whose rights are protected?

A summary of the knowledge that contributes to dictatorships is presented in the PEEK box to the right.

P E E K	
AT DICTATORSHIPS	
Politics	**Economics**
- security of the regime (or those in power) considered the most important - use of constraint to achieve goals	- production and consumption goals determined by the elite - economic system serves the interests of the elite
Environment	**Knowledge**
- need to protect the regime from outside opponents (e.g. Stalin's fear of Western influences)	- belief in inequalities among people - conflict is natural among people, so strong government is needed to achieve the goals of the regime
Field of Action	
- you will read about the fields of action of Nazi Germany and the USSR in subsequent chapters	

Types of Dictatorships

Conflicts for power are often deadly serious; the strong survive and the weak don't. In countries without organizing principles to support consensus and compromise, competing elites will try to limit dissent. If an elite group is in power for purely material reasons, it may use brute force to suppress change. A military dictatorship run by a South American drug lord is an example of how violent this kind of elite can be. Those in power are most interested in accumulating wealth or privilege. They seldom promote a particular social philosophy. As a result, they don't waste time preaching or teaching. Instead, they use fear and physical force to maintain the privilege of their power. This kind of government is devastating to people who need education, health services, and peace.

There are three basic types of dictatorship in the modern world: military, one-party, and totalitarian.

All dictatorships provide protection for the security of the regime. It is important to remember, however, that each type engages in different political practices in the field of action.

There are few countries that are actually pure examples of one type of dictatorship or another. Most have features common to all types, with an emphasis on one type.

One-Party States

One-party states limit power to one or two groups or elites. Powerful elites may try to repress dissent and control the media. The use of physical and psychological coercion is common in one-party states.

An example of a one-party state is South Africa. Here the National Party has supported the policy of apartheid since 1948. Apartheid is a system of racial segregation in which the ruling white elite withholds power from the Black people who have the larger population in South Africa. Chapter 6 looks more closely at apartheid in South Africa.

El Salvador's Christian Democrat alliance forbade opposition in the 1980s, claiming that foreigners were trying to undermine the country. More than 50 000 Union leaders, reporters, and Catholic priests were rounded up and killed. Newspapers that published opposing views were shut down. The 14 families that controlled El Salvador (plantation owners and business leaders) ensured that their security was intact, at the expense of the population at large.

Military Dictatorships

Military dictatorships are basically governments that have declared war on the people. Military dictatorships come into being when an elite or even the majority of the population (a democracy) fails to control the military. Often this type of dictatorship emerges when a one-party state collapses and the elite in power flee,

leaving the military as the most powerful group. Sometimes an elected leader is eliminated or mysteriously disappears.

In 1973, General Augusto Pinochet led a successful **coup d'état** in Chile. What followed included 15 years of conservative economic measures and harsh suppression of political dissent. With his executive powers unchecked by a parliament, Pinochet's government was able to execute and torture its opponents by the hundreds. The Catholic Church estimated that, by the mid-1980s, 80 per cent of the population needed psychological counselling.

In 1988 Pinochet asked the people to elect him president until 1997. They refused. In 1989 elections were held for a democratically elected president.

Totalitarian Dictatorships

In one-party states that are economically underdeveloped, often the government claims exclusive authority to implement economic and development plans. Other one-party states claim special authority based on moral, religious, or political programs. The longer elites hold power the stronger their influence. These states become totalitarian one-party dictatorships. Nazi Germany under Hitler and the USSR under Stalin are examples of totalitarian one-party dictatorships.

Most one-party states have a tenuous existence. There is constant conflict with other elites within the country, and these states are unstable. Often one party can hold power for only a short time before another rises to challenge it. In a desperate attempt to keep power, often these groups adopt the practices of totalitarian regimes, such as psychological manipulation and the re-education of dissidents. Anything that will force total commitment to the regime's goals and leaders is possible.

Dictatorships are hard to categorize. There are no pure one-party states, totalitarian states, or military dictatorships. For example, in Libya, Qaddafi holds

Josef Stalin's rule was a harsh and oppressive one. Stalin did not tolerate opposition, and used force and coercion to control political factions in the USSR.

In 1969, Muammar Qaddafi led an army coup d'état that deposed Libya's King Idris I. His leadership combined elements of religious, socialist, and nationalist ideals.

the respect of a large segment of the population and has much of the authority to make decisions. However, there is no official political party. The 1400 peoples' committees across the country send representatives to a national congress. These representatives support the dictatorship. The military holds power because it protects Libya's nationalist economic interests in oil development.

Qaddafi's power is not total, however. When he tried to enforce compulsory military training for women, the reaction was interesting. Islamic religious leaders organized their followers through local peoples' committees and blocked the move at the national level.

They forced Qaddafi to back off. It is difficult to know for sure where the power lies in Libya. Libya has both the qualities of a military dictatorship and a one-party state. Qaddafi calls his organizational structure a "mass party," where everyone in the country is a member. Combined with the personal **charisma** of Qaddafi, Libya's system seems to work for Libya.

SUMMARY

Although there are many types of dictatorships, all have several common ideas. Each holds a structure of knowledge and a set of beliefs based on the idea that history is a series of conflicts. And, each believes that people need to be controlled and organized by the elite in power. Each provides order and security by giving control and authority to an elite group.

Dictatorships rise when conditions support the need for a powerful elite group to come to power. Many thinkers, for a variety of reasons, have supported the need for strong, elite leadership. Democracies or dictatorships are merely ideas until they are acted upon. As you have learned, the practice of these theories takes place in a field of action.

The next chapter shows the development of other types of dictatorships in Nazi Germany and the USSR. The PEEK box models will show how differences in the field of action contributed to the growth of both.

GETTING ORGANIZED

1. List five countries that have not been focused on in this book. Find out if they have a dictatorial or democratic government.
2. Honestly answer the first four questions under the section ''Theories of Dictatorship'' on page 58. What did you learn about yourself?
3. List the three most charismatic people you know. What makes them so special? Would you want to be any of these people? Why or why not? How would life change for you if you and one of those people could exchange lives?
4. Read more about any one of the people mentioned in this chapter. List five interesting things you learned.

5. Imagine that a powerful, but very kind dictator took over our country. What changes would occur? What would life be like? Could it work? How would it impact you?
6. Debate the following question: Should Canada establish friendly political relationships with dictatorial governments?

REACHING OUT

1. Search the news for a country that is undergoing civil war or a major internal political struggle.
   (a) Using Pareto's idea of reactionaries and revolutionaries, identify those who represent each group. Name the leaders and identify their sources of power in the country.
   (b) Use a large world map for display purposes. Update the struggle between these groups on a regular basis.
2. Read the novel *Animal Farm*, by George Orwell (an animated movie version is available as well). Does the situation in *Animal Farm* parallel Pareto's claim that societies often see struggles between two fighting elites? Outline similarities and differences.
3. George Orwell's *1984* showed what a totalitarian dictatorship might look like. Most video stores have the movie version (under the same title). View the film as a class and construct a PEEK box that summarizes the society depicted in the film.
4. Organizing for your class graduation ceremonies or prom night may be underway in your school now. Identify the students who are involved in the planning. Do they represent an elite in your school? How were they chosen?

Chapter Six:

TWENTIETH CENTURY DICTATORSHIPS

GETTING IT STRAIGHT

1. How did Nazi Germany represent a totalitarian dictatorship?
2. How are glasnost and perestroika leading to the collapse of totalitarian dictatorship in the Soviet Union?
3. What was life like under the dictatorship of the Ceausescus in Romania?
4. How does apartheid in South Africa represent elements of both a one-party state and a military dictatorship?

Why do dictatorships emerge? Conditions in the field of action contribute to situations where a dictatorship is likely to come about. In this chapter, we will study the growth of four dictatorships: Nazi Germany, the USSR, Romania, and South Africa. As you will see, dictatorships are not all the same.

Totalitarian Dictatorship in Nazi Germany

Adolf Hitler

Few people who live in the twentieth century are unaware of the story of Adolf Hitler (1889-1945). Hitler was not a political thinker in the strict sense, yet he successfully drew together the ideas of others and carefully re-interpreted them in relation to the troubles that plagued Germany after World War I. Hitler's political and economic ideology was one of totalitarian **fascism**.

Hitler, who changed his name from Schicklgruber, had an unremarkable childhood in Austria. Reports are that he was a bit of a snob. He avoided getting a job because he thought that working with his hands was beneath his talents. When he fought for Germany in World War I, he was wounded, and he received the Iron Cross. When Germany surrendered, Hitler fumed. Under the 1919 Treaty of Versailles, Germany was forced to ''accept responsibility for all the losses and damages'' of the war. The Allied Forces, especially the French, pushed to make Germany pay. Germans' resentment and bitterness over the harshness of the treaty boiled over when France took a valuable part of German land, called the Ruhr Valley, because Germany failed to make its war payments.

In 1920 Hitler and other nationalists founded the National Socialist German Workers' Party (NSDAP), more commonly known as the Nazi Party. He led the party from 1921 until the end of the war.

In 1923, in one unsuccessful coup d'état the NSDAP attempted to overthrow the government of Bavaria. Hitler was imprisoned for this and it was there he wrote the famous book *Mein Kampf* (*My Struggle*).

Once out of jail, Hitler created the Storm Troops, recruiting teenagers and veterans of World War I. He also worked to elect Nazis to the German Parliament. The Nazis made little headway however, until the devastating stock market crash of 1929. This economic crisis provided Hitler with opportunity and he seized it quickly.

In the 1930 elections, the Nazis gained the balance of power in the parliament. Conservative groups who wanted to limit the power of **left-wing** groups like the Communists supported Hitler. With the support of Nazis and other right-wing parties, Hitler was declared chancellor on January 30, 1933.

Adolf Hitler's unique charismatic appeal, his understanding of human nature, and Germany's economic problems created a large and loyal following for Hitler and the Nazi Party. List some other charismatic leaders, past and present, and the political ideologies they represent.

HITLER'S RISE TO POWER

Knowledge of the events preceding World War II is important in understanding the development of Hitler's ideas. Hitler's Nazism was a specific form of fascism unique to the German environment at the time. Hitler used the following ideas to formulate his policies. These became the rungs on his ideological ladder. The structure of German fascism included four beliefs.

1. **Social Darwinism**
2. **Racism**
3. **Nationalism**
4. **Imperialism**

1. SOCIAL DARWINISM

Alfred Rosenberg, Reich minister for the Occupied Eastern Territories, was Hitler's main source of ideas about the nature of humans and social organization. Rosenberg believed that the **Aryans** were a superior race responsible for most of the progress throughout history. Rosenberg also believed in Social Darwinism. This theory is that societies compete for scarce resources and that "survival of the fittest" enables only superior people to gain wealth and power.

Rosenberg believed that Aryans were a superior race whose racial purity needed to be protected from inter-racial mixing with inferiors. Because inter-mixing has taken place throughout human history, Rosenberg's claims about the racial purity of Aryans are absurd. Although Rosenberg's conclusions were invalid, he used them to support a special claim to authority. They became part of an ideology that fit the circumstances of that period of history.

2. RACISM

Arguing that races were different by nature led Hitler to conclude that racial chaos ought to be avoided. As part of Hitler's political agenda, social policies were developed to limit the opportunities of what he called the inferior races and promote the opportunities of the so-called superior race. So that the Aryan race would not be diluted, Rosenberg and Hitler restricted German soil to Aryans. Deporting those with undesirable racial characteristics from German land became the political solution.

Before World War II began in 1939, the plan was to resettle Jews in Madagascar. As history has shown, the Nazis chose other, more terrible, steps. Millions of Eastern European and Soviet Jews were executed in extermination camps along with Slavs and other people such as Gypsies and homosexuals. Hitler had a special hatred for Slavic people and he dreamed about destroying their countries.

Hitler's objective was to make Germany a "community of physically and psychologically homogeneous creatures."

3. NATIONALISM

As a direct consequence of the myth of the Aryan race and its destiny to dominate history, German nationalism was encouraged. Discontent about the Treaty of Versailles, **inflation**, and the threat of outside interference from France in the Ruhr Valley led to a rise in nationalism. The German population was re-educated to be more loyal to the Reich. They were also educated about the

continued

continued

need to sacrifice and make the state stronger.

Nationalism taken to extremes involves two main ingredients: fear of outsiders and excessive pride in some past or future glory. Hitler encouraged both. High school textbooks in Nazi Germany showed maps of Europe with Germany surrounded by fully-armed enemy states. In many ways, fear of other countries was encouraged.

In his last political statement before his suicide, Hitler wrote about his pride in the soldiers and the youth who died serving the Reich. Hitler died "with a joyful heart" because the National Socialist State "represents the work of centuries to come and obliges each individual person to serve the common interest before his own advantage." Hitler's nationalism had the same ingredients of all countries that are nationalistic, even Canada. He drove fear and pride to extremes. The fear and pride felt by citizens of Nazi Germany is easy to see in this oath sworn by young soldiers your age:

> *I swear by God this sacred oath, that I will render unconditional obedience to Adolf Hitler, the Führer of the German Reich and People, Supreme Commander of the Armed Forces, and will be ready as a brave soldier to risk my life at any time for this oath.*

4. IMPERIALISM

One part of Hitler's Nazi ideology was to show the German population the need to control its own resources. The fact that Germans felt out of control was an important ingredient in Hitler's ideology. Following the re-occupation of the Rhineland in 1935, Hitler began to re-arm Germany and conscript troops. Hitler warned the German people that, without a struggle, they would be squeezed out of history. Hitler stated: "We National Socialists want to love our Fatherland and learn to love it alone, and to tolerate no other idols beside it!"

The ideas that shaped the structure of Nazi philosophy were put into practice in politics and economics that dominated Europe from 1933-1945. Hitler's hope was to make Germany safe for Germans alone and to begin the spread of the Aryan race across the face of Europe. At the same time, Hitler emphasized Germany's need for territorial expansion and the threat of outsiders. The fear of extinction encouraged the German population to commit themselves to Hitler's vision for the German state. Hitler's actions have become a lesson in how fascist totalitarianism can work.

The German people provided the dedication and commitment to the regime's programs because they were convinced by Hitler's re-education, propaganda, and disinformation. Hitler's actions show a key difference between totalitarian regimes and traditional dictatorships. Traditional dictatorships rely more on force to constrain the population than do totalitarian regimes.

Hitler's unique interpretation of human history and the ideal nature of social organization was not a rational or logical theory. Hitler said this himself. He also understood the human will better than many other twentieth-century leaders. He knew that people could believe whatever they wanted to believe. Hitler was able to justify almost any policy based on his view of history and human nature.

Hitler's ideology was important to the development of his political policies. Nazism was a political system created by the elite that surrounded Hitler. However, it was Hitler's personal appeal and his series of quick political successes that drew the support of so many people.

Hitler's Charisma

Charisma is the ability of a political leader to develop devotion and unquestioning support from followers. Max Weber, who lived in Germany (1864-1920), was a sociologist and political economist. He studied leadership in different societies, and believed that charisma was a powerful form of authority that differs from other forms of authority based on tradition, law, or the democratic ideal of consensus and compromise. Charisma is especially important in dictatorships because it places the ideas of the leader above all other forms of authority.

The effects of charisma can be seen in any social system. Rock musicians or movie stars often develop a loyal following. However, their appeal is in a small area of human activity. A "Wayne Gretzky for Prime Minister" campaign might be fun, but it would gain little serious momentum. When political leaders gather charismatic support they also gain authority. At first, Hitler did not have the political support of the majority, but his charisma allowed him to manipulate the unstable republic and gain power.

The PEEK box model demonstrates how a variety of elements came together to create Nazism. Hitler's

PEEK	
AT NAZI GERMANY	
Politics	**Economics**
- security of the Nazi regime most important - use of force and indoctrination	- private enterprise with massive public works directed to achieve the goals of the regime
Environment	**Knowledge**
- Germany humiliated by defeat in WW I; French occupation of the Ruhr Valley in 1923 - stock market crash of 1929	- belief in Aryan superiority - nationalism - fear of internal and external enemies
Field of Action	
- a totalitarian regime that responded to economic and political challenges (e.g. the depression) through the use of force and indoctrination	

personal charisma was a key. Strong support for the ideas of an elite race, nationalism, and imperialism combined with economic problems and Hitler's personal charisma to launch him into power.

Hitler's dictatorial regime in Germany is seen by many as similar to the regimes in the Soviet Union, but such a view is short-sighted. Hitler came in quickly and left just as quickly. His elite gained and held power for a short time through violence, and lost power through the same violence. Historians also suggest that it was Hitler's charisma that led to his downfall.

Hitler came to believe he was beyond advice. He failed to listen to his advisors, and insisted on his personal interpretation of events even in the face of counter evidence. Eventually he lost control. History is full of examples of similar situations. Saddam Hussein's decision to invade Kuwait in August 1990, despite the advice of key people in his government, is an example of a leadership style based on charisma.

The Rise of Dictatorship in the Soviet Union

Vladimir Ilyich Lenin

The USSR is a vast country that occupies 11 time zones. Its geography matches its diverse history. The Soviet Union has undergone many historical changes. Some were violent, some were not. Recent changes in the Soviet government show how a ruling elite can attempt to make changes without resorting to violence.

Until the early twentieth century, the tsars attempted to repress the freedom of the people. In November 1917, the famous Russian Revolution took place. Vladimir Ilyich Lenin (1870-1924) led a coup d'état that overthrew tsar Nicholas II. The tsar's entire family and servants were executed and people loyal to the royal family were left without the symbols of the tsarist regime. Lenin led the Communist Party and it became the ruling elite in Russia. A one-party state was established. Land became the property of the state. Factories, banks, and railroads were **nationalized**.

Josef Vissarionovich Stalin

Lenin died in 1924, and a more repressive dictator, Josef Stalin (1879-1953) emerged as party leader. Stalin's grandfatherly looks were not matched by his

behaviour. Stalin purged or executed most of his military, cultural, and political rivals. Prison camps in Siberia were filled with men and women who disagreed with the government. To read about life in a Stalinist labour camp, you might look at books by the Nobel prize winner, Aleksandr Solzhenitsyn.

THE DICTATOR BUYS NEW BOOTS.

What is the point of view on dictatorships put forward in this cartoon?

Stalin led the Soviet Union through World War II. The war was devastating for the Soviet people. Although Hitler's attack was eventually repelled (with the help of the harsh Soviet winter), the German advance to Moscow left a path of misery and starvation which the Soviets remember to this day.

When World War II ended, the Soviet Union helped form Communist governments throughout Eastern Europe. It set up a large zone of occupation, formally constructed under the Warsaw Pact in 1955, in response to the alliances formed by NATO. After Stalin died, other Communist leaders ruled over the Soviet Union with unequal success. One large problem the Soviets faced was **economic stagnation.** Successive agricultural failures and problems in efficiency and management have plagued the Soviets for decades. In chapter 11, you will read more about the Soviet Union.

The Decline of Totalitarian Dictatorship in the USSR

In 1985, Mikhail Gorbachev came to power. Gorbachev is different from previous Soviet leaders. He is younger, travels widely, and is more open to change. Gorbachev exemplifies a new generation of Soviet politicians. Reforms in the Soviet Union drastically altered relations between the Soviet Union and the world. Two of these changes are called **glasnost** and **perestroika.**

Radical changes occurred in the Soviet Union in the late 1980s and early 1990s, many of them encouraged by Mikhail Gorbachev.

Glasnost

In the late 1980s, a new openness appeared under the rule of Gorbachev. Glasnost means openness. It allowed citizens more freedom to participate in politics, culture, religion, and business, and to affect changes in their own lives. People were granted a greater voice in choosing government representatives. Political changes have allowed for more than one candidate to run for elective office. Previously, Soviet citizens could vote, but there was little or no choice at the ballot box.

Now, Soviets can criticize the government without retribution. Journalists have more freedom to report events at home and abroad. And, if they can afford it, Soviet citizens are now able to travel to other parts of the world. These freedoms are new to the Soviet people.

This cartoon is fairly typical of the attitude of many people inside the USSR and abroad to political and economic changes in the Soviet Union. What conclusions might you draw about the relative importance of politics and economics to humans?

Perestroika

Perestroika means a reorganization that changes the existing system. Perestroika was another accommodation of the wishes of the Soviet people. Perestroika responded to traditional problems of the Soviet economy like the lack of technological progress, production costs, poor quality and limited supply of products, and worker indifference. In an attempt to make the economy more efficient, the Soviet government listened to the demands of consumers. People were now able to sell goods at a profit and had more personal freedom to operate businesses. Consumers looked forward to more quantity and quality.

Perestroika intends to restructure the Soviet economy without changing the central ideas of the socialist approach, like public ownership of production and the belief that people should not become rich by taking advantage of others. Perestroika is seen as a way to break down the cycle of stagnation in all walks of life.

While holding fast to some of the tenets of socialism, Gorbachev called for recognition of consumer needs, less state interference in business, and economic reform. These reforms promise to replace the traditional form of the Soviet command economy with a more open, supply and demand economic structure. The hope is that perestroika will increase the Soviet standard of living and provide greater opportunities to develop and apply personal skills in all areas of life in the USSR. Specific goals of the reforms are to provide every family with a home or apartment, increase incomes, and improve health and education levels.

Without a change of the ruling elite in the Soviet Union through revolution, sweeping changes still took place. The Gorbachev government saw its main job as building trust between the government and the people. If perestroika fails then socialism will also fail, the government believed. Changes within the Soviet Union hold great interest for observers in the West. The effects of Gorbachev's charisma reached across the East-West barrier: in the late 1980s, Gorbachev was more popular in many Western countries than "local" presidents and prime ministers!

Regardless of his personal charisma, Gorbachev's success has always rested on the ability of the Soviet economy to improve itself. It if improves, the Soviets will have an economy and a political life more like those of us in the West. The promise of change raises an important question: if the Soviet Union becomes more Western in economy and politics, can it retain the organizing principles of socialism? Can democratic-style economics and politics succeed only by rejecting the basic ideas of the socialist system? Time will tell.

Life under the Ceausescus in Romania

Nicolae Ceausescu came to power in Romania in 1965. He and his wife Elena led one of the most corrupt and hated regimes in Eastern Europe for 25 years. Romania was supposedly a one-party state led by the Romanian Communist Party. The actual rulers were a small elite group, a regime consisting mostly of Ceausescu family members.

Elena and Nicolae

When Elena and Nicolae Ceausescu were executed on Christmas Day 1989, it is estimated they had accumulated more than $1 billion worth of property and spoils from the Romanian people. They owned 40 homes. The main residence, Primavera, was lavishly decorated with gold-plating. Even the towel racks

This Muscovite family can now enjoy a Big Mac and a milkshake. Some say the influx of Western commercialism throughout the world is not necessarily a good thing. What do you think?

and toilet paper holders were gold-plated. Elena owned 40 fur coats and 2000 gowns.

Elena Ceausescu considered herself both an intellectual and an accomplished scientist. She never got past grade four, but that did not hinder her academic career. It is now believed that her doctoral work was completed by others hired to promote her image. Chemical compounds were named after her because it was claimed she discovered them. A former chief of intelligence in Romania doubts that Elena had the ability to read a newspaper.

Elena promoted herself at home and abroad. The international community accepted her. Elena was awarded 72 honorary degrees by universities at home and abroad. She was awarded an honorary membership in the British Royal Institute of Chemistry in a diplomatic move to improve relations between Britain and Romania.

Why did the Ceausescus have so much power and influence in Romania and internationally? The Ceausescus appeared to be good allies for the West. After World War II, Romania managed to steer a relatively independent course from the Soviet Union. Although a communist, Nicolae Ceausescu was seen by American diplomats as "Our Man in the Eastern Bloc."

Friendship and diplomatic support from Western countries was one of the biggest contributing factors for the success of the Ceausescu regime, according to the former king of Romania, Michael. He said, "They gave him too many honours and too much prestige . . . For 40 years I've tried to explain what was going on. No one wanted to listen."

This was the skill and charisma of the Ceausescus. A tyrant at home, Nicolae made speeches abroad about cutting arms expenditures globally and forgiving the debts of poor countries. The West was concerned about the influence the Soviets. Ceausescu was seen as an effective buffer against Soviet influence in the Eastern bloc; countries like the US and Canada had extensive links with the Romanian dictatorship.

The career of Nicolae Ceausescu helps us understand how dictators achieve, maintain, and abuse power. Ceausescu was the son of peasants and one of 10 children. He was a shoemaker's apprentice after leaving elementary school. Jailed because of anti-Nazi activities in 1936, he was released in 1944 when the Soviets took control over Romania after Hitler's defeat. One of about 800 members of the Communist Party in Romania, Nicolae had risen in status to become secretary general of the Union of Communist Youth. This was an important position from which to launch a political career. In 1947 opposition parties were dissolved, and the country became a one-party state.

Party positions became sources of great privilege. Housing, furniture, the best groceries, and domestic servants were provided to the party elite, called the *nomenklature*. The party met to endorse the policies of the small elite with which Ceausescu surrounded himself. Throughout the last years of the regime, Elena remained very involved in the Communist Party—no one could discuss policies without her approval.

The Regime

The power of the Romanian regime had few limits. One in three citizens was a secret police agent at one time or another. Strikes and protests were brutally crushed. People did not have friends outside of family members—they could not trust each other. An Antitotalitarian Forum was organized to protest government policies: only three families joined. People lived in poverty and fear.

A ROMANIAN CITIZEN SPEAKS OUT

As you read the following excerpt from the *Globe and Mail*, consider this question: according to Nicola Leon, how did Nicolae Ceausescu regulate personal lifestyles and freedoms?

Mr. Leon is a 34-year-old mechanical engineer living in Bucharest. The following is taken from an open letter to Romanian leader Nicolae Ceausescu. It was published five days before the Ceausescus were executed.

Mr. President, you do not represent either the will of the people in the name of which you speak or that of the (Communist) Party. The millions of party members, people who became members for an advantage or out of obligation, do not establish the policy of the party. They are ordinary citizens who, like everyone else, cannot criticize the policy you implement in their names because all these millions are only string puppets in your hands.

They do not even have the courage to defend their own families, they do nothing to ensure for their children a better future; on the contrary, through their silence they contribute to the further destruction of the country and the Romanian people.

I know quite well that all these party members have a double personality, that during free discussions with their families or friends they all criticize your policy and the methods you use, and that they are all dissatisfied with the way in which you lead the country.

Now the country has reached the end of its tether; people are impoverished, at a loss, hungry and in need. Our parents were told that they were the sacrifice generation, that they should sacrifice themselves so that we could live better, but our life is much worse than theirs, and our children's even worse than ours.

The old regime had educated people who knew that the struggle between opposites is the motor of development, and that is why it permitted the existence of several political parties. Why don't you permit the existence of opposites in our country as well? Don't you wish Romania to develop and become one of the civilized countries? Do you think that you have the monopoly of absolute truth?

Bribery and intimidation were used even within the party. Elena had the bedrooms of high party officials bugged with microphones and used an extensive collection of bedroom tapes for blackmail. In the dying years of the regime Elena and Nicolae ousted more than 40 high ranking officials and replaced them with family members. The use of coercion and repression was so widespread that in the end, the party became a victim of its own policies.

The social and economic policies of the Ceausescu regime were largely ineffective. Economic reforms that included collectivization of agriculture achieved the goal of depopulating rural areas and increasing urban growth. In 1960, 65 per cent of the work force was in agriculture. In 1985, this was down to 29 per cent. Five year plans to achieve 34 per cent growth rates between 1986 and 1990 failed.

In 1986 one reporter described life in Romania as a result of the Communist Party's reforms: "the country's 23 million people lived like cold, starving beggars . . . . Private cars were banned due to a fuel shortage. Streetlights were kept off because of an energy shortage. People hurried home to unheated, unlit apartments. The last showing at cinemas was at 5:00 PM, and television ran for only two hours a night." This was in a country that is rich in minerals and agricultural potential!

Obsessed with paying Romania's foreign debt, Ceausescu funnelled off income from sales of agricultural products and petrochemicals. Food and heating fuel were rationed, but the Ceausescus lived in luxury.

In 1982 the Program of Scientific Nourishment was started. This involved allocating food to segments of the population based on the calories they would consume doing their respective jobs. In other words, caloric consumption was decreed by the state! One result of this policy was that in 1989 many 10 year old children had never seen a banana or an orange. These foods were not allocated to this part of the population.

Another policy was the population development plan. The regime stated that economic growth depended on a growing population. Its plan was to grow from 22 million to 30 million people by the year 2000. Abortions were outlawed. Security police investigated every miscarriage. They carefully monitored pregnant women; they followed them and tapped their phones. No aspect of their life was unexamined if they were suspected of considering an abortion.

The Ceausescus offered the babies of single mothers for adoption as a business venture. Newborns were given blood transfusions to stimulate their growth. Sometimes this blood was contaminated with the Aids virus. It gave the newborns a death sentence. Despite advice that this plan was destroying the fabric of Romanian society, Elena insisted the Ministry of Health continue the "pro-family" policy.

PEEK	
AT ROMANIA	
Politics	**Economics**
- security of the Ceausescu regime paramount - use of force, intimidation, and bribery	- five year plans - collectivization of agriculture - increase of urban growth - program of "Scientific Nourishment"
Environment	**Knowledge**
- friendship and support from Western countries (e.g. US and Canada)	- "truth" as determined by the elite (e.g. program of paying off foreign debt, no matter what the consequences)
Field of Action	
- a dictatorship that relied on brute force and a complex web of corruption to maintain its power	

December 1989

By December 1989, the Ceausescus became the victims of their own delusions. They had isolated themselves even from the support of their own party apparatus. When the population faced severe food shortages and ethnic unrest, protests spread quickly. Army units joined the protesters, and the Ceausescus tried to flee. They were captured and executed. Just days after their deaths, all posters, signs, or public reminders of their existence had disappeared. The Ceausescu era ended.

Living with Apartheid in South Africa

South Africa is an example of a country which is hard to categorize. South Africa has been a dictatorship where roughly one-fifth of the population (white people) have dominated and controlled the society. It has been a blend of one-party and military dictatorships. Apartheid, or the segregation of racial groups, was first instituted in South Africa in 1948.

Apartheid in South Africa meant more than racial segregation. Blacks were restricted in many ways. They could vote only for people of their own racial group. Black government leaders had very limited powers. Blacks could not vote in national elections. They were permitted in ''white South Africa'' only to work. These are but a few examples of the restrictions which were faced by the majority of South Africans.

The Land Act of 1913 gave 18 per cent of the population control of 87 per cent of South Africa. The remainder was left as homelands for the Black population. From 1948 to 1990 the policy of apartheid was officially endorsed and defended by the white-dominated government. In 1961, South Africa withdrew from the Commonwealth, an association of countries formerly under British rule. The country became the Republic of South Africa. The new parliament had three chambers: one each for whites, coloureds, and Asians. The four provinces and ten homelands have vastly different standards of living. Inequality has led to many difficulties.

PEEK
AT SOUTH AFRICA

Politics	Economics
- security of racial minority promoted - three chamber parliament and homelands help constrain non-white population	- great inequality of wealth - a country with vast wealth - trade increasingly difficult after sanctions imposed

Environment	Knowledge
- international pressure to abolish apartheid mounts very slowly	- racial inequality accepted as ''natural'' - belief that apartheid prevents social chaos - attitudes changing

Field of Action
- a ''one-party'' state (several white-controlled parties working together) to protect the interests of a racial minority

The distribution of the resources in South Africa is unequal. In 1984, for example, the average monthly income for Black Africans was 273 rands (South African currency) and for whites it was 1834. Black Africans held only 1.6 per cent of managerial jobs while whites held 94.6 per cent of these positions. The ratio of students to teachers was 407.7 to 1 for Black Africans, and 18.9 to 1 for white Africans.

CASE STUDY:

THE YOUTH OF SOUTH AFRICA

Adapted from an interview which appeared in the New Internationalist, *May 1986.*

The people who live in dictatorships are a lot like you. They go to school, they have friends, they have plans for the future. Think about this while you read the Case Study about two South African students.

Julia Molokwane (15) is at Thomas Mofolo Secondary School in Soweto. Her mother is a domestic servant and only comes home occasionally. Julia lives with her father and she has the responsibility of running the house. She has to clean the house, shop for groceries and cook and do the family washing.

"I wish all these troubles would come to an end. We would all like to go to school and carry on with our lives in a normal way.

"But how do we go to school when the army is there arresting us and accusing us of being trouble makers? If there is a meeting to discuss student grievances like corporal punishment and crowded classrooms and lack of proper facilities they say we are instigators and take us to jail.

"Now that we are not in school a lot of things are going wrong. Young children are going to she-beens and becoming drunkards. It is because of boredom. There is nothing else to do except housework and going to church.

"Most young people do not believe in the church because it does not address itself to the problems of the people. They tell us fairy tales. If this is a Christian country why do they send the army to kill babies?"

Lehlohonolo Mokoena is a 19-year-old student at Thomas Mofolo Secondary School. He comes from a family of five. His parents and brothers are factory workers. He has not made up his mind what job he would like to do when he leaves school, but he wants a well-paid one.

"There is no way we can avoid violence. The police and the army who are in the townships are violent. You can get arrested for just walking in the street. You can get shot too.

"The Government makes us pay high rents and general sales tax so that they can buy arms for the army to kill us. What are we supposed to do? Just stand there and look? Even when we are at school we are not safe. The army comes in and whips us and bundles us into vans.

"There will be no end to violence in the townships until the army is removed. Only when this violent Government is removed will violence end."

QUESTIONS:

1. What is the nature of the dictatorship that exists in South Africa?
2. How does living in a dictatorship affect these two young people? Create a sample PEEK box for these young people.
3. In what ways does living as a citizen in a democracy compare with living as a citizen in a dictatorship? Make a list of five important differences. Are there any similarities? What are they?

It is not easy to control large populations unless physical force is used. During a major riot in 1976 more than 600 people were killed in Soweto. Since then, scenes of violence between young people and the police have frequently filled the world's television screens. Forbidding demonstrations, speeches, and political organizations is a common practice of all dictatorships—one-party, military, and totalitarian. In 1991, the South African government surprised the world by announcing the end of apartheid. One reason may be that police are less able to contain demonstrations that surround each new burial of a victim of police violence. Perhaps Bishop Tutu was a prophet when he remarked that the young people of South Africa did no longer fear death. He said, ''They all think they are going to die.''

Apartheid Slowly Failing

In 1986 a state of emergency was declared that gave great power to the police. Until the resignation of P.W. Botha in 1988, there were few changes in the regime. In 1989 F.W. de Klerk assumed office, with a promise to ease the worst effects of apartheid.

Many feel that it is only a matter of time before the South African regime collapses under the tremendous internal pressure for change. In spite of personal danger, 2 million Black workers staged a nation-wide strike in June 1988. Increasingly South Africa has been under the scrutiny of the international community. Since the 1986 state of emergency Western nations have increased pressure to abolish apartheid. Most, including Canada, supported a trade embargo that has caused great economic hardships to the white community and caused political embarrassment to the regime. The government is learning a hard lesson: that nations cannot hope to be immune to the influences of the global political environment.

President P.W. Botha's resignation, the release of African National Congress leader Nelson Mandela, and the commitment to change within and outside the country are significant signs of hope that the abolition of apartheid will be successful. In February 1991, F.W. de Klerk's government introduced legislation that will end some of the worst aspects of apartheid. Although the Black population is still barred from voting, when the legislation was introduced, a brutal backlash from many white people resulted.

CASE STUDY:

THE ROLE OF THE CITIZEN SEEKING CHANGE

As you read this Case Study, think about how events on the other side of the world affect us. What happens in Canada affects others, too. This is true in the environment, in economics, and in politics.

What is happening in South Africa is an example of international interaction. Canada has played a role in supporting the struggle for justice there. Canadians have participated in the politics and economics of South Africa without leaving Canada.

How?

AWARENESS was the first step. Trying to understand the one-party system, learning about the economics, and listening to leaders such as Steve Biko, Desmond Tutu, and Winnie Mandela.

SANCTIONS were instituted first at the grass roots level, and later by the Canadian government in the form of boycotting **consumer goods**. These products included fruit, diamonds, and wine.

continued

CASE STUDY continued

DIVESTMENT was another form of pressure to change the apartheid laws. Canadians refused to deal with banks and companies that loaned money to South Africa, or had business dealings with companies there.

SUPPORT for the fight against apartheid included sending money, sponsoring speaking tours of South Africans, sponsoring students who came to study in Canada, publishing and buying books, plays, and music that told the story of the struggle.

QUESTIONS:
1. Which of these would be considered the most radical?
2. Which political pressures would be most likely taken by a supporter of economic measures?
3. Which of these actions involves global cooperation?

SUMMARY

In this chapter you have seen Nazi Germany, Leninist and Stalinist USSR, Romania, and South Africa, examples of different forms of dictatorships. The leaders of these countries were clever at understanding the way people react to power. Charisma, propaganda, psychological terror, and brutal physical violence are tools dictators use. You also know something about the events in these countries in the recent past. You have seen how these events were affected by politics, economics, environment, and knowledge.

Now that you are familiar with these and the structures discussed in previous chapters, you are ready to understand some economic structures. Chapter 7 begins with a basic introduction to economics.

GETTING ORGANIZED

1. In a dictatorship, two elements of leadership often seem to work together. These are charisma and the ability to gain and use power. Why do you think these two elements are so important to dictatorial leaders? Can you identify examples of these elements in current world leaders?

2. Review the brief outlines about Nazi Germany, the Soviet Union, Romania, and South Africa. Using the information in the text, list some hypotheses about the environment that would encourage the growth of dictatorships.

3. South Africa is currently undergoing political changes. The system of apartheid is breaking down. What changes have taken place since this book was written?

4. How is a country best led? If you were to ask people which they thought was more important—a powerful leader or a strong constitution—you might be surprised at the answers. Design a questionnaire and survey a dozen people. Study your results. What generalizations can you make from the answers?

5. In North America, we have a strong tradition of democracy. Visualize what might happen if a dictator came to power. How would it impact you? What environmental changes in Canada would have to occur for a dictator to come to power?

6. In chapters 3, 4, 5, and 6, you have studied both democracies and dictatorships. In what ways does leadership in democracies compare with leadership in authoritarian states?

REACHING OUT

1. Amnesty International has worked tirelessly to expose the violations of human rights in modern dictatorships around the world. Amnesty is a network of volunteers that writes letters to raise awareness and pressure governments to stop repression. It includes citizens from all walks of life: doctors, students, workers, and business people. Amnesty provides updates on human rights violations and information of value to all students of international politics. Write to Amnesty for more information.
Contact:
Amnesty International,
Suite 900, 130 Slater Street,
Ottawa, Ontario
K1P 6E2

2. Dictatorships, like democracies, have a common set of political practices. Listed below are political practices that dictatorships share. Identify one or two examples of these in action. Use one example from the text and one from current events.
   (a) controlled elections
   (b) an imbalance in the influence of interest groups
   (c) use of force (physical and psychological)
   (d) regulated media with limited access to information
   (e) repression of minorities
   Give your chart a title. Use photos and clippings from the newspapers to illustrate these practices in action.

3. Human rights organizations have catalogued countries that violate human rights and extensively practice the five elements common to dictatorships which we have listed in question 2. Some of those countries are Angola, Burma, Ethiopia, North Korea, and China. Develop a research plan to study these countries by examining the following questions:
   (a) What background questions need to be answered in order to get an understanding of how dictatorship emerged?
   (b) Where might I get information on these countries?
   (c) What are the likely patterns I might find in terms of the political practices of those dictatorships?
   (d) What form could the final research take—oral, written, visual, or other?

Chapter Seven:

WHAT IS ECONOMICS?

GETTING IT STRAIGHT

1. What is economics?
2. How are economic decisions made?
3. What is scarcity?
4. What are the three factors of production?
5. What is the difference between needs and wants?
6. How do people make economic choices?
7. How do countries make economic choices?
8. What is a global economy?

Economics is the study of how people and societies use their resources to meet needs and desires. We all know something about it. Since childhood you have made economic decisions. For example, you have experienced the frustration of window shopping and seeing millions of things you want, but not having enough money to buy them.

As young children, you wished your parents would buy everything you wanted. Sometimes you were angry when they didn't. When they did buy you things, they probably gave you little choice about what you received. If your parents were like most, they bought what they thought was best for you, using the resources they had.

When you were older, you started to buy things by yourself. You had the opportunity to choose, on your own, an ice cream bar or a fudgesicle from the youths peddling their product in your neighbourhood. To young children, these are big purchases. To make sure you had enough, you double-checked the price and re-counted your money. Finally, you bought your product and consumed it on the spot.

These early economic decisions seem like small potatoes now. As we grow, our needs and desire for funds grow, too.

Your economic education probably developed slowly. As you grew older you realized your parents had to budget their resources. There was a finite amount of money to buy what was used in your household. In your teens, you probably started to branch out economically. Maybe you got a part-time job and started to make your own economic decisions. Choosing what goods and services to buy and how to get the money to buy them is the way we all participate in economics.

What are Production and Consumption?

Although you didn't know it when you were growing up, the things you wanted to purchase came in two economic categories: goods and services. Goods are products like designer jeans, sports cars, and food. Services are things that people do for you, like car repairs, hair cuts, or ski lessons.

You probably learned there was never enough money to get everything that you wanted. Even with a part-time job, there were goods and services you did without. You had to make economic choices. Most of your income probably went to purchasing things you thought you really needed, like gas for the car or a

winter jacket. Maybe you decided against buying a CD player. You experienced the economic concept called **scarcity**. Economics is the study of how people resolve the problem of scarcity.

Some of you may be already living on your own. Sooner or later, the rest of you will be forced to make your own economic decisions, with no help from other adults. When you leave home, the first part of your income will buy food and housing. The remainder of your income will buy clothing, transportation, and incidentals.

These teenagers in Japan study well-stocked shelves before making an economic decision. A variety of choice affects consumers making economic decisions.

Needs are both real and imagined. Advertising convinces us that many goods and services are essential. Can you name some examples? You must set priorities and decide what you want most. What you consider less important will be purchased later, or forgotten. These decisions are a natural part of the economic system in which we live. Every Canadian is the same. We make economic choices about what to do with our resources (our money). In an economic sense, Canadians are fortunate to have many choices and great variety from which to choose. Almost like a political election, money allows us to choose from among a wide spectrum of candidates, or goods and services. We elect the goods and services we want by voting with our dollars. Each dollar is a vote, and we cast these economic votes every day.

Economic Choices

For wealthy people, choices about what to consume are almost endless. Any giant shopping mall in any large Canadian city is an example of some of the choices that exist. New products and services are invented every day. Where do these ideas for products and services come from?

With all the choices available, have you ever wondered why certain products are in the stores and other products are not? How are decisions made that bring these products to market in the first place? They aren't there by accident. Companies promote certain goods rather than others. There is more profit to be made in processed food than in unprocessed food, for example. As a result, most advertising dollars promote processed products.

Individuals in our society can choose from a wide variety of goods and services. We can also choose where we will sell our own skills. Some individuals and societies are not so fortunate. They have few choices, especially in buying goods or services. Many also have few choices when selling their own skills or services. In these societies the choices are often made for the

CASE STUDY:
HOW DO YOU MAKE AN ECONOMIC CHOICE?

What criteria do you use to make a consumer choice? In this Case Study, you will explore this important question.

Do you think consciously about your choices every time you face the store shelves? Producers, advertisers, and store managers do.

You want to buy something that you need. On a sheet of paper, list a few things you think you need to buy. Next list the choices that you have. Consider quality, price, and style. Try to list at least five criteria. Write how you expect to choose. If there is a relationship between price and quality, will you choose higher quality and the higher price, or will you choose lower quality and the lower price?

QUESTIONS:

1. Consider two of the most important consumer choices you have made in the past year. Is there a pattern in your own choices?
2. Do you have enough money to buy everything on the list? Which will you buy first? Which will you leave until later?
3. Are you guided by a consumer ideology? If so, what is it?
4. Can you make a generalization about your consumer ideology?
5. Create a 30-second radio commercial that uses the generalization you have listed in question 4 in a way that might convince you to purchase a product you want. Would you find it hard to resist your own sales pitch? Why or why not?

individual by a government agency. This agency acts in much the same way your parents did for you when you were younger. The choices they provide to the people are usually much less than what we have in Canada.

Economic Resources

Anything that is used in the production of goods and services can be classified as a resource. Traditionally, there are three categories: **land**, **labour**, and **capital**.

These construction workers may have chosen this field of work because it pays well or for the satisfaction it gives them. Our society permits us many career choices.

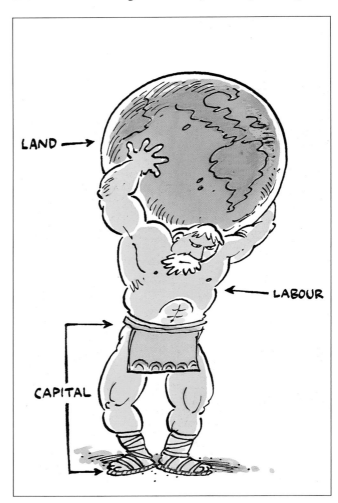

Land, labour, and capital are the ingredients of production. How does this cartoon differ from the cartoons you have seen previously in the book?

Land includes all the natural resources used in the production of goods and services. Some examples of land resources are mineral deposits, water, fish, farm land, wildlife, forests, and areas available for building houses.

Labour includes all human resources, which means any work done by humans. It includes the physical work done by labourers on oil rigs or in mines. It includes posing for Sunshine Girl or Sunshine Boy photos that appear in newspapers, and the work of the photographer. It also includes the work of your teachers when they grade your tests on this unit of social studies. It includes your work at McDonald's restaurant and the mental and paper work done by professionals such as petroleum engineers and company presidents. It includes the knowledge you have which affects your ability to get a job.

Capital includes all the money, equipment, and inventory used in production. It includes the money used to purchase goods and services to start a business. It includes all the machines that make products, as well as the buildings in which that machinery is housed. It includes new high tech equipment that may make our jobs easier, or may even replace us. It also includes inventory such as furniture, light bulbs, twinkies, or the supplies that oil companies have on hand to sell to gas stations. It includes the pencils, papers, and computers used by a business to track sales. Capital even includes the free coffee your real estate agent serves as you look for a place to live.

When General Motors developed their new Saturn car, they used a computer to help them. They spent $5 billion to develop the design and set up an assembly line. Of this $5 billion, $2 billion was spent on computers and software. They needed people with computer skills (labour) and computers (capital) to help get the job done.

The computer, adding machine, and office supplies shown here are all capital. Examine the capital of a business with which you are familiar.

Land, labour, and capital are the ingredients of production. If you discover oil on your farm (and own the mineral rights), you may start a company to enable you to market it. You will require the services of many people: bankers, outfitters, rig workers, office personnel, and so on. You will require many goods, too, everything from a derrick to a desk. Your success will be influenced by whether or not all your neighbours have done the same thing. In the same way, the structure of a nation's production and consumption is influenced by the physical environment and the international situation.

Scarcity

Because our resources are always limited (scarce) in some way, we must learn to make economic choices. We are constantly trying to solve a basic problem: to get what we don't have. This means that we have a scarcity, or an inadequate supply, of capital to fulfill

CASE STUDY:

YOUR OWN BUSINESS?

In this Case Study, you will find some of the questions you will need to ask if you decide to set up your own business.

Rather than work for an established business, many students begin their own. Successful companies include t-shirt companies, baby-sitting services, music D.J. services, and odd job companies that provide painting, yard work, or cleaning services.

You may wish to interview an entrepreneur or invite a young business person to speak to your class. Some questions you might ask include:

QUESTIONS

1. What are the biggest problems in dealing with the labour component of your business? Do you have a staff?
2. Business people often have good ideas but lack the capital to make these ideas reality. Where do you start?
3. What have you learned that you regret not knowing when you first started?
4. What is the best thing about owning your own business?

our wants. Some people argue that, even with tremendous resources, those with money still want more. Wants seem to be unlimited for many people.

Scarcity can exist even if there is enough for everyone. World famine is an example. According to experts on food production, the problem is not the quantity of food available, but rather the distribution of food. There is more than enough grain and other food to provide all humans on earth with their nutritional requirements. A large part of the problem of scarcity is that the rich industrial nations hoard food. It takes four or five kilograms of grain to produce a half kilogram of hamburger. In order to conserve grain, are you willing to stop eating at your local hamburger joint?

Scarcity also relates to production. Our desire for goods and services is greater than the resources available to meet these desires. This is true both on an individual and on a societal level. Governments decide how to use available resources to meet the needs and

wants of society. In the same way you or your parents decide how to use your resources to meet the needs and wants of your family. It doesn't matter whether it is you, your parents, a business, or a government. Decisions about the best way to use scarce resources are similar for all levels of society.

The Differences between Needs and Wants

How do we know the difference between our needs and our wants? Needs are the basic things we must have to survive from day to day. They include food and protection from the elements (shelter and clothing). Fulfilling these basic needs helps us stay alive.

They are the minimally acceptable requirements to sustain our lives until tomorrow.

Wants are our desires which we think will make our lives easier or happier. After we obtain food, shelter, and clothing, we extend our wants. We start to make choices based on criteria other than just staying alive. If you are like most Canadians, you may have a variety of clothing, some seldom worn, just to stay in fashion. You might want to go home tonight and count how many pairs of shoes and boots there are in your home. What is the average per family member?

Choices to satisfy personal desires are made not only by young people. Adults may decide to buy a newer, bigger home even though their children will soon leave and they no longer need the space. They may choose to buy a new car although the old one is not broken. Wants also include Hawaiian holidays at Christmas break, or a sports car to drive to school. We can all live without fulfilling these wants and it would make little difference in our lives. Still, many of us strive to attain them. Why? Because we live in a society that believes in obtaining material goods.

In our society, some wants have become so common that we believe they are needs. Many of us think of cars, telephones, flush toilets, radios, and refrigerators as needs. Most of us have grown accustomed to the quality of life these conveniences bring us and would find living without them troublesome.

As we fulfill these desires we come to expect a certain standard of living. Our standard of living includes all the comforts of life we enjoy. We buy things because we think they make our lives easier. Our society's structure of knowledge tends to promote a belief in convenience and material happiness. In some societies a government agency may decide what the citizens should have, actually deciding needs and wants for individuals.

HOW DO YOU SPEND A DOLLAR?

Assume you have a part-time job and work 25 hours per week at minimum wage. (If you actually do have a part-time job, use your real income.)

List the goods and services you want to buy. Put them in order of priority. If you are saving for something, be sure to include savings on your list.

Divide your list into needs and wants.

1. Are your needs at the top of your list?

2. Are your needs actually needs, or just things that are so common to you that you believe they are needs?

3. Would your list change if the scarcity of your personal resources (money) changed? If you were able to get a better paying job, or you won some money, or you were given a large inheritance, how would your list be different?

There are different definitions of "needs" and "wants." This marketplace in China illustrates that our "need" to shop at a large grocery store with a multitude of different products might be considered a "want" in some other cultures.

The Economy and the Environment

No economic system exists in isolation. Each is influenced by complex factors, many which are out of the control of individuals. In non-industrialized countries economic choices are limited and human energy is focused on obtaining the necessities of life.

The wealth of a nation usually depends upon the resources available and how these resources are used to create wealth. The difference between an industrialized country and a non-industrialized country may simply be the luck of the draw. One country might have a huge deposit of oil; the other may not. The structure of the environment deeply influences the structure of the economy.

TRADING PARTNERS

When one country has a scarcity of one resource, but an abundance of another, it trades for the scarce resource.

Some countries have few natural resources but a large supply of cheap labour. Our economies are global in nature, with one country depending on another for certain resources. One example is Iraq selling oil to countries that don't have enough. In return, Iraq bought high tech equipment and military goods.

Some countries allow their corporations to establish factories in other nations to help ensure a steady supply of the resource they need.

Take a look at where your clothes or other personal possessions are made. Why do you think they were made there?

Give other examples of our global economy.

Making an Economic Decision

There is no such thing as a purely economic decision. One choice is usually made at the expense of another. This is true both for families and societies. For example, when your parents were deciding whether to fix the old car or buy a new one, they may have decided to fix the old one because they wanted to take the family on a winter holiday. Buying a new car might have been their first choice, but the rest of the family wanted to go on the winter vacation.

When your family makes choices, you ask yourselves a basic economic question: Who should make economic decisions? Should one person decide alone, or should that person consider others' desires? The choices and decisions we make are about scarcity of resources. However, they are also about power and the society's beliefs.

You may make such decisions for yourself, like deciding to buy a designer leather jacket instead of going skiing with your friends. Or, you may skip buying the jacket so you have more money to buy a special outfit for graduation. People make different choices because they have different priorities. Each person satisfies wants in a unique way.

If you oppose killing animals, you will choose not to wear leather. Perhaps you might choose to buy a less expensive coat and send the money saved to help people in the Third World. The choices we make every day become patterns of beliefs. These patterns become lifestyles. Lifestyles become structures of thinking.

Economic Decisions of Businesses, Communities, and Countries

There are many levels at which economic choices are made. Some are ethical choices, but many are simply practical. A business executive must decide how much to pay full- and part-time employees and how many workers are needed to serve customers, while still making a profit. Is it more profitable to hire one full-time or two part-time employees? How will the difference between part-time and full-time workers affect service, staffing requirements, and paid benefits? Will a business lose customers if it doesn't have the staff to provide a particular service?

Each community must also decide how to spend its resources. Should it build a new school or improve roads? Parents might want a new school. Those without children might want a golf course. The decision made, and who decides, is as much about political power as it is about economics.

Countries must also decide how to use available resources in their respective environments. Do they provide resources to all citizens, or do they require that individuals purchase their own resources? Do they determine what goods and services are produced or do members of society decide?

Since different people and societies want different things, and because wants are greater than available resources, every society's economic system makes decisions about production. Although the choices are different, every economic system works to answer three basic questions. The answers to these questions are the organizing principles governments employ to decide how to use economic resources and how to organize their system. The basic concerns for all economies are production, consumption, and distribution.

The three basic economic questions each society addresses are:

1. What goods and services should be produced? (production-consumption)
2. How will these goods and services be produced? (production)
3. Who should decide how goods and services are distributed or allocated? (consumption and distribution)

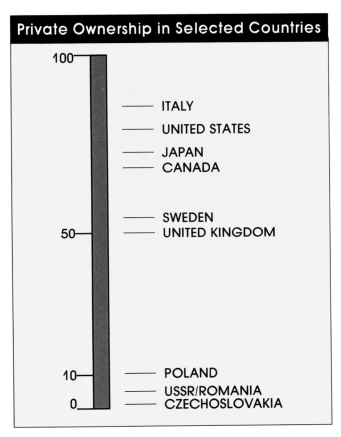

Private Ownership in Selected Countries

- 100 —
- ITALY
- UNITED STATES
- JAPAN
- CANADA
- SWEDEN
- 50 — UNITED KINGDOM
- POLAND
- 10 — USSR/ROMANIA
- 0 — CZECHOSLOVAKIA

As this chart shows, the percentages of private ownership or investment in the world's economies in 1990 varied tremendously. No economy had total government ownership or investment. Czechoslovakia came closest of those sampled. Interestingly, the United States, thought to be the home of free enterprise, had less private investment than Italy.

Societies answer these questions by considering their political ideologies, resources, and structures of knowledge. Individuals in some societies have a large part in the decision-making process. In other societies, economic experts decide how citizens will benefit from the system. All societies, regardless of their political ideology, face one over-riding political and economic problem. They must deal with problems of scarcity in relation to human needs and wants. Although this concern is mainly economical, factors that help address it come from all four sides of the PEEK box.

SUMMARY

As you learned in chapter 1, all humans, alone or in groups, take part in political and economic life. The chapters that follow continue with the focus on economic elements that shape the structure of production and consumption.

Economic questions are also political questions. Can humans survive? Can we ensure our own basic needs? As we have discussed, when individuals can take care of their own basic needs, the desire to satisfy wants begins to surface. This process is almost universal. Humans can satisfy their needs and remain unsatisfied.

In this text, we have emphasized several universal points. Needs and wants fall into two economic categories: goods and services. The attainment of these goods and services raises the standard of living in a society. But here lies the economic problem. Usually, there aren't enough goods and services for everyone. Economic needs and desires abound, but the ability to fill them all is limited. Humans live in a world where scarcity exists.

Because there is scarcity, either created naturally or by intentional human actions, societies set up economic systems to address the problem and deal with production, consumption, and distribution. If there were an overabundance of the items we need and want, and the items could be freely distributed, there would be less need for an economic system to answer the economic problem of scarcity. Answers to economic problems can be different, but the three economic questions are the same. What are the goods and services that a society should provide for its people? How should these goods and services be produced? And, who should get them once they have been produced?

Later chapters will look at specific economic structures that countries have developed in relation to their unique ideological, political, and environmental contexts.

GETTING ORGANIZED

1. List 10 things you own, but really don't need. List 10 things you own that you need most. Compare your lists with your classmates'.
2. Consider your spending habits over the past week. List your purchases. Categorize your list into goods and services.
3. What economic problems or issues does Canada face today? Consider the way in which your federal and territorial or provincial governments are addressing the issues. Given their actions, what do you think are the priorities of the governments? List the top five government priorities.
4. Do you budget your money? How do you make economic choices? Estimate how much money you will spend during the next two weeks. List the goods and services you expect to buy and estimate the cost for each. Can you afford them? How will you decide which things to buy? Divide your list into needs and wants. When do you think wants become needs? Are your needs different from your classmates' needs?
5. What skills do you have to market? What skills do you hope to obtain after graduation? Do different skills cost different amounts of time and money to acquire? Imagine two different scenarios about your future work life. Outline the cost, in terms of time and money, of both of these scenarios.

6. Review this introductory chapter on economics. List five main ideas or key points from the chapter. Write these on a wall chart for your classroom. Look at what each of you has written and list each different point that you regard as important.

REACHING OUT

1. The line that distinguishes between needs and wants is a blurred one for most people. Things you thought you needed sometimes turn out to be of less importance once you have them.

   (a) Imagine you could go back in time and meet yourself as you were in grade 9. What three goods or services that you really wanted in grade 9 seem of little importance to you now? What three things still seem important to you?

   (b) What advice would you give your grade 9 self about needs and wants? Consider such things as purchasing decisions or jobs. How might you look back on yourself in three years?

   (c) Do you think your priorities in your early twenties will be the same as they are now? Why or why not? Write a letter to yourself about your priorities now, and what you think they will be when you are 25. Share your letter with others in your class. What similarities and differences are there? You may wish to keep your letter until you *are* 25.

2. Make a collage of pictures from news magazines that display these concepts: Making Choices, Scarcity, Land, Labour and Capital.

Chapter Eight:

THE STRUCTURE OF THE MARKET ECONOMY

GETTING IT STRAIGHT

1. What is the market economy?
2. How did the structure of the environment encourage the growth of the market economy?
3. What are the essential features of a market economy?
4. How does a monopoly differ from an oligopoly?
5. How does the "invisible hand" encourage production of goods and services?
6. What is a market?
7. What is consumer sovereignty?
8. How are the three economic questions answered in a market economy?
9. How does the market economy relate to the individual?
10. How does the market economy fit in with the PEEK box?

Every time you buy something, from a package of chewing gum to a car, you are contributing to the forces of supply and demand.

A **market economy** is one governed by the forces of supply and demand based on price, in which private business people produce goods and services that people want. Market economies evolved as a way to simplify business transactions between individuals who owned resources. Although market economies have a long history, the Industrial Revolution and the construction of large-scale factories marked the beginning of modern **private enterprise**. Large factories not only changed the way work was done, they changed the way people lived and thought about life. Until the Industrial Revolution, the workplace was dominated by crafts people. Slow, steady, high-quality work was admired and rewarded. Young people apprenticed for

CASE STUDY:
CHANGES AT THE VOLVO FACTORY

Factory owners are always trying to improve their production process. This is because factory work is often tedious, and boring. As you read this Case Study, think about how Sweden's Volvo car factory is attempting to make their Volvos better.

Volvo is modifying the assembly line approach it has used for years. The company hopes to be able to give customers their orders more quickly and efficiently with a new approach which gives the workers more responsibility and say in the production of cars and the politics of the factory.

Several small work teams work together to produce complete cars. Members take turns representing the group at factory meetings. Every team member learns how to assemble the entire car. The workers no longer take their place on a long assembly line where they repeat a simple job over and over again. They now must become more skilled workers, facing approximately 3500 parts needed for assembly. The time needed to build a car is not made known to the team, but the team is encouraged to work as hard as it can. The interesting result is that the teams can build cars faster than the factory anticipated. Volvo workers seem to be working harder, and enjoying it more.

QUESTIONS:

1. Do you think the work teams are more efficient than assembly lines? Why or why not?
2. Do you think the people in the work group would get to know one another better than they did on the assembly line?
3. What might be some results of this different working relationship? In what ways might the factory benefit? In what ways would the workers benefit? Do you think that eventually workers would begin to specialize in some work on the car?
4. Pretend you have been called on to advise the owners of the Volvo factory. Write a short report either supporting or not supporting change for the sake of change. As you write this report, consider what you know about the nature of humans.

Henry Ford pioneered assembly line technology and changed production methods drastically. Today, Volvo has changed the way its products are assembled.

years with masters of a trade. The factory system made machines the masters. It allowed people with limited craftsmanship, but who were ambitious and hardworking, to get rich.

Assembly line production was an innovation that quickly out-paced the production of skilled artisans working with hand tools. Instead of making a large profit on one product, a small profit was made by selling many products. Individuals who were fortunate enough or smart enough to invest at the right time in new steam-powered equipment became wealthy. The assembly line created a division of labour and made businesses and workers more specialized and interdependent. Today's car manufacturer depends on miners to mine the iron ore, on steel makers to turn it into steel, and on sheet metal fabricators to form the car frames and doors. Car manufacturers must also rely on a host of other businesses, or sub-trades, like the rubber manufacturers that provide tires to put on the car, and truckers to take the cars to market.

The Structure of Knowledge, Production, and Consumption

The essential features of a market economy include:
1. the individualism of competition
2. the private ownership of property

BIG MAC TO GO

Can you think of a good example of assembly line production? One modern example of assembly line production you probably know a lot about is McDonald's. The cashier takes your order and your money. One person cooks the burger. Another puts on the special sauce. Another wraps the burger and places it on a rack. The cashier bags your burger and gives it to you. You get your own straws and napkins. With this method of production, if people did not perform their assigned tasks, the Big Mac would not be the hamburger you expect. The fact that every Big Mac in the world tastes the same only proves how well assembly line production works.

3. the incentive of making a profit, and
4. the workings of supply and demand on the free market.

These features do not operate independently. They are integrated, and interact with one another.

P E E K	
AT A MARKET ECONOMY	
Politics	**Economics**
- government provides a secure background for economic exchange - laissez-faire	- specialization - market operates according to supply and demand
Environment	**Knowledge**
- growing global interdependence - disappearance of national boundaries as barriers to trade	- self-interest motivates human action (**invisible hand**) - strong belief in individualism
Field of Action	
- you will read about the fields of action of the USA and Canada in subsequent chapters	

Economic Individualism

Individualism is one of the organizing principles of a market economy. It means that the individual decisions of buyers and sellers shape the economy. People, as consumers, may choose what they wish to buy, where they will buy it, and what price they are willing to pay. People may choose not to buy a product that is too costly. Instead, they may choose a cheaper item similar to the more expensive one they really wanted. Producers, or **entrepreneurs,** can freely enter the **marketplace** with any product they think will sell and that meets government standards.

A market economy is based on a number of organizational structures. People are individually free to choose where they will work. Businesses are free from being interfered with by others, including the government. And, people are free to own and exchange property, including money. These are all part of individualism. Market economies could not function without individual initiative and hard work. Market economies encourage the individual dreams of opportunity, creativity, and wealth. The theory of the market economy is, *if people are willing to work hard, they will be able to improve their positions in life.*

Market economies are based on a belief in self-reliance. This belief implies that most people can and should take care of themselves and that individual initiative should be encouraged. It is based on the theory that each person should work to realize personal goals. In a market economy, the collective goals of society are equated with the individual goals of people. The theory is that if individual goals are met, the whole society will benefit.

Competition

A belief in economic individualism implies competition between people and products in society. Competition occurs when more than one business sells similar products in the same marketplace. Each business wants to make money. This profit motive encourages businesses to sell products at the lowest price they can afford to charge and at the greatest price they think the buyer will pay.

If a business were the only seller of a particular product or service in the marketplace, it would have a **monopoly**. An example of a monopoly is Alberta

Government Telephones, which exists as the sole Alberta-wide telephone company. If there are only a few sellers of a similar product in the marketplace, it is called an **oligopoly**. An example of an oligopoly is in the soap products market. Only three companies produce most of the soap products available. Sometimes oligopolies compete with one another, but they also compete against themselves.

Competing against yourself might not sound like a good economic practice, but it can be very rewarding. A soap company produces three laundry soaps and advertises, for example, that soap *a* washes cleanest, soap *b* washes brightest, and soap *c* washes whitest. No matter which soap the consumer buys, the soap company makes money. The growth of oligopolies in the marketplace has been a major trend in Canada. Examples also include the beer industry, newspapers, and automobiles.

Well-known Scottish economist Adam Smith (1723-1790) spoke of competition as the "**invisible hand**" which encouraged the production of goods and services for the benefit of the consumer. According to Smith, if people in business want to satisfy their desire to make money (profit motive) they will be forced to produce goods that consumers want. He said that this process was both natural and logical, and worked in the best interests of everyone in society. Smith suggested that all economic actions are carried out for personal reasons. Still, the economic logic of the system works so that everyone in the society gets what they want and need.

Constant change and the love of novelty make up the backbone of capitalism. The invisible hand leads to the creation of entirely new and different products each year. Toys are probably the best examples of rapid innovations. Pet rocks emerge one year, skateboards the next, and World Wrestling Federation figures the next. The home appliance market also shows how new items can catch the public's fancy. The microwave oven, unheard of a generation ago, was named the most popular home appliance of the 1980s.

The cartoonists have simplified the concept of the invisible hand (competition) to make their point. From what you have read, what important factors might the cartoonists have left out or added? Is the cartoon accurate?

G.I. JOE

Adapted from the book,
Toyland: The High-Stakes Game of the Toy Industry
(©1990) by Sydney L. Stern and Ted Schoenhaus

In a market economy, any individual can create a product or sell an idea to a company. Stanley Weston, a toy inventor, had an idea to sell. Against the popular opinion of the day, Weston believed that boys liked to play with dolls almost as much as girls did. But what boy wanted a Barbie Doll?

Because Weston played with toy soldiers as a kid, he decided that other boys would like a military doll too. He interested the Hassenfeld brothers, of Hasbro Toys, in his idea. For $52, Stanley built a demonstration model complete with military insignias and paraphernalia. After a complex series of negotiations, Weston and Hasbro Toys settled on the huge sum of $100 000 for the rights to his G.I. Joe concept. Weston was overjoyed. A $52 investment turned into a huge profit.

With toys, the normal fee for inventors or developers is five per cent of the profit. But, because the idea seemed risky, Weston was especially happy with the $100 000 payment. You might already know what happened to the doll. It became a big seller.

Would Stanley Weston make the same deal again? By 1987, the G. I. Joe line had total sales of over $250 million. At a royalty of five per cent, Weston's share would have been $12.5 million! Does he regret his sale to Hasbro Toys? As a true entrepreneur, he doesn't. He said, "Even though a lot of people think I'm a fool, I'll take those odds—100 000 to 52—any day!"

Private Ownership of Capital

In a market economy, also called a private enterprise system, the **means of production** are owned by individuals and not by the government. Private ownership works on the premise that people care more for what is theirs than for what belongs to someone else. It is believed that when individuals own or control private property, their interest in its success is maximized. Individual ownership carries with it the freedom to decide when and if to buy and sell goods and services. This freedom includes the sale or purchase of all resources. Private ownership does not prevent the government from owning or controlling public companies like the Canadian Broadcasting Corporation or public services like Canada Post.

The belief in owning private property reflects the individualist attitude of the market economy. If property is owned by many people, all owners maintain limited economic power. If economic power is to work best, it should be decentralized (not concentrated in the hands of a few). Those who believe in a market economy and political democracy believe property and power should not rest in the hands of a few people.

The Profit Motive

The idea of making a profit on a business transaction is an idea that originated with merchants in ancient Greece. Why should an entrepreneur begin a business? The answer is easy: to produce goods and services consumers want, and to make money. The desire for profit is the motivation for entrepreneurs to start any business, operate it efficiently, and continue to change and improve the business.

One general truth of capitalism is that it takes money to make money. In any business, producers must spend capital to produce a product. Producers then try to sell what they make for more than it cost to make the product. The profit is the money left after production cost is subtracted from the selling price.

For example, a local gas station owner hires workers. She hopes that the price she charges the consumer for gas will be enough to cover her costs of operation and make a living for her family. The equation is very simple. If she is going to make a profit, she must sell enough gas to pay for staff, the cost of doing business, and her own salary.

Many people become wealthy doing business in a market economy. Some people go bankrupt. No one who starts a business is assured success. Sometimes, for all sorts of reasons, products just won't sell. Sometimes people in business read the market incorrectly. Sometimes there is too much competition, even for the really good ideas.

Not all people who are very rich or very smart can make a go of a business. People in business may make all the right decisions, but something out of their

Many teenagers work at part-time jobs after school and on weekends.

control (like a new fad, a hurricane, or civil war in another country) creates problems they cannot overcome. In a market economy, anyone who cannot make money in business will be forced to close.

CASE STUDY:
THE JOB MARKET

This Case Study has two parts. As you read the first section and answer the questions about the supply and demand of labour, think about the choices you can make as you enter the job market.

PART I

If workers match their skills to market needs, they will find a job and make a good salary. But, if too many people enter the work force with the skills formerly in short supply, wages will decrease, especially for new workers.

As part-time workers, students usually discover what skills are required to fit into the workplace. They tend to work for low wages, often minimum wage. This keeps wages lower for full-time workers.

An example of how supply and demand affects skilled workers is found in Alberta's oil business. In the early 1980s, oil rig workers were in high demand. The wages offered by oil companies increased as they attempted to attract more workers to the oil field. As workers moved into Alberta from other

continued

parts of the country in response to the job needs, wages levelled off. As an even greater supply of workers became available, the demand dropped and competition for jobs among workers began. Some workers began to sell their services for less than the rates offered for these jobs.

QUESTIONS:

1. How does supply and demand affect the job market in your area?
2. What happens to wages if the supply of workers increases but the demand for them stays the same?
3. What happens to wages when the demand for workers increases while the supply stays the same?
4. In your community right now, what is the demand for workers your age? What is the supply?

PART II

JUGGLING SCHOOL AND A JOB

As a teenager completing high school, you may be trying to juggle your desire for good grades and your desire to have money. In 1990, over 400 000 high school students in Canada (almost two out of five students) worked part-time.

Students who work are forced to make difficult decisions. For example, Susan is pleased to have a job as a gas station attendant. She makes her own money. She has time between the end of the school day and the beginning of her work day (8 PM) to complete her homework. The drawback is that she works until 3 AM four times a week. She knows her school work is suffering.

Anne is in Susan's class. She works hard to balance a part-time job in a drycleaner's with a full load of coursework and after-school sports. To balance school and work, Anne doesn't do the day-to-day homework, just the big assignments. ''It's driving me crazy,'' Anne says. Anne admits that she lives at home and doesn't need the money, but she likes her job, the people she meets, and the extra money she earns.

Why do so many high school students work? Part of the reason is the strong Canadian economy. Help Wanted signs are almost a permanent sight in store windows. Part of the reason is the change in the Canadian social climate. An increase in the number of single-parent families means that more students must work to support themselves or to supplement their family's income.

Some sociologists suggest that there is a *youth culture* that places importance on money. In order to be acceptable in society, youth must have money. Some young people spend a lot of money every month to acquire the latest fashions. Others want money because they feel the need to be independent.

The result of part-time work is more than just money in the jeans. On the plus side, students are learning valuable skills. They learn money management, time management, responsibility, and gain practical work experience. On the negative side, working students are often tired, can lose touch with their families, and may develop poor health habits. Academic life can suffer. Some teachers ask about the sense of assigning homework that students

continued

CASE STUDY *continued*

won't, or can't, do. All in all, when high school students work part-time, many changes take place within the family, the school, the workplace, and the community.

QUESTIONS:

1. Why do so many high school students work part-time? Do you have a part-time job? Why?
2. How widespread is part-time work among high school students in your community? What are some of the difficulties it causes? Do you think it is worth it to work part-time? On what criteria (values) do you base your answer?
3. If a large number of students work part-time, how might this affect the economy and the social structure of your community and province or territory?
4. Do you believe there is a youth culture that encourages high school students to work? If you do, list some of the values of this youth culture.
5. Write a 250-word essay, from the perspective of a teacher, with the title: We have confused the need to work with the desire to have money.

During the 1970s and early 1980s, people from throughout Canada moved to Alberta to work for high wages in the oil industry. Later in the 1980s, many of these people had to accept lower wages. Some were out of work. The job market had changed.

The Free Market of Supply and Demand

A market is any place where buyers and sellers come together: a hamburger joint, a farmers' market, a department store. A free or open market means that both business and labour, and producers and consumers, operate under the law of supply and demand. This means that producers try to provide what consumers want. However, the producers can also affect the types of consumer demands with effective advertising.

Most often, **consumer sovereignty** determines what products will be produced and how much can be charged for them. In theory, consumer sovereignty works much like an election. As you have read, the idea is that when you buy, you vote for the product you buy and against the product you don't. For example, every time you purchase a new shirt you are saying that the business that made the shirt should continue to do so. If the business sells enough shirts to make a profit, they can continue production.

Supply and demand are constantly changing. Demand tends to increase when consumers are encouraged to buy more. They may respond to falling prices or the fact that they have more money to spend. Supply increases when producers see an opportunity to make a profit.

Supply and demand work together to set wages and salaries in much the same way as they increase or decrease the number of goods and services on the market. Wages and salaries are paid to workers in exchange for services provided to businesses. If a particular skill is needed but workers with that skill are in short supply, the wage offered in exchange for the skill usually rises.

CHALLENGES TO THE MARKET ECONOMY

CHALLENGE 1: Specialization in Modern Factories

Assembly lines, with their division of labour, are repetitive, routine, and highly specialized. Often workers obtain little satisfaction from their work. They seldom complete a product or even see the finished product. Cost cutting occurs in an effort to remain competitive and maximize profit. Sometimes, safety standards are reduced. When this happens, quality is sacrificed for profit.

How can a market economy produce cheaply and safely?

CHALLENGE 2: Is a Clean Environment Compatible with Profit?

Critics of market economies name pollution as one of the biggest problems. Pollution is often the result of industry's desire for quick profit. Some companies argue that they would go broke, and create unemployment if they had to work pollution-free. Critics say long-term consequences for society are more important than short-term gain. Canadian and American governments are attempting to come to an agreement to stop sulphur emissions from US plants. But the problem of acid rain continues.

One example of how companies attempt to solve problems as easily as possible involved the failed attempt to control pollution at the nickel mines in Sudbury, Ontario. The mines were ordered to stop emissions that caused acid rain. Their response was to build one of the highest chimneys in the world. The result is that acid rain was moved from Sudbury to towns and cities downwind of the plant.

How much is a pollution-free environment worth?

CHALLENGE 3: Rich and Poor: Who Gets the Goods?

The inequity of incomes between rich and poor is another problem of the market economy. Critics suggest that the market economy creates a situation where the rich become richer while the poor live without opportunities to better themselves economically. Although the market economy proudly points to examples of people who rise from rags to riches, more typically the wealthy gain their wealth not from intelligence or hard work, but through inheritance. It is easy for those

continued

continued

with wealth to become even richer. The numbers speak for themselves. The rich are only a small percentage of the people in Canada, yet they control most the country's wealth.

How important is it for Canada to narrow the gap between rich and poor?

CHALLENGE 4: Is Survival of Big and Strong the Best?

In market economies, business is becoming more and more concentrated in the hands of fewer and fewer people. Theoretically, the market economy works well when millions of small businesses compete with one another. In Canada, an example of the concentration of business in the hands of fewer companies is the Hudson's Bay Company. The Bay owns many stores and Zellers and Simpsons, as well.

It appears the Free Trade Agreement between Canada and the United States has spurred large companies to purchase smaller companies or merge with other large companies in order to compete in larger US markets. Molson's breweries has merged with Carling O'Keefe, which is owned by the Elders Company of Australia. These takeovers and mergers decrease competition and real consumer choice.

How important is it for Canada to help keep smaller businesses in operation?

CHALLENGE 5: The Tax System: Who Pays? Who Profits?

Economic power brings political power. Newspapers report that large companies often influence government decisions. Ordinary people become alienated from government, especially when individual income tax rises with no rise in the rate of corporate taxes. In 1987 alone a total of 93 405 businesses making profits of $27 000 000 paid no tax on their earnings. In Canada and the United States, the middle income worker carries the greatest burden of income tax. Many poor people and many rich people pay little, if any, tax.

How important is it that the rich carry a heavier burden of taxation?

There are some problems with the market system. Businesses sometimes sacrifice pollution controls and worker safety in order to make a larger profit.

SUMMARY

To those who study them, market economies seem to be part ideology, part myth, part magic. But these facts cannot be disputed: market economies have fostered great creative genius, wealth, economic abuse, and poverty. Like other political or economic ideas, there are both good and bad elements. Those who take huge risks can win great riches. They can also lose everything. The free and independent open market of the market economy is supported strongly by some, and hated thoroughly by others.

A society with a market economy would answer the three economic questions in this way:

1. What goods and services should be produced?

   Businesses produce those goods and services demanded by consumers. The profit motive drives the businesses to give the consumers what they want. If businesses don't meet consumers' needs, they won't be able to sell their products.

2. How should goods and services be produced?

   Businesses produce goods and services in the least expensive and most efficient way possible. The fear of losing business to other producers forces those in business to carefully monitor their methods of production to keep prices down, quality up, and supply and demand in equilibrium.

3. How should goods and services be distributed?

   Businesses sell the goods and services they produce to those who can afford to pay for them. In the individualist society where the free market thrives and prospers, only those consumers who pay for the product can have it.

The theory of free enterprise includes some very specific beliefs about how the economy should work. In practice in any one country, the way those beliefs are applied can be considerably different. The knowledge or beliefs about how things are supposed to work must be adapted to accommodate ongoing changes in the environment, politics, and the economy. These factors may be difficult to predict. As you read about individual countries in the remaining chapters of the text, remember that no economic system can be understood in isolation. All four sides of the PEEK box must be considered.

In the next chapter, you will read about a country where the market economy is practised: the United States.

GETTING ORGANIZED

1. List some novelty items you have purchased or been given. How did the invisible hand lead the producers to produce them? During the 1991 Gulf War, some companies in the United States increased profits—such as companies which produced greeting cards. Why would greeting card companies be able to make such a huge profit in a time of national stress?

2. List the places of employment in your community. Which are privately owned and which are publicly owned? Is the manager of the privately owned business the owner? How many of the places of employment have the worker as the owner?

3. How do you get your money? If you work for someone, how do they know how much to pay you? How do they know how much to charge for their products or services?

4. When you walk into a retail store (a record or book store, for example), you can often see items selling at about one-tenth the regular price. You may be lucky enough to find a book originally worth $24.99 for   Why would the store reduce prices this much?

5. Most economies in the world are mixed economies. Even in a market economy, there are businesses that are not run on the principles of the open market. Think of a business that is not run on open market principles, such as a phone company, post office, or library. What would happen if the business suddenly began to operate on open market principles? What would be some problems? Could it work?

6. Answer the question: To what extent should governments encourage consumers to use credit

REACHING OUT

1. Invite guest speakers in your community to come into class and talk on the issues listed on pages 99-100, *Challenges to the Market Economy.*

   For example, invite a union leader to speak on the issue "Rich and Poor—Who Gets the Goods?" Invite a business owner to speak on "The Tax System—Who Pays, Who Profits?"

   In each presentation, identify the following:
   (a) statements of fact versus statements of opinion
   (b) the speaker's main assumptions and beliefs about individualism

2. Write a letter to your boss or a former employer explaining how changes might be made to the work site based on the Case Study on page 91, *Changes at the Volvo Factory.*

   Recommend changes you would suggest to improve labour and management relations.

   After you have written your letter, predict your employer's response.

   What differences are there between you and your employer in terms of beliefs, attitudes, and motives? Are there grounds for mutual benefit in the spirit of reciprocity?

3. Shoplifting in Canada is costly. Every day, Canadian retailers lose $3 million to customers and $2 million to staff. (Retail Council of Canada, May, 1991—Broadcast News)
   (a) How might one explain the motivations of shoplifters in terms of the values and beliefs promoted by the market economy? Do you think these beliefs are justified?
   (b) Invite a local store owner to your class to explain his or her point of view on the prosecution of shoplifters. Compose a paragraph that summarizes the arguments presented in class.

Chapter Nine:

THE UNITED STATES OF AMERICA

Bordered on the east by the Atlantic Ocean and on the west by the Pacific Ocean, the United States comprises 50 states. Of these, 48 are joined together into one large land mass bordered on the north by Canada and on the south by Mexico. Alaska, west of the Yukon, and Hawaii, halfway to Japan, are the other two states. The United States is one of the wealthiest countries in the world. It has rich agricultural land, an abundance of water, and other natural resources. The "melting pot" culture includes a variety of ethnic origins and a generally affluent population.

The American Economy

In the United States, government intervention in the economy reflects the American political ideals (organizing principles) written into the Constitution. The US Constitution states that each individual has the right to "life, liberty, and the pursuit of happiness."

THUMBNAIL FACTS

Area: 9 393 909 sq. km (including all areas under US jurisdiction)

Population: 241 504 825

Density: 26 people per sq. km

Chief Cities: Washington, D.C. (capital), New York City, Chicago, Los Angeles, Philadelphia.

Type of Government: Federal Republic

Per Capita Income: $14 080

Most Important Industries: motor vehicles, aircraft, industrial machinery, electrical equipment and appliances, chemicals, petroleum products, fabricated metals, railroad equipment, processed foods.

Agriculture: wheat, corn, rye, barley, oats, soybeans, cattle, dairy products, cotton, tobacco, hogs.

Minerals: coal, petroleum, natural gas, iron ore, copper, uranium.

Most Important Trading Partners: Canada and Japan.

GNP: $5.640 trillion

The United States has an economy which reflects its political ideals.

Changing international environment, political tensions, and economic necessity have led to increased government involvement in the US economy. This involvement began in the late nineteenth century when large corporations started to buy up their own competition and build monopolies. Government involvement increased further during the Great Depression of 1929 to 1939. During this time of economic turmoil, nearly one-third of the US labour force was unemployed.

To get the nation working again, Franklin Roosevelt's Democratic government began massive public works programs and regulated the American banking system. During the depression, the US government stimulated business, redistributed income, and provided economic security for those who could not manage on their own. Because of this government intervention, the United States does not have a pure market economy (nor does any other country).

In chapter 4, you read about the democratic government in the United States. The US Constitution outlined different tasks for both state and federal governments. The US government plays two roles in the economy. It regulates economic activity, to ensure economic stability and growth. It also provides services.

Americans value political and economic freedom, equality, and national security.

Early in its history, the US government was reluctant to become involved in the private sector, except in transportation. When the US Constitution was written in 1787, the political leaders who wrote it were influenced by Adam Smith's ideas of **laissez-faire** and the free market economy. Politically and economically, the US believed in private ownership and that business should be guided by the natural forces of supply and demand.

BUSINESS ORGANIZATIONS IN THE UNITED STATES

CORPORATIONS

A corporation is a large number of people working together; it has an interesting legal status. Since ancient times in Greece, corporations have been considered individuals. Most corporations in the United States are privately owned by large groups of people who buy shares as an investment on a stock exchange. These people are rarely involved in the day-to-day activities of the corporation. Instead, the corporation is run by a board of directors which has the legal power to make decisions for the business as if it were their own.

The owners of shares have only a **limited liability** in the company. If the company goes broke, shareholders lose only the money they have invested in their stock purchases. On the other hand, if a corporation goes broke, people or companies to whom the corporation owes money are out of luck.

American corporations control much of the wealth of the country. More than 25 per cent of all US business is done by large corporations. Some examples are General Motors (GM), International Business Machines (IBM), and General Electric (GE). General Motors' annual sales exceed the GNP of more than 100 countries!

PRIVATE ENTERPRISES

Private enterprises are usually quite small. In these businesses, the individual owner is totally responsible for all debts incurred and receives all the profits. One advantage of these businesses is that owners can make quick decisions, without having to consult others. Private enterprises also pay fewer taxes than corporations. In the United States, small businesses usually survive by meeting local needs and providing the personalized service that large corporations cannot.

PARTNERSHIPS

Partnerships are businesses formed through agreements between two or more people. These legal agreements specify the amount of money each partner has invested and the duties each is to perform. If the business goes broke, the partners are liable for the debts. Partnerships are able to pool the talents of two or more individuals and, like private enterprises, enjoy tax breaks that corporations do not. The federal government formed the Small Business Administration as a way to help small businesses with financing and management. In the United States, partnerships are common in medicine, law, real estate, and retail stores.

FRANCHISES

Franchises are popular in the US. Large companies, like Bonanza or Wendy's, sell the right to use their names and ideas. Individuals who purchase franchise rights can rely on the parent company to help market the product and to provide supplies and facilities. The person buying the franchise accepts sole responsibility for losses or profits. Franchise holders benefit from and contribute to the large advertising budget of the larger firm. Most franchises exist in the restaurant business.

Providing services to all people within the USA places a heavy demand on government funds. The population of almost 250 million people is driven by the principles of a market economy, and hopes to fulfill its own wants and needs.

Americans tend to expect a high standard of living. The US government tries to care for its citizens by working actively to promote the growth of business and job creation. But, like any society, the demand for government funds is always greater than the funds available. The US government must deal with scarcity.

Political decisions dictate how funds are to be spent. Each year, the president of the United States presents a federal budget to the Congress. This budget outlines how tax dollars and other revenues will be spent.

Positive Features of the American Economy

There are many advantages to a market economy. Consumers have economic freedom and choice. The government is uninvolved, other than to support free enterprise and to monitor the safety of products.

Consumers can make personal choices in shopping and choose the best buy. Producers can produce whatever goods they choose, and of whatever quality they desire. Competition encourages producers to be efficient and innovative. Wise consumers want the best value for their dollar and the highest quality at the lowest price. Producers who can meet this need usually are successful.

Americans enjoy a greater wealth of product choices than anyone in the world. Consumers influence the economy by choosing how to spend their money. If consumers spend money on cars, more cars will be produced. The same is true with clothing, CD players, and all other marketable goods and services. Companies will make whatever consumers will buy. But, if consumers do not buy a product, the producer will either close down business or start to make and sell something else. By freely choosing to buy or not to buy, consumers determine whether companies succeed or fail.

American consumers are free to buy whatever they wish, as long as they can afford it.

In the US market system, people are free to live anywhere in the country and apply for the job of their choice. The market economy also encourages consumer responsibility. Unless products are defective or unsafe, buyers must accept the product as it is. Advertising can be seductive, and individuals must purchase carefully.

Negative Features of the American Economy

Because the market is decentralized or not controlled by a central plan, the US economy is hard to control. Producers manufacture whatever the consumer is willing to pay for, even if the product may be harmful. Examples include cigarettes, alcohol, and cars that waste gas and pollute the air. The potential for abuse raises an important economic question: How much government intervention should there be?

The goal of pursuing a profit can conflict with the goal of government to serve its constituents. Businesses do not take responsibility for the environment. As a result, streams and beaches are polluted with toxic wastes. The air is polluted, and the rain is filled with acid. To businesses, profits are the top priority.

The job of government is to consider long-term goals. Conservation today will bring profits tomorrow. Should government force businesses to clean up their own pollution? Or, should governments use public funds to help businesses adopt new pollution control devices? These are not easy questions, especially for a government which wants to preserve economic freedom by staying out of the economy as much as possible.

Although the United States is a wealthy country, some Americans cannot afford even the basic necessities of life. For these people, security and survival are daily problems. Some Americans starve to death or die because they lack proper medical attention. These are economic problems, but they require political solutions. In a market economy, should the rich be concerned about the poor? Is it the moral duty of the government to ensure that everyone's basic needs are met?

There are some negative features to every economic system. Not all are as obvious as this! What are some other aspects of the American economy which are not positive?

CASE STUDY:

MEDICAL CARE IN THE USA

Hospital care is costly. In this Case Study, consider the American system of health care.

Dan is 47 years old. He owns and operates the corner store. Business has not been good for the past two years and Dan has been forced to cut both personal and business expenses just to make ends meet for him and his family. Dan was especially worried when he heard the news that another bigger convenience store was going to be built at the end of the block.

Partly caused by his heavy work schedule and partly from the stress and worry, Dan suffered a heart attack and was rushed to the hospital. He was admitted and treated. Dan's doctor had told Dan that he must stay in the hospital, but Dan was only there for five days before he checked himself out.

Even though his doctor protested strongly, Dan had to leave.

Why did Dan leave? One of the cuts Dan made in his business expenses was to allow his private hospital insurance to expire. He was now faced with a bill of over $4000, and he did not have the money to pay it.

QUESTIONS:
1. Why did Dan not have hospital insurance?
2. If you were Dan, would you have stayed in the hospital longer?
3. Should the US provide emergency hospital coverage for people like Dan?
4. Should all citizens of the US be forced to pay hospital coverage?

In free market economies, bigger is often better. Free markets encourage dog-eat-dog competition and, in the survival of the economic fittest, large corporations gobble up small businesses. Large firms do this for one simple reason: they want to eliminate competition. IBM wants to dominate the computer market, and General Electric wants to control the electrical business.

On one hand, the US government does not want to intervene in the natural workings of the free market system. On the other hand, it wants to ensure that competition from many small producers is kept alive. A free market system left alone may allow big firms to devour little ones to the point where there is no competition left.

The answer is a precarious balancing of the market, in which the US government intervenes just a little in an attempt to preserve the element of competition.

The concentration of business into fewer and fewer corporations is becoming a concern. In the United States, the largest 200 corporations hold about 25 per cent of the income-producing wealth of the nation. Often big businesses are strong businesses. But, if corporations become too large, will the government be able to control them? Should government act to keep corporations smaller?

Other Concerns

Market economies distribute goods and services according to wealth. Those with money can buy, those without cannot. In the United States, goods and services are distributed unequally because income is distributed unequally. The top 1 per cent of US households takes home more income than the bottom 15 per cent. The top 1 per cent owns more property than the

People who lack resources often suffer in a pure market economy. What resources do the homeless and the "shopping cart people" of the USA lack?

Why do some people in the USA worry that large corporations control much of the mass media?

bottom 70 per cent. Should government redistribute wealth more evenly through a greater progressive income tax? Should government institute a guaranteed annual income?

In the United States, because money often means power, and power means influence, rich corporations are very involved in politics. Business-sponsored political action committees make substantial contributions to political candidates. If a business conglomerate owns a newspaper, it has the power to print or exclude certain points of view.

Should politicians be allowed to accept political campaign donations from corporations? Should campaign donors' names be publicized, along with the amounts they donate?

Another economic problem is the political control the US exerts over other countries. To protect their home or domestic markets, businesses attempt to persuade their governments to establish political control in the exploited lands.

Large countries such as the United States take advantage of smaller countries which have a large, inexpensive labour force, unexploited resources, and a large population (market). The small country raises cash crops for the dominant country, rather than crops to feed the people. This begins a cycle of dependency, poverty, foreign aid, and sometimes, a ruined environment. Should wealthy countries be allowed to exert political control over other nations?

Perhaps the biggest criticism of a market economy is how it affects people psychologically. Market economies encourage a take-care-of-yourself attitude.

Critics warn that the free market system encourages us all to be more individualistic, uncaring, and selfish. As pop star Madonna sings: "It's a material world, and I am a material girl." Some of us define the success of our lives by what we own.

Market economies raise many interesting questions. Does Michael Jackson deserve $90 million annually, even if you love his music? Should people be paid according to their contribution to society? How should

CASE STUDY:

THE 1990 BASEBALL STRIKE

As you read the following Case Study, think about the contribution of baseball players to society in terms of their labour.

In 1990 the major league baseball players went on strike. In part, the players' argument was simple. There was a lot of money floating around, and they wanted more of it. Specifically, they wanted to obtain a greater share of the millions and millions of dollars that the owners received from television revenues.

But, like all workers, baseball players were also interested in other issues. Should they be allowed to choose where they worked, or should their movement be restricted? Another argument centred on the success of baseball. Who was responsible for its success? Was it the entrepreneurs (the owners) who risked their capital investing in baseball as a business? Or, was it the individual players who made baseball exciting for the fans?

Third, baseball players were part of a union that was concerned about the needs and wants of its members, especially those who were new (rookies) and those who were retired. After a series of threats, postures, and walk-outs, the strike was settled. Both owners and players gave in a little. Baseball games in the United States and Canada were delayed for a few weeks while the two sides negotiated, and when the season started almost everyone forgot the strike had happened.

QUESTIONS:

1. Do you think a baseball players' strike is the result of "capitalist oppressors" (owners) refusing to negotiate with "workers" (players)?
2. Do you think a baseball player who earns $4 million a year is oppressed by the team owners?
3. Do you think a sports figure should be paid such a high salary? Is anyone's skill worth that much? If you represented the players, how would you justify the salaries that baseball players make? How would you argue if you represented the owners? Discuss this in groups.
4. What should be the highest paying jobs in the world? List the three most important jobs and give your reasons for choosing these. How much should people who govern countries be paid?
5. Organize a short debate on the question: Can a democratic society justify paying sports figures millions of dollars while other people in the society starve?

people's contribution to society be judged? Is playing a sport worth millions a year? Even if Bo Jackson knows both baseball and football, is his contribution as great as the president of the United States or the prime minister of Canada, both of whom make less than $250 000 Cdn per year?

Many workers are dissatisfied with their jobs. Many jobs are repetitive, monotonous, and deadening. The drive for an efficient, cost-conscious organization that maximizes profits often ignores the human part of the equation. The assembly line seems to mass produce both products and workers. Pride in workmanship often disappears when tasks are piecemeal and repetitive. Marx called this the alienation of workers from their jobs.

PEEK
AT THE UNITED STATES

Politics	Economics
- government ensures a secure political environment (security of the person and property)	- private ownership - growing concentration of wealth - corporations, private enterprises, partnerships, and franchises
Environment	**Knowledge**
- growing global competition challenges traditional US dominance (e.g. computers, autos) - pollution and depletion of resources are issues	- "life, liberty and the pursuit of happiness" - freedom of choice (if you have money)
Field of Action	
- increasing global competition challenges US business - growing government involvement and regulation	

To What Extent Does the US Government Control the Economy?

The US federal government exerts some control over the economy through the Federal Reserve system. The Federal Reserve Bank controls the flow of money to the banks, and to the people. This is called the **monetary policy**. If inflation is too high, member banks may be required to hold larger reserves. In this **tight money policy**, banks raise interest rates and lend money only to very safe borrowers.

Banks may also require larger down payments. For example, rather than requiring a 20 per cent down payment on a house, banks may require 30 per cent. These increases depress the economy. Fewer people qualify for mortgages, so fewer houses are built, and fewer house builders are employed.

The government can also control the economy through its **fiscal policy**. The fiscal policy controls the economy by adjusting the tax rate. If taxes are high, consumers have less money. If taxes are low, consumers have more. Obviously, tax rates affect consumer spending. The US government may increase taxes to encourage the consumer to spend less, or decrease taxes to stimulate the economy through consumer spending. Using monetary and fiscal policy, the US government tries to curb inflation, fight depressions, and provide employment.

The American construction industry is one of many affected by fluctuations in the economy.

The government also regulates the market by passing laws to protect the rights of consumers in the marketplace. Consumer rights include the right to safety from poorly made products; the right to information about products, especially about nutrition and true interest rates; the right to choice; freedom from price-fixing; and, the right to be heard, especially when expressing concerns about products.

The US government allows monopolies if it feels monopolies are necessary. Monopolies are allowed to make a fair profit, but they cannot raise prices unfairly. To most Americans, these rights seem to be fundamental protections. Ironically, they are examples of how government intervention into the economy limits the freedoms of the market.

To guarantee and protect the rights of constituents, government agencies are needed. The work of these agencies sometimes causes higher prices. This is especially true if an agency forces businesses to build safer or better products. It is always cheaper to produce lower quality goods. If the free market system worked as it should, consumers would not buy dangerous goods and producers would be forced to build quality merchandise. However, the government protects citizens from harm until the natural laws of the market take effect. Typically, the US government limits its involvement in business to protecting individuals from unscrupulous business people.

Should Economic Equality Be a Goal?

The US government intervenes in the lives of its citizens to ensure that they maintain a basic standard of living. Federal and state governments design social programs that are funded by tax money to help redistribute income. During budget debates, federal agencies justify their budget requests by showing how important their programs are to the whole nation.

Entitlement programs represent the largest share of the US budget. They *entitle* people to a respectable standard of living and a decent quality of life. Surprisingly, one of every five people in the US lives below the poverty line. In the US, individuals are defined as poor when more than one-third of their income is spent on food. The gap between the rich and the poor has increased over recent years, even while the American economy was growing rapidly. Poverty is most common among women, the young, the old, and nonwhites.

The US government sponsors an Unemployment Insurance Program for people who are out of work for short periods of time. Employers deduct a portion of workers' wages. If people quit their jobs without good cause, are fired for misconduct, or refuse a job offered to them, they are not eligible for unemployment insurance. Individuals are required to have worked and contributed to the Unemployment Insurance Program to receive benefits. Social security helps provide a minimum standard of living for those who would otherwise be impoverished. Social security is paid to the elderly, the disabled, or to orphans.

Subsidized housing is available for low income earners. Free clinics and crisis centres help the poor obtain medical aid or counselling. These free clinics are usually set up in poorer urban areas. Wealthier Americans buy private medical insurance or pay, if necessary, for their own medical treatment.

Education and job retraining programs have been set up to help people gain the skills to find better paying jobs. The government hopes that, through training or retraining, individuals will no longer need assistance. Despite government help, some individuals have a difficult time. Food banks and charitable organizations which distribute clothing answer some of the needs of these people. These services are sponsored by private donations and run by volunteers. People who make contributions can deduct them on their income tax at a "fair market value." Charitable organizations are becoming more and more important to people in need. Recent governments have tended to cut social legislation budgets and to redistribute money to the military and to support big business.

There are also ways in which the government assists working people. Both employers and employees must contribute to a federal retirement system. The elderly are eligible for full pension upon retirement at age 65, but may retire at age 62 with less pension.

Most union contracts include retirement pensions. Many unions have also bargained for medical benefits. Medicare was added to the Social Security Act in 1965 for people 65 and over. Hospital coverage is automatic through medicare but coverage of doctor fees is optional. People wishing to have medical coverage pay a monthly premium.

Both pensions and free education are examples of government programs established to give all citizens equal opportunities.

Education is provided free to elementary and secondary students. Post-secondary students must pay tuition to schools, and purchase their own textbooks and supplies. But tuition does not pay the entire cost of the schooling. At public universities, the government subsidizes the rest. Interest-free student loans and grants are available to those who qualify, according to need.

Americans believe that equality means, in part, equality of income. And, like other societies, the United States uses taxation to help bring about greater equality of income. Taxation does not create wealth, it merely transfers it from one person to another. US tax rates are progressive, which means that the higher your income, the more tax you pay. Because of the lower tax rates in the United States, most hockey players in the National Hockey League would rather play for a US team than a Canadian team. If they play in the US, they keep a higher percentage of their income. Generally, taxes in the US are lower than in countries, like Canada, which provide more social services.

SUMMARY

The free market economy of the United States answers the three economic questions in the following way:

1. What goods and services should be produced?

    The desires of the consumer affect which goods and services will be produced. The producer who sells what the consumers want at a price they will pay makes a profit. Government is involved in this process through regulation and monitoring of business.

2. How should goods and services be produced?

    There are four types of business ownership. For each of these, the producer decides how to produce goods and services. Usually goods and services are produced in the least expensive and most efficient way. By keeping prices low, producers hope to control such a large market share that other competitors will not produce similar products. The effect of corporations' production methods on the environment is now an important issue. Another issue is the use of the resources of other countries by US corporations.

3. How should goods and services be distributed?

    Goods and services are distributed to individuals willing and able to pay for them. Sellers in the marketplace will sell to make a profit. Today, many corporations have grown to a very large size, and control much of the country's wealth.

GETTING ORGANIZED

1. List local businesses that are corporations, privately owned, partnerships, and franchises. Which of these are Canadian owned, and which of them are American owned?

2. Why do sports figures or media stars make so much money? What principles of the US open market system allow their huge wages to exist?

3. You have choices in almost everything you buy. Do you prefer to buy from a small, privately owned company or a large corporation? Why?

4. Research one of the very large American corporations. List the businesses they own or control under different names.

5. The United States has an extensive social welfare system, although this system seems to be getting smaller (providing fewer services to fewer people). Write a scenario that might occur if the US cancelled all of its social welfare programs. List all the people who would be affected and how they would be affected (both for the best and for the worst). Can you see any possibility that social welfare programs could be cancelled? What would have to happen before that decision would be considered?

6. Answer this question by making a list of supporting points: Should individuals be held responsible for their own economic well-being?

REACHING OUT

1. Imagine if a scouting party of aliens was to land in a typical American home. Their mission is to collect five items that would show the folks back home the basic structure of the American economy. These items must be symbols or what anthropologists call "icons." After examining these five items, the aliens would have a good understanding of how the American economy answers the economic questions: What is produced? How is it produced? For whom is it produced?

   Be sure to assess and evaluate your selections carefully. Your items need to represent the key features of a highly specialized market economy.

   (a) Have fun with this—present your collection to the class and defend your choices. Your class could rate the items on a 5-point scale. Do the items:
   - exhibit some of the values that contribute to the knowledge of American society (e.g. materialism, consumer convenience)?
   - reflect parts of the structure of the economic system of the US?
   - help the audience (of aliens) infer how the US economic system responds to the three economic questions (what to produce, how, and for whom)?

   (b) Would your choices for a Canadian home be different? Why? Why not? Your class might make a full session out of this exercise with class members listening to the presentations as if they were an alien culture.

2. There are four types of business organizations listed on page 105: Corporations, Private Enterprises, Partnerships, and Franchises. Design questions for business people around the issues raised in this chapter. Sample issues might include: What limits should be placed on the activities of business development in our community? Should business owners be asked to contribute more of their earnings to the tax system? It is important to generate questions relevant to your community or individual interest.

   (a) Invite a member of the business community to speak to your class. He or she should represent one of the four types of business organizations.

   (b) Have members of your class interview one of each type of business person.

Chapter Ten:

THE STRUCTURE OF THE PLANNED ECONOMY

GETTING IT STRAIGHT

1. What is a planned economy?
2. How did the ideology of the planned economy come into being?
3. How did Karl Marx contribute to the planned economy?
4. What are the main elements of the planned economy?
5. How do universal programs help create equality?
6. How does the planned economy relate to or affect the individual?
7. How are the three economic questions answered in the planned economy?

Planned economies are those directed by a central government. Economic decisions are made by a central planning committee. Another term for planned economy is command economy.

Planned economies must be examined in relation to political systems. In this chapter, we will describe a theoretical pure planned economy. In chapter 11, we will give an example of how planned economies work in the Soviet Union, a country with a dictatorial form of government.

A democracy which chooses to have a planned economy usually makes that choice because the pursuit of economic equality among all individuals is desired. A dictatorship which chooses a planned economy usually does so in order to protect the collective power of the state. In a democracy, power is shared among the people. In a dictatorship, power is concentrated in the hands of a few. Both democratic command economies and dictatorial command economies seek to provide economic security and growth, usually through a cooperative system, in which people and government expect to work together for the good of everyone.

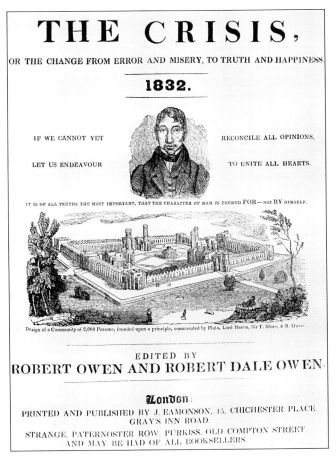

This photo shows the cover of a tract published by Robert Owen and his son. It shows an illustration of the cooperative community, New Harmony.

The Rise of Planned Economies

It is important to consider the historical environment that helped to shape socialism. Planned economies came about because some people felt that other economic systems were constructed so that one group of

ROBERT OWEN'S MILL: ## A COOPERATIVE SYSTEM

As you read the following Case Study, think about how Robert Owen's ideas could apply to an entire nation. Also, see what characteristics of a cooperative structure you can recognize in his story.

Robert Owen (1771-1858) was born into a poor family in Britain. He became the owner of a spinning mill. His ideologies about life guided him in operating his business. He believed that there was no conflict between happiness and prosperity. If people were happier, they would work harder and produce more. Specifically, he advocated the eight-hour working day and, unlike others of his time, he believed that children under the age of 11 should not work at all. He believed that people were naturally good, but that a poor environment would make them bad. He believed the industrial workplace was an example of a poor environment. His vision was to change this environment so that the best qualities of humans could be brought out. To make this positive change, Owen advocated cooperative ownership of property.

Owen was an interesting man. As the saying goes, he put his money where his mouth was. In his mill in New Lanark, Scotland, he created a new work environment. He provided education for children and taught his workers good health habits. He offered them medical benefits, a shortened work week, higher minimum wages, and job security. He even showed his faith in the workers by paying their wages when the plant was

continued

CASE STUDY *continued*

shut down. Many people thought he was crazy, but to their surprise, Owen's profits rose. His mill became a curiosity and was visited by other industrialists. Although many came to see his innovations, few followed his example.

Owen extended his ideas to North America. He built a cooperative community called New Harmony in Indiana. Owen invited the "industrious and well disposed" from all over the United States to come to live and work in New Harmony. But many who showed up were neither. Owen was not present to oversee the operation, and the experiment failed.

Although New Harmony was not harmonious, Owen showed that a work environment could be built in which workers were not exploited. His attempts suggested that governments were not able to solve every economic and political problem. Owen left behind a legacy of democratic socialism. He helped set up trade unions in Britain. He also showed that mutual consideration and communication between workers and employers would increase profits for both groups.

QUESTIONS:

1. What did Owen believe would make workers work better?
2. What effect do you think a shorter work week would have on workers?
3. Why do you think other industrialists did not follow the lead of Owen and try to reform their workplaces?
4. Considering what you know about your own personality and the personalities of your friends, answer the following question: Would most workers work harder for owners like Owen?

people attained greater privilege or power than another. Specifically, the idea of the planned economies came about as a response to the problems of industrialization in the eighteenth century.

The industrial growth of the eighteenth century provided an environment that favoured the rich and exploited the poor. Workers were expected to do backbreaking jobs with little monetary reward. The typical factory worker of the Industrial Revolution was faced with poor and often dangerous working conditions, long hours of work (up to 16 hours per day) and low wages. Not only adults suffered these conditions; children as young as eight were also workers in these factories. The rich really did get richer, and the poor really did get poorer.

The problems of the Industrial Revolution did not stop at the factory gates. Workers returned home to them after every shift. Living conditions for most were crowded and unsanitary. If the job didn't kill them, the dirt and disease in their homes would. As a result of poor living conditions, there was much social alienation, drunkenness, theft, squalor, and unemployment. Anyone who has read Charles Dickens' books or seen the film *A Christmas Carol* will have an idea of this life. All of this, some people concluded, was the result of one problem—the exploitation of the workers by the wealthy.

In the midst of these difficult conditions, some people wanted change. But these people believed that the changes could not be small ones. Merely changing the conditions in the workplace was not enough. A greater transformation was necessary. This transformation had to be in the form of a revolution. Everything had to change.

The only way to heal the system was to wrestle the means of production away from the rich and place it in the hands of someone, or some group, more concerned about the needs of the common people. These people believed that if a government controlled the economy and chose what should be produced, how it should be produced, and who should get it after it was produced, there would be a greater economic equality. Only in the hands of the government could industrial growth benefit all of society. This belief was the beginning of the idea of a command, or planned, economy.

The Ideology of the Planned Economy

Karl Marx

German philosopher and revolutionary Karl Marx (1818-1883) is probably the most well known advocate of the planned economy. He was greatly moved by the problems caused by the Industrial Revolution. Marx did not believe that gradual change was possible. He said that the workers must replace the ruling class through revolution before things could improve. Marx also believed that human lives were largely determined by economic relationships. Those who controlled the means of production determined the course of society. Those who lacked property lived according to the whims of

others. He felt that human history was the story of **class conflict** between workers and the capitalist class or those who owned the means of production. Marx and his friend Friedrich Engels co-authored *The Communist Manifesto* which detailed these beliefs.

In Marx's ideal communist society, people would be free. However, this freedom would be of a different type than in a capitalist society. There would be freedom from exploitation and economic insecurity. This freedom would allow people to develop their creativity and improve their talents and interests. In the economic system Marx envisioned, the interests of the individual would be best served when the whole

" WELCOME TO THE POTATO CANNING COLLECTIVE! HERE YOU ARE FREE TO DEVELOP YOUR OWN TALENTS AND ABILITIES — PROVIDED YOU DO IT WHILE CANNING POTATOES."

What are the cartoonists saying here about the nature of work in a Marxist society? Do you agree or disagree with their point of view?

country benefited. Society would be based on cooperation, not competition. To build this society, force would not be used. Instead, mutual trust and common goals would be the natural ideal.

Marx felt that workers in a capitalist society were deprived of their economic rights and that profits ("surplus value") should belong to the individuals who created the product and gave it value. It was not right that all the profits went to the entrepreneurs. Capitalists were naturally driven to seek maximum profit and to minimize costs. Marx felt that profits were maximized through exploitation of the workers.

Marx believed that all capitalist societies must follow a natural course of events. Because the capitalist oppressors would never negotiate, workers had no choice but to revolt. They would overthrow the existing order through revolution and implement a new classless society, which would provide goods and services equally for all, "from each according to their ability, to each according to their need." Marx believed that there were enough goods and services available for all. The problem with capitalism was that it did not put the available goods and services into the hands of all consumers. He envisioned large warehouses where people could get what they needed and wanted.

Marx also believed that workers were alienated from themselves and each other. This alienation helped business people exploit and degrade the workers. Alienation was caused by the division of labour where workers completed only small portions of the total product. They never saw the final product. Because work was so specialized, workers never felt attached to it or pride in the completion of the product. Workers were set away from each other with very little interaction.

How would you fix these problems of industrial society? Marx had dreams of an ideal society where all people would be able to earn a decent standard of living. There would be freedom from exploitation and economic necessity. Economic differences would continue to exist, but no person would be able to amass enormous wealth while others lived in poverty. Everyone would be provided equal opportunity.

Marx thought the economy would be administered by officials who would periodically collect information to help assess what should be produced to meet citizens' needs. Private property and the profit motive would be abolished. The interests of the individual would be served best when the whole society benefited. Society would be based on cooperation, not competition.

What Are the Elements of a Planned Economy?

Planned economic systems have come a long way since Marx first had visions of a new society without capitalism. Remember that elements of a planned economy can be found in democracies as well as in dictatorships. There are many elements which help a command economy function, including cooperation, **public ownership** of property, equality, and central planning.

Cooperation

Cooperation means that individuals or groups work together for the common goal. Individual workers use and develop their own talents and abilities in ways that will benefit the group. The incentive for individuals comes from using their unique skills to benefit their society and the people in it.

Cooperation also means that the individual is not fitted into the job, like squeezing a square peg into a round hole. Rather, the job is molded to take advantage of an individual's unique abilities. Developing personal talents means more fulfilling and rewarding work. Charles Fourier (1772-1837) was a French socialist philosopher who taught that as people within the society use their talents cooperatively all workers will feel good about their work. They will begin to work, not just for profit, but for the love of their job.

These organizing principles of a planned economy differ quite radically from the principles used to mold market economies. Competition and the profit motive are not the driving forces behind the production of goods and services in a cooperative society. Cooperation and equality are the driving forces.

In a planned economy, the government considers the needs of the community, and then determines what goods and services are needed by the people. As products are needed or wanted, they are produced.

In summary, the ethics of the collectivists (those that believe in cooperation) rest on the simple logic that the collective is more important than one individual.

Collective farms are common in the Soviet Union, although that may change in the 1990s.

WHAT IS COLLECTIVISM?

In theory, collectivists believe that if everyone works together as a group, the entire society will benefit. The task of the government is to enforce the decision of the majority concerning the individual's duties and responsibilities. These include consenting to the decisions of the majority or the central authority and contributing to society by working.

Planned economies believe that collectivism provides individuals with a number of benefits. First, collectivism provides greater equality for people than the individualist market economy. The government provides equality by intervening to control the economy and help protect the rights and freedoms of all members of society. The government ensures that economic, social, and political barriers will not interfere with a person's ability to participate fully in society. In other words, discrimination due to race, sex, or religion should not interfere with the development of the individual.

Most collectivists are humanitarians. They believe that society should operate in the best interests of all its members. No society should benefit just a few fortunate people. Collectivists are concerned with social welfare and economic equality. They believe in providing a basic standard of living for each person, regardless of that person's contribution to society. Collectivists would likely contribute to charities such as Santa's Helpers or the Food Bank. They would believe in the welfare state, the idea that the society should look after the citizens of the state throughout their lives, even if they were not contributing to society by working.

Public Ownership of Property

Public ownership of property means that production is communally owned and controlled by the state. State ownership allows governments to control all natural and human resources.

Public ownership of property rests on the philosophy of collectivism. If ownership of property is centralized and placed in the hands of the government, it can help ensure that the collective property of the state will bring the greatest benefit to all citizens. In a planned economy, individuals cannot purchase or control large amounts of property. Even if some private property is allowed, the rights of the individual who owns that property are always subordinate to the rights of the community.

Equality as Incentive

Different societies hold different ideological positions. Each also defines basic ideas in a different way. The term *equality* is one of those. In a planned economy, equality means that all members of society should have the same opportunities and benefits as everyone else. All people should be guaranteed economic security. Even if people are unable to work, they should not be allowed to starve. They should be provided with basic social services that allow them to maintain the minimum standard of living as defined by the state.

These social programs should also be **universal**. Every person in society should be entitled to the same services. An example of a universal social program in Canada would be the medical care program. Currently, all citizens and landed immigrants in Canada are entitled to the same medical attention, no matter what their income or position in society. It should be noted that some provinces, like Alberta, demand that a medicare

These Soviet students' education will be completely paid for by the state. Because only the very best students are accepted into university, many of these children attend evening lessons to help them raise their marks. Their parents must pay for these lessons.

premium be paid to the government to help support this system.

Socialism is the belief in equality of opportunity. This means that citizens should be allowed to take part in all the activities of their society. People are considered equal regardless of race, sex, or age. There is no prejudice by birth, and all people are allowed to contribute according to their ability to do so. For example, no one would be denied a post-secondary education because they lacked the money. Education is a basic right, and this right is supported by the government. In most planned economies, people are given free education. However, this doesn't mean that a person without ability or intelligence can become a doctor or a teacher. People are generally placed into the educational system based on their abilities.

A flaw in this system is that when economic decisions are made by those with political power, friends and family of the politicians may acquire more privileges. Whose children will go to the best schools, or get the best jobs? There is always the possibility of privileges being used for personal advantage, especially when vast power is concentrated in the hands of a few people.

Central Planning

Central planning requires a group of economic experts who carry out the goals of the government. These experts study the economy and then advise the government about the best way to meet its goals. Public control of property, and some form of price and wage controls are essential to central planning. In a centrally planned economy, major production and consumption decisions are made by those in political office. They are not made by individual corporations or consumers.

Central planning provides governments with the opportunity to plan ahead and carry out long-term national goals. Market economies are seen as shortsighted, based sometimes on the ever changing desires of a fickle public. Supply and demand is not as important in a planned economy as it is in a market economy. After considering the alternatives, the central planners make conscious decisions about goods and prices. The consumer has little say about what is produced. Production and consumption are organized to achieve the needs and wants defined by those in political office.

In theory, because the state controls the means of production, it is quite easy for central planners to adjust their decisions if they wish. Central planners try to make decisions that help maintain a steady economic growth and advance their economy at a quicker rate than would a market economy.

One reason centrally planned economies can advance more quickly than market economies is that they can allocate a substantial portion of their nation's resources to building up a particular sector. Many communist governments use what are called five year plans to emphasize some part of the economy at the expense of the other parts of the economy. For example, agricultural production might be a top priority, while factory modernization lags behind.

There is usually a certain kind of relationship between leaders and workers in a planned economy. What point are the cartoonists making? Is their point fair?

CASE STUDY:

FIVE YEAR PLANS

As you read the following Case Study, try to determine the effectiveness of five year plans.

In theory, five year plans can be very effective ways to stimulate the economy in centrally planned economies. Central planners use their power to institute five year plans to build a particular sector of the economy quickly. Stalin's five year plans worked because he had the power and political will to institute them at all costs. His five year plans built up the industrial strength in the Soviet Union in the late 1920s and 1930s. Because his power was complete, he was able to take land from wealthy farmers (kulaks) by harsh and heavy-handed means. Many kulaks and their families were sent to work camps. Others were left to starve after Stalin took their grain.

With the land Stalin confiscated, he helped feed the industrial workers. He also sold grain to obtain money to purchase industrial equipment. Stalin justified what he was doing by stating that his actions would help the entire population instead of a chosen few. Now the country would be able to obtain the capital goods necessary to produce consumer goods.

Stalin's five year plans were interrupted by World War II. Khrushchev, who became leader after Stalin, also employed five year plans. Khrushchev planned to increase the amount of farm land and, therefore, production. But his plan was unsuccessful. The land he attempted to bring into production was marginal and not very good for agriculture.

The difference between political theory and economic practice has been felt inside and outside the Soviet Union. Sometimes the five year plans have worked well, other times they have failed. It is difficult to prosper in times of drought, flood, and other natural disasters. Sometimes humans have brought internal conflicts and revolutions. Central planning is not a fail-proof answer to economic problems.

QUESTIONS:

1. Stalin believed that "the end justifies the means." Do you agree? Is it right for a government to use drastic measures to provide a better life for the people of the country in the future?

2. Do you think command economies have an advantage over market economies because of their ability to direct their nation's resources and fulfill a nation's goals more quickly?

3. How might a market economy develop one sector of its economy faster than another without the drastic tactics used by Stalin?

4. Many factors make it difficult to meet goals set by five year plans. List some of the human or natural problems that might conspire against such plans.

Central planners, by controlling the resources, can establish a greater control over the economy. The result is that planned economies can reduce unemployment problems and maintain low rates of inflation. Some planners even decide what work individuals will do, where they will work, and what they will receive as wages. All these decisions are made in the best interests of the society. Those ''best interests'' are defined by those with political authority.

PEEK

AT A PLANNED ECONOMY

Politics	Economics
- government plans and controls the economy - government provides for all needs of all citizens	- market operates according to central plan - public ownership - freedom from exploitation

Environment	Knowledge
- Industrial Revolution and technological change threatened to dehumanize people - Many centrally planned economies are moving toward a market system in the 1990s	- problems of industrialization - workers can be exploited by capitalists - alienation - alienation and exploitation need to be solved

Field of Action
- a society where collective action is desirable in order to protect the individual's economic and political security

CHALLENGES TO THE PLANNED ECONOMY

CHALLENGE 1: Getting People to Work Hard

Criticisms of planned economies focus on the lack of incentives. Critics believe that people will not contribute to the best of their abilities because there is no economic incentive. Even if people do work harder, there are few personal rewards. Critics believe that personal rewards usually encourage greater success because humans are basically selfish. Working together in a cooperative community is a pipe dream that doesn't work. Because people live in cold, hard economic realities, they need cold, hard economic ideals. Greed and power fuel more fires than collectivism and cooperation, critics say. They add that most people believe they should be free to make their own decisions.

Most people care more about their personal economic futures than about the economic future of the whole society. People cannot be trusted to work cooperatively.

Can planned economies also encourage personal initiative and hard work?

CHALLENGE 2: Lack of Technological Progress

In a planned economy, technological progress may be hampered. If state economic planners make all the decisions, new inventions and breakthroughs tend to come slowly.

continued

continued

Shutting down a plant to re-tool means production quotas won't be met. When central authorities make the plans, the people will not take the same risks as people in market economies. Governments tend to be conservative. They focus on basic needs rather than the production of those novelty items that often spur inventive and creative technological advances in the market economy. Individual initiative is needed.

How can technological innovation be encouraged in a planned economy?

CHALLENGE 3: Bureaucracies

Planned economies require huge bureaucracies. Both state and individual agencies are large. As bureaucracies expand, more people are required to keep the government running. As the number of administrators becomes larger, the government reacts even more slowly to changes and the business of governing becomes increasingly more tedious. Departments become more specialized and communications between them are slow. The ordinary person is isolated from government.

Is it possible to have a centrally planned economy without bureaucracy?

CHALLENGE 4: Black Markets

Since consumer sovereignty is not important in planned economies, many goods and services desired by consumers are not produced. Black markets, underground markets not sanctioned by the state, often provide goods to people who can pay for them. These black markets disrupt the basic purpose of the centrally planned economy because they place a greater stress on people to get more money. Goods sold cannot be purchased from regular markets. An example of a black market activity was the sale of Levi jeans in the USSR. In the 1970s these jeans were unavailable in stores, and commanded a very high price.

How can planned economies consider consumer demands of non-basic items?

CHALLENGE 5: Loss of Individuality

Another criticism of the planned economy is that individuals are forced to conform. When people are made to act and live in the same way as everyone else, they often lose their individual personalities and become part of the crowd. As a result, conformity reduces individual freedoms. People cannot buy what they wish, nor can they work at jobs they choose. They work where they are told to work. The result is that people tend to become placid, with little drive or creativity.

How important is the opportunity for individual goals and choice of work?

CHALLENGE 6: Who Can Plan the Future?

Planning and attempting to fulfill the goals of the state can be done except that one ingredient of any plan remains a mystery—the future. Economically and politically, the future global scene can only be guessed at. No matter how carefully the plan is made, a war, a famine, civil unrest, drought, or disasters, such as the Chernobyl meltdown, can change the plan overnight.

How can centrally planned economies deal with an unknown future?

BEAUTIFUL! MARVELOUS! THE STATE WANTS 500 MORE OF THE SAME!

True or False: the cartoonists are saying that centrally planned economies encourage individuality.

challenges. A society with a planned economy would answer the three economic questions in this way:

1. What goods and services are produced?

   This is seen both as a political and an economic question. The central planning authority controls production, reflecting the goals of the state. The perceived needs of the people are considered by these planners, but individual goals are secondary to state goals.

2. How should goods and services be produced?

   Central planners decide how the goods and services are to be produced. There is collective ownership of the means of production. The planners also consider the amount and type of resources that are available, and they regulate wages and prices in order to control unemployment and inflation.

3. How should goods and services be distributed?

   No one should do without basic goods and services, and all individuals should contribute according to their abilities. Goods and services are distributed according to what the government believes the people within the society need or should have.

SUMMARY

Planned economies do not offer consumers a wide variety of choices or the opportunity for entrepreneurs to make a great deal of money. Central planning, which may work well on paper, often faces difficulties and

GETTING ORGANIZED

1. In Canada there are a number of social programs at work to help Canadian citizens and residents. Find out if the government pays Family Allowance for you. Find out how much it is. If the government stopped paying it, what would happen? Find out if your grandparents receive an Old Age Pension. Would you be able to live on the average Old Age Pension?

2. List publicly owned companies in your community. What types of businesses are they (service, production, etc.)? Is there a reason why publicly owned businesses do the work they do?

3. Think of businesses that hire students. Do you think the employers are concerned about working conditions, hours of work, or the age of employees? Imagine you are being treated unfairly at work. What can you do? What would be the advantages and disadvantages of your options?

4. Health care is a basic need in any community. Find out the average daily cost of hospitalization, and how much doctors receive for delivering a baby, fixing a broken leg, or performing a heart transplant. What do doctors take into consideration when prescribing treatment?

5. Is everyone entitled to free education? Who pays for the education you are receiving? Who decides how you use the educational materials you have? How different would education be if it followed the free market design? Do you think it could work?

6. Consider the following question: To what extent should a government control the area of health care (both preventing and treating illness) of its citizens? Instead of answering the question directly, generate a list of sub-questions you would need to answer if you were going to answer the main question.

REACHING OUT

1. Review newspapers for the next two weeks looking for news from countries in Eastern Europe trying to adapt their economies away from centrally planned models. Using the *Challenges to the Planned Economy* section on pages 125-126, identify the challenges reported in the news articles. Summarize the challenges facing planned economies. Is there a pattern?

2. Canada's Charter of Rights guarantees political, but not economic, freedoms. For example, freedom of speech is guaranteed but not freedom from hunger or poverty.
   (a) Write an "Economic Bill of Rights" as if Canada had a planned economy.
   (b) Who would pay for these rights to be guaranteed? Research in your library for constitutions of planned economies like the USSR up until 1990. These constitutions might reveal some ideas for an Economic Bill of Rights.
   (c) Rank order your "Bill of Rights" from most important to least important. Are some rights more important than others?
   (d) Some environmental groups have proposed that an "Environmental Bill of Rights" should be included in Canada's constitution. They argue that legal rights and freedom from discrimination are important, but so are the rights to clean air and water. Compose such a list of environmental rights.

   What arguments could be put forward in opposition to such a bill? Would those arguments originate from supporters of a market or a planned economy?

Chapter Eleven:

THE SOVIET UNION

GETTING IT STRAIGHT

1. How did the present economic system of the USSR come about?
2. How are manufacturing and agricultural economic decisions made in the USSR?
3. What part does the individual play in the economy of the USSR?
4. What is the difference between state farms and collective farms?
5. How have glasnost and perestroika changed the Soviet economy?
6. What are some advantages and disadvantages of the Soviet economic system?
7. How does the USSR answer the three economic questions?

The Union of Soviet Socialist Republics, or the Soviet Union, is the world's largest country. Its land area covers over one-sixth of the Earth's surface. The Soviet Union is a federation of 15 republics. Its economy is organized around the principles of socialism. After the United States, the Soviet Union is the world's greatest industrial power. Within its borders lie huge treasures of minerals, especially iron ore. Because of its size and strength, the Soviet Union is a world political leader. Until recently, it dominated the affairs of many other states in Eastern Europe, which were treated almost like political and economic colonies of the USSR.

Red Square, located in Moscow, the capital of the USSR, is the centre of the Soviet government.

THUMBNAIL FACTS

Area: 22 402 236 sq. km

Population: 280 442 000

Density: 13 people per sq. km

Chief Cities: Moscow (capital), Leningrad, Kiev, Tashkent, Gorky.

Type of Government: People's Republic

Most Important Industries: steel, chemicals, timber, fishing, petroleum, motor vehicles.

Agriculture: wheat, rye, dairy products, cotton, tobacco, sugar beets, potatoes.

Minerals: coal, iron ore, chromite, platinum, tungsten.

Most Important Trading Partners: Bulgaria, Poland, Hungary, Czechoslovakia, Germany, and Japan.

GNP: $188.9 billion

The Soviet Union is a northern country. Most of the land area lies about 50 degrees north latitude. At its westernmost part, it borders Europe. At its easternmost part, it comes within 5 km of Alaska. Inside its borders a great variety of ethnic groups live in diverse geographical climates and landforms. To most North Americans, the Soviet Union seems like a unified country, with a centrally planned economy and a dictatorial political system. In reality, it has been difficult to unify the diverse ethnic groups and prop up an economy that has often sputtered from poor grain harvests and difficulties in distributing goods and services. The Soviet Union's seemingly powerful central structure may in fact be falling apart.

Recent political and economic reforms in the Soviet Union make it difficult and exciting to write about. Until recently, the Soviet Union has had a planned economy. The organizing principle was the belief that government should make economic decisions for the collective good of the whole society. In setting economic priorities, addressing group needs was more important than allowing individual advancement. The Soviet government believed that economic growth, equality, stability, and individual security were best achieved by providing effective controls on the national economy and by distributing the resources of the land equally.

The Planned Economy

The Soviet economy was born during World War I (in November of 1917) when Vladimir Ilyich Lenin led a revolution to overthrow the corrupt and inefficient tsarist government. His rallying cry was ''Peace, Land, and Bread.'' The tsarist regime was never able to supply either the soldiers or the people with basic

Lenin led a highly organized group of revolutionaries called the Bolsheviks.

items like food or clothing. Industrial workers fared no better. They suffered low wages and poor living and working conditions. These problems escalated during the war.

Lenin promised to end the war, divide the land among the peasants, and give control of industry to the people. He promised economic growth, public ownership of industry and agriculture, and individual security. Lenin brought the ideas of Karl Marx to the Soviet people. First he nationalized private property, often without compensation to the owner.

Nationalizing industry was relatively easy because workers liked the idea of owning the factory where they worked. The hardest private property to nationalize was agricultural land. Many peasants wanted their own, private plots of land. Lenin believed that building the country was a cooperative effort, equally shared by farmers and workers. Lenin planned for people to "contribute according to their ability and receive according to their need." He decided that most land in the USSR would be collectively owned.

Lenin's dream was that the Communist Party would be a party of the workers, a "dictatorship of the **proletariat**." The means of production were to be put into the hands of the people. Like Marx, Lenin believed that history was dominated by the struggle between the owners of the means of production and the workers. If this were true, shared public ownership would eliminate one reason for conflict.

Economic Decisions

The Politburo (Political Bureau) conducted the business of the Communist Party. The Party dictated policy and the government carried it out. Basic economic policy decisions were made by the government. It first decided whether to produce consumer goods or capital goods. Consumer goods were used directly by the people. Capital goods, such as machinery, produced consumer goods. In this way, capital goods were used indirectly by the people to improve their quality of life.

Once an economic decision was made, it was implemented by the central planning agency (Gosplan).

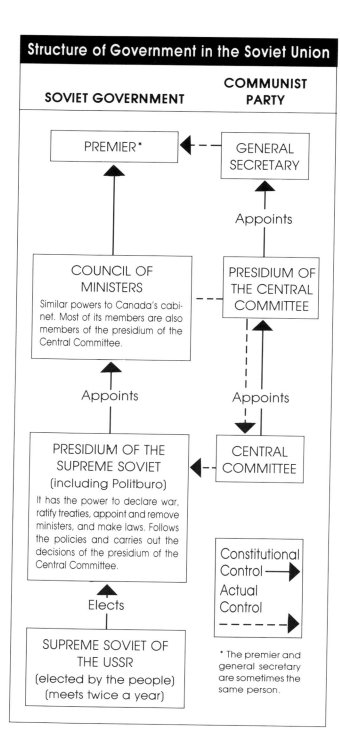

Structure of Government in the Soviet Union

SOVIET GOVERNMENT

COMMUNIST PARTY

PREMIER*

GENERAL SECRETARY

Appoints

COUNCIL OF MINISTERS

Similar powers to Canada's cabinet. Most of its members are also members of the presidium of the Central Committee.

PRESIDIUM OF THE CENTRAL COMMITTEE

Appoints

Appoints

PRESIDIUM OF THE SUPREME SOVIET (including Politburo)

It has the power to declare war, ratify treaties, appoint and remove ministers, and make laws. Follows the policies and carries out the decisions of the presidium of the Central Committee.

CENTRAL COMMITTEE

Elects

Constitutional Control ➝

Actual Control ---➝

SUPREME SOVIET OF THE USSR (elected by the people) (meets twice a year)

* The premier and general secretary are sometimes the same person.

The Gosplan was made up of economic experts, statisticians, and engineers. It relied on the Central Statistical Administration to collect data about the production capacity of factories, types of labour, number of machines, and available natural resources. This central Soviet agency decided how best to use the scarce resources of the society.

" ALTHOUGH BATHTUB PRODUCTION IS UP, I CANNOT SHOW YOU HOW MUCH BECAUSE, AS YOU CAN SEE HERE, PRODUCTION OF CHARTS AND GRAPHS IS WAY DOWN."

What are the cartoonists trying to tell us about Gosplan? What are some of the problems of a centrally planned economy?

After the Gosplan received information, it estimated the resources required and set goals for the economy. The Gosplan knew what resources were available and attempted to balance the demand for goods with available resources. For example, the Gosplan may have decided that new housing was a priority. It knew that lumber, glass, and bathtubs would be needed. It estimated the resources required to fill quotas and determined how an increase in the production of lumber or bathtubs affected the rest of the economy. If too much lumber was needed for another project, housing projects were scaled down.

After overall targets were set, Soviet planners broke down the plan into individual quotas. For example, the Ministry of Construction issued a production quota to each bathtub construction plant. The plant manager studied the quota and made a list of all the resources (land, labour, and capital) required to fulfill it.

The plant manager replied to the Ministry of Construction who then sent the reply to Gosplan. Since bonuses were based on output, it was in the plant manager's best interest to underestimate his or her plant's capacity to meet the quota and win a bonus. Ministry leaders and members of Gosplan met to negotiate quotas and required resources. These negotiations were difficult and sometimes unfriendly. Any adjustments to quotas were made at this time. Gosplan then made the final decision about the national economic plan. The plant's quota was sent back to the plant manager who contracted for resources and sold directly to wholesalers and retail outlets.

Until the late 1980s, military goods and heavy industry were economic priorities in the Soviet Union and received most of the country's resources. Consumer goods were often placed at the bottom of the priority list.

Economic Incentives

In the Soviet Union, plant managers were very concerned about meeting quotas. However, they often did not care how a quota was met. Meeting quotas was more important than making quality products or using resources efficiently.

In the perfect planned economy, love of work would be the only incentive a worker needed. However, like Canadians, most Soviet workers want something material to hold in their hands and call their own. In a recent response, the Soviet government set up incentive systems. Managers receive bonuses based on a percentage of their salary for meeting a quota. Some may receive a car, special vacations, preferred housing, or access to preferred places of shopping.

CASE STUDY:
SOVIET HOUSING

As you read, think about what *preferred housing* might be.

In the Soviet Union, a house with a plot of land of approximately 500 square metres generally costs between 8000 and 10 000 rubles. The average Soviet citizen earns 240 rubles per month. Few houses in the Soviet Union are built for individuals, and most are built by the state. Some private homes are built by cooperatives in order to lower the selling price.

It is more common for Soviet people to live in apartments than in single-family houses. It is also more common for the Soviet government to build apartments for its people. In total, there were 2.1 million apartments built by the state in 1986.

QUESTIONS:

1. Canadian mortgage companies indicate that a person should not pay more than one-third of their gross income toward a mortgage over a 25-year period. If these same figures held true for the Soviet Union, would the average Soviet wage earner be able to afford one of the new cooperative homes?

2. Do you live in a single-family dwelling or in an apartment? Do you think living in an apartment rather than a single-family dwelling changes the way a person thinks about home? If so, in what ways?

Plant managers can now earn more money if their plant runs efficiently and makes a profit. Managers also receive bonuses if they can find a use for products that were formerly discarded. These bonuses began as a way to control the waste of resources. State inspectors travel from plant to plant to test product quality. The need for "State Acceptance" has made factory workers more interested in creating quality products.

In the past, Soviet central planners made economic plans for the entire society. The system was efficient because the government could determine what goods and services the nation needed. On the other hand, citizens lacked the economic freedom to purchase what they wished. It was difficult for Gosplan to plan the

What Are Some Criticisms of Central Planning?

Like other economic systems, central planning has problems. The Soviet economy is particularly difficult to change. One problem lies in adapting new technology to industry. In the past, there was little incentive to use new technology. Placing new technology in a Soviet plant took time and often resulted in the plant not meeting its quota. The long-term increase in a plant's productivity was sometimes lost in the rush to meet quotas.

Housing is important to people everywhere. How might this need be filled through central planning? What problems might this cause?

economy completely. Consumers sometimes would not purchase products, no matter how inexpensive they were.

Consumer goods were sometimes produced by different state enterprises, but consumer demand did not influence the supply or the price of the product. Product prices were usually set by the central planners. Price controls enabled the government to accomplish its goals more easily. For example, the government charged high prices for luxury goods, like cars, to discourage consumer demand and to build up other sectors of the economy. Recently, the Soviet government has worked harder to balance the production of capital goods and consumer goods.

Soviet central planning was slow to respond to consumer decisions, and there was no efficient way to replace items that sold out quickly. Shortages resulted. Often Soviet plants produced goods no one wanted simply to fulfill a quota for bonuses. There was no incentive to discontinue production. Soviet planners were also notoriously slow to pick up market signs and hesitated to change established quotas. Unwanted products usually sat in government warehouses or were disposed of at very low prices.

Plant managers worried more about meeting quotas than about the cost of production. Often, resources were misused or wasted because it was easier to fulfill a quota if resources were plentiful. Plants seldom worked cooperatively. Instead, they often hoarded resources. Sometimes they estimated lower output capabilities than what they could actually provide, to meet targets more easily and receive bonuses. Central planners are now responding by trying to make plants more efficient and providing incentives based on plant profits.

Agriculture

Agriculture has always been the lifeblood of the Soviet Union. When Josef Stalin took over the leadership of the Soviet Union in 1928, he **collectivized** agricultural lands. Stalin recognized the need for industrial growth and, like Lenin, believed that industrialization should be partially financed by agriculture. But Soviet agriculture was inefficient.

Poor farmers worked mostly by hand. Wealthy farmers (kulaks) produced more, but demanded high prices for their products. Stalin's highly unpopular solution was to place all farms under state control. Many who disagreed with this plan were sent to Siberian work camps. Some kulaks destroyed their machinery and killed their livestock rather than giving them to the state. These actions drastically reduced agricultural production and famine occurred. Millions died, while the grain produced was exported to pay for industrialization.

Stalin finally gained control of Soviet agriculture and created collective farms by putting smaller farms together. Individuals kept their homes and animals, but machinery was owned by the group. An elected management board decided what to produce, what machinery to use, and who would use it at which times. A farmer's income was based on the farm profits and the amount of work the farmer did. Agricultural production was further increased by farming more land.

State and Collective Farms

State farms were also introduced. Management boards made all the production decisions for these farms. All produce and profits went to the state. Some state farms were set aside to research and develop better farming techniques. Stalin's ideas worked. Agricultural production increased as farming became more mechanized and efficient. Today, slightly over half the cultivated land in the Soviet union is farmed by the state. These state farms pay wages that are not based on profits.

Still, collective farms are more productive than state farms. Farmers who work on collective farms are given incentives to increase production. Workers' salaries are based on profit. Unfortunately, no matter how hard farmers work, the Soviet weather can be unpredictable. Weather and farm profits go hand in hand. If the weather is good, hard work is rewarded and farmers can make higher profits. If the weather is bad, no amount of hard work can save the harvest.

Not all land is controlled by the government. Three percent of all cultivated land is allowed for private use. Currently more is being allotted to individuals. Farmers may sell their livestock and produce at local collective farm markets. These private plots are intensively farmed and are very productive. They provide about half a farmer's income and almost half the fresh vegetables and meats available in the Soviet economy. Farmers' markets in the Soviet Union are much like farmers' markets in Canada, and the prices of produce are based on supply and demand.

Critics of the Soviet system wonder if, since the Soviet Union usually must import grain, state farms should be turned into collective farms or whether workers' wages should reflect the profits of the farms where they work. Critics also suggest that, if farmers owned more land, Soviet farms might become more productive.

Private Enterprise

The small, private plots of farm land were not the only private businesses found in the Soviet Union. Soviet law allowed some small businesses run by individual peasants and artisans. These businesses were mainly in the service industry. The general principle was that people could run their own businesses as long as they did not employ, and therefore exploit, others. These businesses could not sell goods produced by others. Businesses that were privately owned included watchmakers, jewelry makers, taxi drivers, tailors, and restaurant owners. Under the Gorbachev government, more individually owned businesses were allowed.

Concern over the ''exploitation of the worker'' no longer prevents small businesses from becoming more common in the Soviet Union.

PRIVATE TAXI CABS IN LENINGRAD

If you are one of the lucky people in the Soviet Union who owns a car, there is always a way to make an extra ruble. Individuals who own cars in Leningrad and have had a license for at least three years without a traffic violation may moonlight as cabbies. Some part-time drivers work four hours after their day jobs to increase the number of taxis operating on Leningrad streets.

These part-time drivers charge the same fares as the drivers who work for state owned cabs. Private drivers pay a monthly tax on top of their insurance, gas, and repairs. They are some of the most active private entrepreneurs in the Soviet Union.

Meeting Basic Needs

Social services, supplied by the Soviet government, are not included in wages, but represent about one-third of a person's average monthly earnings. The government also offers sick leave, pregnancy leave, and state-sponsored funerals for the poor. Soviet men may receive a pension at 60, women at 55. To receive a full pension, one must work 25 years. Pensioners are encouraged to work past their pensionable age. If they choose, they can work shorter hours and shorter work weeks.

Maternity leave is granted to a mother for up to 18 months. Mothers receive full pay for 70 days and a portion of their income for the rest of the time. Mothers also receive paid leave for 14 days if their children are sick. Parents on low incomes receive allowances for children up to 12 years of age.

The Soviet government offers a wide range of social services to its citizens. Everyone in the Soviet Union has the right to health, housing, education, and cultural benefits. The government actively encourages citizens to use health services. The Soviet health care system was so thorough that it was used by the UN's World Health Organization as a model for other health services. Still, the Soviets felt they needed improvements like the construction of new hospitals and clinics.

Education is free from the first day of school to the end of post-secondary education. All Soviet students must attend school for 10 years. The goal of schooling is to help students feel at home in their diverse world. University students do not pay tuition. They are given free textbooks and low-cost housing. Most students also receive a stipend each month to help pay their living expenses.

Students in the Soviet Union, like those in other countries, work part-time. Students work an average of five hours per day and use the money to buy luxury goods like motorbikes and stereos. Soviets see part-time work by students as "labour education" and believe it helps young people develop a positive attitude toward work.

Low-cost housing is offered to low income earners. The state builds 70 per cent of all housing. Rent costs about 3 per cent of a worker's monthly earnings, less than the average Canadian family pays for a mortgage. Private dwellings are located in rural areas because the government has not permitted private housing in urban areas. The wealthy can build their own homes or be part of cooperative housing developments. Cooperative homes are usually expensive, but are quite desirable. They are much like condominiums in Canada.

CASE STUDY:

THE RIGHT TO HEALTH

In this Case Study, you are asked to consider whether or not giving every resident a thorough medical checkup will help prevent disease.

In the Soviet Union, doctors work quite differently than doctors in Canada. To guarantee everyone the right to health, Soviet doctors go to their patients to give them regular checkups. Soviet doctors believe that disease prevention is more important than disease treatment. What these doctors have found is interesting. People in apparent good health between 45 and 50 years suffer from many ailments, including heart disease.

Although the idea of seeking out patients and treating them before they go to a doctor is expensive, the Soviet government feels that the expense is justified and will save money in the long run. Medical checkups include x-rays of the lungs, a cardiogram, and an examination by a dentist. It is less expensive to prevent or treat disease in an early stage than it is to try to heal a person who is very ill.

QUESTIONS:

1. Why do Soviet doctors give healthy people checkups?
2. What are the advantages of preventative health care? What might be some disadvantages?
3. Write a 250-word essay either agreeing or disagreeing with the following statement: Canadian doctors should practise preventative medicine.

Although many Soviet families can now afford to buy apartments, the government does not yet have the ability or materials to meet the demand for new apartment buildings.

The Soviet government attempts to reduce income inequality by pricing products to help accomplish economic goals. Central planners set low prices for books

WHAT DOES ECONOMIC EQUALITY MEAN IN THE SOVIET UNION?

Karl Marx believed people would work for the love of working and contribute to society "from each according to his ability, to each according to his need." Today Soviets believe that workers should be paid for what they do. The Soviet system attempts to distribute income equally, yet offers higher wages to workers in jobs that require greater skill or are dangerous. Salary is also based on how much a person contributes to society. Plant managers, government officials, scientists, hockey stars, and doctors earn the highest salaries. Labourers are at the bottom of the wage scale.

The supreme goal of socialism is to encourage the well-being of the people and to satisfy their material and cultural needs. The Soviet government works to ensure that all citizens maintain a decent standard of living and quality of life. Like many countries, the government provides services through social programs. Because private property is limited and profits are highly taxed, there are few millionaires in the Soviet Union.

to promote education, low prices for clothing to encourage larger families, and low prices for food because everyone, rich or poor, must eat. On the other hand, luxury goods, such as cars and caviar, are expensive.

Taxation also provides some income equality. The Soviet government pays for social services through taxation. Profits on state businesses provide most of the money for social programs. A sales tax, called a turnover tax, accounts for much of the government's income. This tax changes from year to year and is used to control spending, much in the way that Canada, the United States, and Sweden use fiscal and monetary policy. The tax is decreased during slow economic times and raised when the economy is strong.

Income tax is part of the Soviet economy. Like that of Canada and the United States, Soviet income tax hits middle income earners more than low or high income earners. The Soviet income tax rate is one of the lowest in the world, approximately one-third the tax rate of the United States. Attempts at income equality have not narrowed the spread between the high income and low income earners. Skilled workers make about three times more money than the unskilled in the Soviet Union.

Glasnost and Perestroika Change the Soviet Economy

As we discussed in chapter 6, the new openness or glasnost has appeared recently under the rule of Mikhail Gorbachev. Glasnost allows individuals more opportunities to make decisions about their daily lives. People have greater political choice because more than one party member is nominated for election. Within reason, people may criticize the government. Reporters may freely express their opinions about politics and life. If they can afford it, citizens may travel to other parts of the world.

Perestroika means to restructure or reform. It came as a response to some of the problems in the Soviet economy like slow technological progress, inability to cut costs of production, poor quality products, poor supply of products, and indifference of the workers. Perestroika is an example of the Soviet government trying to accommodate the wishes of the people.

Perestroika allows Soviets to buy and sell goods at a profit. In an effort to meet the constant demand of the Soviet people for new and different products, businesses have been given more operational freedom. Workers have also been given more freedom to choose where they want to work. With perestroika, Soviets hope to abandon command economic measures and allow greater independence in both industry and agriculture. The goal is for industries to become self-supporting and profitable. This radical economic reform

The Soviet Union and Canada have teamed up to open a McDonald's in Moscow. Vladimir Malyshkow (left) and George Cohon (right) are shown here at the opening. Most of the young workers pictured behind them are part-time workers.

CASE STUDY:

PART-TIME WORK AT MCDONALD'S

McDonald's golden arches have hit Moscow. Not only are the Big Macs new to the Soviet people, but the company has brought with it a large number of part-time jobs. As you read this Case Study, consider the result of a McDonald's opening in the Soviet Union.

Moscow's McDonald's hired 630 workers out of an application avalanche of 25 000. Most were from the University of Moscow. Why were so many hired for only one restaurant? This McDonald's is the largest in the world. It has a seating capacity of 900.

The salary for part-time workers is one ruble, 50 kopecks per hour. This translates into about $2.15 Cdn. A Big Mac, fries, and a soft drink cost five rubles, 60 kopecks—about a half day's wage at the average monthly salary of 240 rubles.

QUESTIONS:

1. How much do McDonald's part-time workers earn in Canada?
2. Compare the cost of a Big Mac, fries, and a drink in Canada to those in the Soviet Union. If this dinner cost a half day's pay in Canada, what would it cost? At that rate, would you eat at McDonald's?
3. If education is paid for by the state, why do you think students at the University of Moscow are looking for part-time jobs?
4. Do you think there is a difference between students looking for part-time jobs in Canada and in the Soviet Union? As you think about your answer to this question, consider the basic differences between a capitalist and a command economy.

is designed to transform the economy from a centralized, regulated system to one balanced between centralism and consumer sovereignty. The Soviet government wants the economy to use resources more efficiently and pay closer attention to the demands of consumers.

As well as allowing more private business, Gorbachev hopes to modernize the marketplace. Formerly, an individual who bought a product at a state store had to wait in three line-ups. The first was to find out if the item was still available. The second was to pay for it. The third was to present a receipt to a salesperson to get the merchandise. New Soviet stores work much like stores in Canada. A consumer can pick out the product, take it to the cashier, and pay for it.

Other Soviet reforms allow businesses to operate with less government regulation. Plant managers will not be as strictly controlled by the central planners. They can plan their own economic strategies, develop new products, improve present products, expand or reduce, and set salaries. The goal is to make a profit. Now, for example, the Lada automobile factory may buy parts from anywhere in the world and sell anywhere in the world.

Joint ventures between Soviet companies and foreign investors are becoming more common. These changes spell a new approach to Soviet economics. Only time will tell if these changes will make the Soviet economy stronger.

CASE STUDY:

JOINT VENTURES IN THE SOVIET UNION

In the following Case Study, you will read about opportunities that Gorbachev has created with new economic reforms. Think about how these opportunities may benefit Soviet companies and the Soviet Union's economy.

Economic reforms in the Soviet Union have greatly increased the flow of investment between the Soviet Union and other countries. Canada is only one of many countries to benefit.

Canadian investors are finding that competition can be tough. They have to compete with investors from Japan and other countries throughout the world. One Canadian company, the Seabeco Group from Toronto, is heavily involved in joint trade between Canada and the USSR. Seabeco's business is to arrange the transfer of goods and services between the two countries. The company also acts as a general contractor in engineering, construction,

and equipment supply. One of Seabeco's projects is to develop a world-class recreational facility on the outskirts of Moscow. Initially, this facility will serve the 30 000 foreigners who live in Moscow.

QUESTIONS:

1. Describe the economic reforms referred to in this Case Study.
2. Could Seabeco's ventures have gone ahead before the new Soviet reforms?
3. Do you think cooperation between Canada and the Soviet Union will lead to greater understanding between us? List three reasons to support your answer.
4. Why might Seabeco's new recreational development be designed for the foreign people in Moscow and not for the Soviets? List two things foreigners would have that Soviets would not have.

Gorbachev has called democracy the soul of perestroika. Perestroika is meant to increase the standard of living and provide greater opportunities to develop and apply personal skills in areas like sports, music, and recreation. The government hopes to provide every family with an individual home and improve health and education. It also hopes to double industrial output and incomes by the year 2000.

Economic reform is not always smooth. Conflicts still exist between central planners and independent businesses. Some people fear that perestroika will not work. Like all people, Soviets feel comfortable with tradition and fear unknown changes. The Gorbachev

government sees that it must build trust between the state and the people. Some feel that, should perestroika fail, Soviet socialism will also fail.

Advantages of the Soviet Economic System

One advantage of planned economies is that government can allocate scarce resources in the best interests

PEEK	
AT THE SOVIET UNION **(until early 1990s)**	
Politics	**Economics**
- security of the party's goals and interests - elite protects its interests	- economy controlled by the government (Gosplan) - Central Statistical Administration to advise - factories fill quotas
Environment	**Knowledge**
- foreign opposition to Lenin's 1917 revolution - Soviet Union attacked from outside (e.g. 20 million killed in WW II)	- desire to eliminate class warfare (between workers and owners) - based on ideas of Marx and Lenin
Field of Action	
- a totalitarian regime with a centrally planned economy that imposed itself on numerous peoples - growing shift toward democracy and private enterprise - eventual disintegration of USSR in the 1990s?	

to improve a particular sector of the economy. For example, in 1928 Stalin expanded the nation's heavy industry capacity and provided more goods and services to the people. The Soviet Union grew to fourth in industrial output in the world. Soviet planners have since used other five year plans to emphasize certain sectors of the economy. Most have been successful.

The Soviet Union was able to industrialize quickly because central planners focused the means of production into one sector. Other economic systems, particularly market economies, cannot build up one sector because their systems are decentralized. In market economies, businesses make their own decisions and cannot mobilize all the factors of production together.

Stalin's five year plans provided hydro-electric power, tractors, and railways at the expense of housing, food, clothing, and other consumer goods. In the 1970s, the economy focused on military equipment, again at the expense of consumer goods. Recently, however, consumer goods have gained priority. A period of friendly relations between the two superpowers, the United States and the Soviet Union, has helped decrease military spending and increase consumer spending.

Employment in the Soviet Union is high. People are expected to make individual contributions to society, according to what they do best. Individuals are provided with the necessities of life, and their standard of living is maintained.

Disadvantages of the Soviet Economic System

Consumer sovereignty has often been overlooked in the Soviet Union. Economic decisions by the government have sometimes conflicted with what Soviet consumers want. The Soviet government believed that

of society. It can provide economic stability and growth, while ensuring that citizens maintain an acceptable quality of life. The Soviet Union has been able to decide which sector of the economy needs improvement and to work systematically to improve it.

Since the days of Stalin, increasing capital was the highest priority. Stalin instituted five year plans to increase the production of capital goods. In these plans, the government allocated the majority of its resources providing goods and services and setting the price of products was more important than consumer sovereignty. The Soviets paid little attention to economic ideas like supply and demand.

Until recently, few incentives existed in the Soviet Union for innovation or the invention of new industrial technology. Bureaucracy slowed down the work of the economy. As bureaucracy increased, individuals felt more alienated from government. The Soviet economy was very complex and the number of experts or officials needed to organize the economy was great. Gosplan could not anticipate the consumers' wants, could not react to changes in the demand of products, and could not quickly change the prices of products.

An increasing income difference exists between skilled and unskilled workers. Although the government attempts to redistribute income to gain economic equality, the gap widens. Also, the Soviet economy continues to have production problems. The USSR has abundant resources but the economy is relatively weak. The standard of living for Soviet citizens is not

Individual consumers have not always been the highest priority in the Soviet economic system. Line-ups are a common sight at most stores.

as high as that of other developed countries, even though social services are provided free to the people.

SUMMARY

The government has owned most of the nation's capital and natural resources, and its central planning committee was responsible for the overall economic strategy of the Soviet economy. Mikhail Gorbachev brought economic reform to the Soviet Union. With perestroika in place, people are finding long line-ups and shortages of goods are still common. The economy is not able to provide enough for the consumers. Gorbachev is under increasing pressure to solve the problem.

The Soviet Union answered the three economic questions in the following ways:

1. What goods and services should be produced?

   The government decided what goods and services should be produced based on what it thought best for the collective, and on available resources. It was helped by its economic planning agency (Gosplan). With reform, the Soviet government gave more freedom of choice to consumers. Allowing these choices has become more important to the planners.

2. How should goods and services be produced?

   Central planners decided how goods and services should be produced, based on available resources. This central planning is changing quite rapidly. More initiative is being allowed to individuals to make economic decisions based on available resources.

3. How should goods and services be distributed?

   Central planners decided how to distribute goods and services, based on who they thought should have them. Increasingly, consumers are able to influence decisions based on who can and will pay for the product.

GETTING ORGANIZED

1. Compare how the governments of the Soviet Union and Canada attempt to ensure economic equality.

2. Almost every book that discusses the economy of the Soviet Union talks about Soviet citizens waiting in lines to receive basic goods and services. How would you explain to a Soviet visitor what happens in our country: lines outside music stores the day of a big sale; lines at the grocery store cashier; and the vast array of choices we have?

3. In the Soviet Union, privately owned and operated farms and businesses have been more productive than those owned by the state. Why? Is there a basic human need to control one's life and welfare? If you think so, how might governments or leaders use this basic need to encourage prosperity in society?

4. Sometimes governments take property for "the greater good." Should governments be allowed to do this? If the government said it needed your property for a freeway or to ensure the safety of citizens, would you agree with them? Under what circumstances do governments in Canada take land or other property? How is it possible for citizens to fight the government when this happens?

5. Is Canada really an open society? If glasnost and perestroika came to Canada, what could be changed? What new openness would you like to have? Why? Is your idea practical?

6. Consider the following question: To what extent should governments pursue the common good? Instead of answering the question directly, hold a 10-minute brainstorming session with two others then answer the question: What is the common good?

REACHING OUT

1. Invite a guest who has lived in a centrally planned economy to speak to your classmates. The person may be from China, an African country, Eastern Europe, or the Soviet Union.

   Ask the person to name the best things about living in a centrally planned economy. Ask the person to name the worst things about living there. Summarize the responses. What were the similarities between what the speaker discussed, and the points raised in this chapter?

2. Think back over the last four weeks to the purchases you have made, listing any items over $5.00. How many of these would not have been available in the Soviet Union? Were any of these items what one would consider "essentials"?

Chapter Twelve:

THE STRUCTURE OF THE MIXED ECONOMY

GETTING IT STRAIGHT

1. What is a mixed economy?
2. How did the ideology of the mixed economy come about?
3. How did the ideas of the Utopian Socialists contribute to the theories of the mixed economy?
4. What encouraged the growth of government intervention in the economy?
5. What are the essential features of the mixed economy?
6. What is the difference between direct and indirect government controls?

7. What are the monetary and fiscal policies of a mixed economy?
8. What is the business cycle?
9. Government can control the economy by changing monetary and fiscal policies. Are there other methods government can use?
10. How does the mixed economy answer the three economic questions?

Some economists argue that every economy in the world is, to some extent, a mixed economy because ideas from both a market economy and a planned economy are included. In mixed economies, basic economic questions are answered both by individual buyers and sellers using a free market, and by governments that sometimes regulate the economy. The essential features of the mixed economy are the incentive of equality for all people, public and private ownership of property, and government controls by intervention. Because of the growth of transnational corporations, the opening of trade links, and the rapid changes in technology, all countries seem to be using economic combinations to structure their economic systems.

In chapter 8, you learned that market economies follow the principle that opportunity for ownership should be free from central controls. In short, that governments should not intervene in the economy. To work properly, market economies depend upon natural forces of supply and demand. You learned in chapter 10 that planned economies follow the principle that public ownership of property and central planning are effective ways to meet goals. Central authorities make decisions on production of those goods and services thought necessary for the progress of the state. Unlike in a market economy, goods and services are not produced in a planned economy simply because individuals want them.

How Mixed Economies Come About

A mixed economy is a practical attempt to take advantage of the best parts of both planned and market economies. Since both planned and market economies are based on different ideological beliefs, those who favour mixed economies attempt to create a balance between the belief in collectivism and the belief in individualism. Mixed economies allow both public and private enterprise. The challenge in a mixed economy is to reach the point where both collectivists and individualists are satisfied.

The Utopian Socialists

The **Utopian Socialists** hoped to bring about radical change throughout society. These were people who wrote about working together to create ideal communities, or utopias. Because of their ideals, they were known as Utopian Socialists. Robert Owen, who you read about in the Case Study in chapter 10, was also known as a Utopian Socialist.

Three other Utopian Socialists had far-reaching beliefs. Claude Henri Saint-Simon (1760-1825) was a French social philosopher. John Stuart Mill (1806-1873) was a British philosopher and economist. Louis Blanc (1811-1882) was a French socialist and journalist. All three witnessed the abuses of the Industrial Revolution. The society they saw was a mess. These

Louis Blanc was a Utopian Socialist who worked to make life better for all people. What do you think the cartoonists' ''Blanc Wealth Fertilizer'' sack might contain?

three men believed that for conditions to improve, several things had to change.

The Utopian Socialists believed two changes were most important. First, poverty had to be abolished. Second, equality had to be established. Each believed that changes in society could be made that would benefit all people. The starting point for the new order they envisioned was the belief that human beings were basically rational and good and, given a chance, they would do what was best for everyone.

The Utopian Socialists believed that regulating the private enterprise system could abolish poverty and establish equality, or "redistribute liberty." The Utopian Socialists' ideas differed from those of Marx. They believed that revolutionary change could come gradually within the present political structure through legislation, and that the violent change Marx advocated was unnecessary.

Although industrialism brought problems, Henri Saint-Simon believed it would be the integrating force in a new society. He believed all people should work together to make the most of their resources. Rather than the rich exploiting the poor, both together should exploit nature. Saint-Simon believed that the struggle between the classes could be channelled into a common struggle that would benefit all people—beating nature into submission.

Saint-Simon also believed that people should strive for the greatest good for all the people. One way of doing this was to improve the conditions of the poor by sharing wealth through income redistribution. Industry would be controlled by a government run by scientific and industrial experts. These experts would supervise both the production and distribution of goods. Individuals would be rewarded in proportion to their contribution to society.

John Stuart Mill had previously supported Adam Smith's analysis of the market economy, but changed his thinking as the abuses of industrialization increased.

Mill believed these abuses should be stopped, and that government should take a more active role in controlling the economy. He believed in both economic equality and the efficiency of the capitalist system. Unlike Marx, Mill did not think the market system would lead to class conflict. Instead, he wanted the government to correct the problems of capitalism without altering its essential features. Mill's ideas were instrumental in influencing factory laws in Britain.

Louis Blanc studied industrialism and saw one major obstacle preventing workers from rising out of poverty. This obstacle was competition, and he wanted to end it. In Blanc's mind, strong government was necessary to protect the weak and control industry. Blanc believed that wealth should not be taken away. Rather it should be "fertilized" until it became universal and raised the level of humanity for everyone, without exception. Blanc believed that workers should control industry. He wanted government-financed workshops and profit-sharing for the workers.

The Growth of Government Intervention

In part, the growth of mixed economies reflects the feelings of people who agreed with industrial growth but were dissatisfied with the Industrial Revolution. Mixed economies grew as governments saw the need to accommodate changing economic and social circumstances. One of the first laws governments passed was aimed at giving citizens a minimum standard of living. Other benefits have included pension plans and universal medical care.

Sometimes the international environment required special governmental action. Following the upheavals of World War I and the Great Depression, governments began to take over the means of production, or industry, with or without compensation to the previous owners.

During the Great Depression, government intervention in the economy was seen as a necessary evil. It was especially successful in the United States, where President Franklin D. Roosevelt responded to the needs of the American people by starting a number of social security programs that probably would not have been considered before the depression. He also set a minimum wage and maximum hours employees could work.

As governments began to provide a greater variety of welfare programs for their citizens, they also changed the organizing principles that guided their actions. Many governments began to believe that the state should assume a greater responsibility for the welfare of its citizens. Governments began to nationalize or buy industries, usually those in financial trouble, to maintain the jobs that those industries provided. People also began to believe that economic freedom included taking part in the decision-making of the state, even though property was owned by the government.

CASE STUDY:

HOW ARE ECONOMIC DECISIONS MADE?

The following Case Study looks at the complex economic decisions countries make. As you read, think about the value of making complex decisions based on one simple question: does the society value competition or cooperation?

If a society believes that people, businesses, and governments should compete for the same resources, there is likely to be little government intervention. The highest bidder will usually get the resource. People are not expected to work for the good of society, but only for their own good. By working for their own good, or that of their families, they can satisfy their wants and needs. Competition takes place when people must decide what they are going to buy, especially if they face a limited supply of funds or resources.

If, on the other hand, a society believes in cooperation among people, businesses, and government enterprise, government usually becomes more involved in the affairs of business. This involvement usually means setting government regulations.

Government regulations provide the rules that groups who want resources must follow. They also ensure that money does not do all the talking. Sometimes the group with the most money does not obtain the resource.

QUESTIONS:

1. Why would a government want to intervene in the economy?
2. Do you think governments should make rules about how their economies should work? Would it be a good idea to have a world economic council that made rules for how economies should work? What would be the benefits? What would be the drawbacks?
3. *The government does not influence my personal economic decisions very much.* Do you agree with this statement, or disagree? List two economic decisions for which you would permit outside influence. List two economic decisions for which you would not permit outside influence.

People no longer felt responsible to meet all their own needs from birth until death. Government assumed some of the load. Government intervention was seen as a way to provide for the public good by controlling the factors of production and the distribution of goods and services. If governments did their jobs well, everyone would share in the wealth of the state. The government's position changed from one of non-interference to one of ensuring that property owners and the wealthy shared with less fortunate people.

The Essentials of a Mixed Economy

Incentive: Equality for All

Mixed economies work on the belief that all people should have equal opportunity to all public services. This equality is made law. Economic equality does not mean that the government will control all production and stop people from accumulating wealth. It does mean that the government will establish regulations to ensure that citizens will have their basic needs supplied.

The goal of a mixed economy is to allow all people to maintain a good standard of living. The economy is controlled when necessary, in the best interests of the whole society. As in a planned economy, people are provided with social welfare programs to help maintain a minimum standard of living.

Mixed economies seek equality by attempting to redistribute individual wealth. The most popular form of redistributing individual wealth, other than social welfare programs, is the progressive income tax. The progressive income tax allows people with a smaller income to pay less income tax. The greater your income, the greater the proportion of tax you must pay.

This is a familiar scene in Canadian households each spring. The funds collected from income tax provide the revenue for government social programs.

For example, people earning $20 000 a year may pay 15 per cent of their income in tax. People earning $50 000 a year may pay 30 per cent of their income in tax. In taxing people's incomes progressively, an essential feature of the market economy, the profit motive, is encouraged. At the same time, the planned economy's ideal of equality for all is also maintained.

Balancing Private and Public Ownership

In mixed economies, a balance exists between public and private ownership. When goods, services, and property can be owned privately, workers feel that they are working for themselves. The feeling of ownership provides incentive. In mixed economies, public ownership is usually limited to industries of national importance like public utilities, banks, and resource industries like coal and oil.

Governments use public enterprise in a number of important ways. If a government believes all people have a right to work, public enterprise can be used to safeguard employment. If a private enterprise is going out of business, a government may decide to take over its operation and keep it in business. Such a move would help keep employment levels high and poverty levels low.

Public enterprise can also be used to create jobs by developing industries in areas of the country that are not attractive for private enterprise. In Canada, the North is an example of an area where private enterprises find it difficult to make a profit, as it is geographically very remote, and transportation costs are high.

In reality, there are never pure private or public enterprises. Both are subject to the market and political decisions that affect every society. In most mixed economies, private enterprise dominates public enterprise.

In Canada, government-owned businesses are called Crown Corporations. Via Rail was an example of such a company. Think of some other companies owned by the Canadian government.

Joint Ownership

In mixed economies, joint ownership of an enterprise is sometimes seen as the best way to run the business. This is private business and government working as partners. Often joint ownership is used to offset high costs of starting production.

Examples of successful joint ventures include the Alberta Tar Sands Project in Fort McMurray or the Husky Oil upgrader project in Lloydminster. In these projects, the provincial governments of Alberta and Saskatchewan, the federal government, and the oil company all contributed money. Without the monies given by the governments (75 per cent of the total cost), the projects probably would not have been feasible. No private business would support a project that was almost sure to lose money in the beginning.

Joint ventures are undertaken when economic risks are great but the project is important. Sometimes the returns on joint ventures may be high, sometimes not. But joint ventures do one important thing. They boost the economy through job creation.

As jobs are created, people earn money to buy goods and services. In Fort McMurray, when oil workers moved into town, they needed places to live. As new construction began, home builders were needed, as well as electricians, plumbers, and carpenters. These people, in turn, earned and spent money on new cars or eating in restaurants. Each expenditure created work and provided income for others, who could also spend money on homes, cars, restaurant meals. The more money circulating in the economy, the more money is spent to keep people working.

Since everyone who earns money pays taxes to the government, the government gets an almost immediate return on its investment. The government gains in another way. Rather than depending on the government for unemployment insurance or social welfare benefits, people become wage earners. Workers take care of their own economic needs.

CASE STUDY:

OVERSTIMULATION

Almost every part of Canada goes through cycles of strong and weak economies, but sometimes one area almost goes crazy. As you will read in this Case Study, Ontario during the late 1980s was an example of an overstimulated economy.

Employment was high and most people earned and spent a great deal of money. Many people moved to Ontario, and houses became scarce. Like all scarce commodities, house prices rose. By the time the economic stimulation had slowed, Toronto house prices had tripled.

Such an economic boost might seem to benefit everyone. However, young adults in Ontario without homes found that house prices were out of reach. The average cost of an apartment was prohibitive to people on a fixed income. People who bought houses in the late 1980s and tried to sell them

in the early 1990s found they lost money. Their $300 000 house was worth only $255 000. They actually owed more money than it was worth.

There is an irony to economic growth. It is almost always good to have a strong economy, but it is sometimes not good if the economy is too strong.

QUESTIONS:

1. Why did house prices in the Toronto area rise? Why did they fall?

2. How would you feel if you bought the house at the high price and still owed more than it was worth? What would you do if you owed more on your house than you could get by selling it?

3. Should the government step in to help people who pay too much for homes? Why or why not?

As the economic picture brightens and people begin to purchase additional goods and services (as they did during the Fort McMurray project) the costs of these goods and services will rise. Higher costs mean inflation. The federal government may then decide to intervene by setting higher interest rates or higher tax rates. While it is good to stimulate the economy, too much economic stimulation can be bad. If prices rise too quickly, people with little purchasing power will be left behind.

Government Intervention

In a mixed economy, many sectors of the economy operate under strict government controls. In this

section, you will read about a variety of forms of government intervention—from actual law-making, to different froms of taxation. John Maynard Keynes' ideas on government intervention are reviewed.

Laws that prevent monopolies are examples of government intervention. Businesses must also follow laws about such things as minimum wages, working conditions, pollution limits, and hiring practices.

Government regulations attempt to improve resource distribution, to alter income distribution to achieve greater economic equality, and to achieve the social goals of the nation. Regulations are put in place to guide business operations. The government in a mixed economy seldom regulates who can own and run a business.

In any economic system, it is important that the government has an understanding of the needs and wants of citizens. What methods might a government use to discover the habits of consumers in a mixed economy?

Governments may also control the economy by regulating spending. Too much spending brings inflation. Not enough spending brings recession. Both are undesirable. When inflation leads to higher prices and forces labour to look for increased wages, a vicious cycle is created.

Governments can involve themselves either directly or indirectly in the economy. Income taxes are an example of direct controls. Governments can control the money supply by raising or lowering the taxes. These government interventions will either take money out of the hands of consumers or provide more money to spend.

Indirect controls include excise taxes on tobacco and alcohol, sales taxes, and all types of **value-added taxes**. The goods and services tax (GST) is an example of a value-added tax in Canada. The government controls the economy indirectly by using taxes to adjust spending rates. These adjustments either add or take money from the economy in much the same way as would decreasing the interest rate or increasing income taxes.

English economist John Maynard Keynes (1883-1946) proposed government controls to even out the highs and lows of the business cycle. He suggested that monetary and fiscal policy should be used to keep the economy at a steady growth rate.

Monetary policy controls the interest rates by adjusting the money supply. If prices rise above acceptable levels (inflation), the economy is adjusted downward by adjusting interest rates upward. With increased interest rates, borrowing money becomes more expensive. Consumer and investment spending decreases and the economy slows down. The level of production of goods and services falls. Keynes believed that by creating jobs, the government could stimulate the economy and manipulate economic growth.

Taxation and government spending together form the government's fiscal policy.

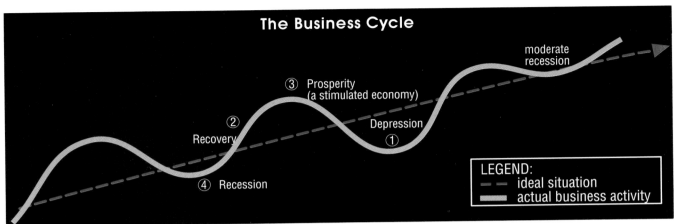

John Maynard Keynes believed governments had a role to play in economies—to help stabilize the peaks and valleys of the business cycle. Someone once said that a recession is when people you know lose their jobs; a depression is when you lose your job. Do you know which phase of the business cycle Canada is currently in?

CASE STUDY:

WHAT IS THE BUSINESS CYCLE?

As you read the following Case Study, refer to the chart above, The Business Cycle.

John Maynard Keynes said that the economy moves in peaks and valleys. Government should help to level out the peaks and valleys in order to make a smooth economy, like the one seen on the checkered line. He said that government could smooth out the economy by spending money in the bad times (the low part of the cycle), and save money or cut spending in the good times (the high part of the cycle).

Government could create more spending by reducing taxes (fiscal policy) or by lowering interest rates (monetary policy). These government actions would give more money to consumers to spend. On the other hand, the government could cut spending by reducing government services, and could

increase taxes and/or interest rates so the consumer would have less money to spend.

Business cycles are patterned movements which consist of recurring periods of prosperity and recession. Normally the business cycle is measured by the industrial growth and production of the economy. Economists have usually divided business cycles into four phases:

1. depression
2. recovery
3. prosperity
4. recession

Depression is the turning point of the lower portion of the business cycle. Prosperity is the turning point of the upper portion of the business cycle. Recession and depression are usually accompanied

continued

CASE STUDY *continued*

by rising unemployment, and a decrease in consumer buying power. Recovery and prosperity are normally associated with low unemployment, expanding consumer purchasing power, and rising prices.

In the short term, the business cycle fluctuates in response to fluctuations in the economy, such as when students return to school. The long-run business cycle involves major movement over the economy over many years, such as Japan's growth to an industrial superpower.

During the period of prosperity, a rise in production occurs. Employment, wages, and profits increase. Businesses are optimistic and expand production. As the upswing in business continues, obstacles tend to slow the further expansion of business. For example, production costs increase, important raw materials become scarce, the ability to ship raw materials or finished products becomes more difficult, consumers tire of waiting for products and cancel their orders, or skilled labour becomes scarce. Interest rates rise and consumers stop purchasing. Consumption falls behind production and inventories start to pile up. Prices fall.

A price decline causes producers to stop production. Workers are laid off. A recession occurs and often with it, a financial panic. Businesses become pessimistic as prices and profits drop. People save money instead of spending it. Production stops and factories shut down. Unemployment rises.

But full recovery finally comes. The recovery might be spurred by new consumer demands, because inventories have been used up, or because debts have been paid off. Sometimes the government purposely stimulates the economy, as in the case of armaments in wartime. Recovery may be slow and sporadic, but it soon gains momentum. Prices rise faster than costs. Employment opportunities increase and workers have more money to spend. Investment increases. People become optimistic and begin to speculate. A new cycle is underway.

QUESTIONS:

1. What action should the government consider at point 1 on the chart? Why?
2. What action should the government consider at point 2 on the chart? Why?
3. What are the two government policies? Define these terms and write them in your notebook.
4. Review your local newspapers or a national business magazine over the past three weeks. Where is Canada on the business cycle now?
5. If the government used its fiscal policy to slow the economy, how would their actions affect employment rates?
6. If the government used the monetary policy to increase spending and stimulate the economy, how would their actions affect employment rates?
7. Does it bother you that the economies of large countries can be "ordered around" by the government? Or, do you think this is a good thing for people? List three reasons to support your answer.

Keynes also noted that governments could spend money to stimulate the economy. He suggested that governments should spend money in bad economic times by creating social programs or jobs. Government programs such as unemployment insurance, create an automatic stabilizer. When the rate of unemployment rises due to recession, government payments automatically rise. Governments should save money in good economic times when most people are working and contributing to the government treasury through their income taxes. Many governments today, including Canada's, follow the ideas of Keynes and attempt to even out the highs and lows in the economy through intervention.

Other Government Controls

Think of some items that you might purchase in the course of a day. How might government controls have affected the prices? What effect did they have on your decision to purchase?

Governments may attempt to control the economy by setting production standards for companies. The higher the production standards, the more it costs to produce goods. If the government wished to encourage the production of a particular product or start an industry, it could relax standards until companies became economically stable.

Government controls could also take the form of **tax incentives** to business. To help a company begin a business in a particular area, or to begin the production of some previously unproduced product, the government could reduce taxes on earnings in that industry for a specified period of time. Often local governments attempt to encourage business investment by allowing private enterprises to operate tax-free for a specified number of years. The private investors who built and own Canada's West Edmonton Mall, for instance, received tax concessions.

Governments often use guaranteed loans to encourage production. The government promises to pay a loan if the company cannot. However, the company is not free from financial obligation. If the company cannot repay the loan, the government can assume control of the business. This happened in 1989 when the Alberta government took over Gainer's Meats after Gainer's defaulted on its loan payments.

Subsidies are another means of economic control. The government pays money (or subsidies) to help certain industries stay in business. One sector of the economy which often receives subsidies is agriculture. At the best of times, operating farms as private enterprises is a risky business. Farmers must wrestle with weather conditions and other natural occurrences they cannot control. One bad year can wipe out a lifetime of work. Since food is a basic need, governments try to intervene quickly.

Marketing boards can be used to control industries such as agriculture. All farmers on the marketing board agree to sell their products at a fixed price. Some may even agree to limit production so the market will not be flooded. Most agree to sell their product to the board as well. Marketing boards act much like miniature planned economies. Economic planners tell producers how much to produce and the price that they can charge for their products.

Agriculture is an important Canadian industry. Since many individual farmers find it difficult to run their businesses at a profit in today's market, the government provides subsidies to keep the industry strong.

CASE STUDY:

THE MILK MARKETING BOARD

As you read the following Case Study, think about what you would do with surplus milk if you were a dairy farmer.

Free milk! Bring your own container! Why would farmers advertise such a great bargain? Why would farmers spill milk down the drain? The answer is more logical than you might think.

Milk producers belong to a milk marketing board and have a contract signed with the board to produce a certain amount of milk at a certain price. They are not allowed to sell their milk to anyone else. If they do not meet the quota, or the agreed-upon amount in the contract, they may be fined. If they surpass their quota, they lose the milk to the board, and are fined.

Because milk producers must have a contract in order to sell milk, these quotas are almost like gold. As a result, it is very difficult to purchase a milk contract and many farmers pass down their milk contracts to their children.

Advocates of the marketing boards believe that the boards ensure that all milk producers will remain in business and receive a fair price for their milk. If there were too many large farmers who produced too much milk, they could force the smaller producers out of business by undercutting the prices.

People who believe in free enterprise insist that only the efficient producers should be allowed to remain in business. If the milk business were run like any other private enterprise, milk prices would fall.

continued

CASE STUDY *continued*

QUESTIONS:

1. Why is there a milk marketing board? Who does the board help?
2. Should farmers lose their excess milk and be fined for over production? Is it ever justifiable to throw away nutritious food when there are hungry people in Canada and the world? If so, what are the reasons? If not, why not?
3. Do you think milk marketing boards are a good idea? Why?
4. What other marketing boards exist where you live?

P E E K
AT A MIXED ECONOMY

Politics	Economics
- government guarantees basic economic "minimums" - political security and economic security are closely linked	- borrows structure from both market and command systems - emphasis on joint private and government ventures

Environment	Knowledge
- response to excesses of the Industrial Revolution - World War I and the depression promoted the need for government intervention	- production and consumption should have social welfare in mind - ongoing experimentation with social and economic policies

Field of Action
- combines principles of democracy and government regulation and/or ownership in the economy

CHALLENGES TO THE MIXED ECONOMY

CHALLENGE 1: Paying the Price for Social Programs

One main criticism of mixed economies is the progressive income tax they generally levy. In some mixed economies, income taxes are so high that the incentive to work hard and earn more money is reduced. The progressive tax system also encourages people to hide their income and attempt to avoid paying tax.

Mixed economies also encourage bartering to avoid paying taxes. Bartering is the exchange of goods and services without using money or documenting the profit from the transaction as income. For example, a mechanic fixes the dentist's car in exchange for a root canal. No money, only services, have exchanged hands. No records were kept, and no tax was paid. While this may seem like a logical and simple exchange of services, it costs the government tax revenues and disrupts the logic of the system.

Is it possible to have a mixed economy without a high income tax?

CHALLENGE 2: Hard Times, Hard Decisions

All economies face difficult decisions. Government spending to provide expected goods and services to the people is growing. Critics suggest that a combination of tax increases and a decrease in government spending is necessary.

Tax increases can lead to a greater separation between the wealthy and the poor,

continued

continued

since tax increases usually hit the middle class harder than other economic groups. Tax increases make it increasingly difficult for the middle class to maintain its standard of living.

Government subsidies to keep people working are often very expensive. Some critics don't believe they are all necessary, because large companies do not really need them. This is especially true when money goes to a company owner who may be losing money in one business but owns other companies that are making a tidy profit.

On what criteria should mixed economies decide to limit or increase spending for social programs?

CHALLENGE 3: Large Bureaucracies

Mixed economies often encourage the creation of large bureaucracies. Government intervention always adds government administration. Government businesses almost always employ lots of managers. People are needed to oversee the industries. People are needed to check to make sure people pay their fair share in tax. People are needed to check to see that the checkers and overseers are doing their jobs! The large number of people needed to check on others usually becomes very expensive.

Is it possible to have strong social programs without a large bureaucracy?

SUMMARY

Every major nation on Earth uses some operating principles of the market economy and of the planned economy. As we have seen in chapter 7, in some countries the market system is dominant and in others central planning is dominant. In a mixed economy, the state controls some sectors of the economy, while individuals control others. However, both are regulated by government. Even when resources are privately owned, the state may intervene to promote economic growth.

Societies with mixed economies would answer the three economic questions this way:

1. What goods and services should be produced?

   Mixed economies produce the goods and services desired by consumers. Mixed economies also produce goods and services which the government determines that consumers should have.

2. How should goods and services be produced?

   Mixed economies produce goods and services in the most efficient and inexpensive way. At the same time, they attempt to maintain a high standard of quality. Mixed economies allow the government to direct how goods and services are produced if necessary. Often these decisions are based on what resources are available and which means of production are the least expensive.

3. How should goods and services be distributed?

   In a mixed economy, the government acts according to the principle of economic equality by providing basic goods and services for everyone. Goods and services are also produced for whomever can pay.

The mixed economy represents a practical choice that societies make about how to organize and answer the three basic economic questions. Unlike the other economic choices, the decision to have a mixed economy is based on practical principles. Economic actions that work are kept in use; those that don't work are discarded.

Now that you have a basic idea of how a mixed economy works, you will read about two nations using this system. Chapter 13 looks at Sweden, and chapter 14 looks at Canada.

GETTING ORGANIZED

1. If you live in a house that is not rented, ask your parents or guardians how much they paid for it when they bought it. When did they buy it? How much is it worth today?

2. List 10 ways a government can redistribute wealth to give greater economic equality.

3. Compare your standard of living with someone your age living in a developing country. What conveniences do you take for granted that the other person would not have? Write a letter to that person explaining why you have such things as a television, VCR, indoor plumbing, microwave, and hair spray.

4. Research the types of government controls used in a mixed economy. Give examples of any that are used to create business in your community, province, or territory.

5. What elements would you include if you designed your own utopian society? What principles would you use to govern?

6. In a short essay, answer the following question: Should governments be held responsible for the economic well-being of their citizens?

REACHING OUT

1. The socialists described at the opening of the chapter had a great impact on the evolution of political and economic thought. Research their backgrounds and ideas.

   (a) Find a standard job application form. Answer the questions on the job application as if you were one of the socialists. Share the results of your research with the class.

   (b) Which of these socialist thinkers would make a good finance minister?

2. Canadian communities are experiencing cutbacks in government services and spending in the 1990s. Make a file of newspaper articles that focus on the issues listed in *Challenges to the Mixed Economy*, on pages 157-58. For example, a newspaper story on cuts to education might fit under the heading *Hard Times, Hard Decisions*. In each article underline statements that indicate differences in goals and values.

3. Your school has a large bureaucracy. Invite your principal to class to review the difficult decisions he or she makes in developing the school budget.

   (a) Which programs will be cut? Which will be encouraged to grow? Why? Write a summary of the principal's comments.

   (b) What role could the students play in determining where school funds should be directed? Does your student council contribute to the decisions? Why?

Chapter Thirteen:

SWEDEN

GETTING IT STRAIGHT

1. What is the structure of the Swedish economy?
2. How does Sweden balance a planned and a market economy?
3. How are economic decisions made?
4. What is indicative planning?
5. How does Sweden balance private and public enterprise?
6. When are industries nationalized in Sweden?
7. When does the Swedish government intervene in the economy?
8. How does Sweden try to achieve economic equality?
9. How does Sweden answer the three economic questions?

The Kingdom of Sweden is one of the most prosperous countries in the world. Located in northern Europe, Sweden is bordered by two other Scandinavian countries, Norway and Finland. Sweden is also a coastal country. It borders on the Skagerrak, the Kattegat, the Gulf of Bothnia, and the Baltic Sea.

Sweden is a beautiful country, with a variety of geographical landforms, from sandy beaches to high, rugged mountains and forests. Low-lying southern Sweden (where most of the population lives) is warmed by the Gulf Stream. The Arctic Circle passes through northern Sweden, which includes Lapland. There, the winters can last more than six months. Sweden is heavily industrialized and exports to many other countries.

Sweden has two main geographic areas: the mountainous north, including Lapland, and the low-lying south. This photo was taken in the south where the climate is less harsh.

THUMBNAIL FACTS

Area: 449 751 sq. km

Population: 8 503 010

Density: 18 people per sq. km

Chief Cities: Stockholm (capital), Göteborg, Malmö.

Type of Government: Limited Parliamentary Monarchy

Per Capita Income: $14 801

Most Important Industries: pulp and paper, ship building, machinery, automobiles, aircraft, toolmaking, iron and steel.

Agriculture: cattle, hogs, oats, sugar beets, potatoes, and wheat.

Minerals: iron ore, and zinc.

Most Important Trading Partners: United Kingdom, Germany, Norway, and Denmark.

GNP: $98.5 billion

Structure of the Swedish Economy

Both public and private enterprise flourish in the Swedish economy. Although the government controls transportation, water power, communication, and iron ore mining, more than 85 per cent of the total industrial output is produced by private enterprise. The Swedes believe that government intervention is often necessary to address specific economic and social problems. The organizing principle of Swedish politics and economics is to turn ethical ideas into practical action. For example, political and economic decisions are often the result of concerns for the welfare of people who fare badly in the market system. More than any other country, Sweden works on the belief that all people should be economically equal.

In order to turn ethical ideas into practical, political programs, the Swedish government attempts to redistribute the country's wealth and provide basic services to everyone. The government's goal is to help people enjoy a high standard of living. Sweden's economic policy stresses full employment, economic stability, economic security, some degree of economic planning, and economic growth.

Government and Economy

The Social Democrats have been the ruling party in Sweden almost continually since 1936. The party started as a popular, grass-roots movement and has continued to work for the common people. Social Democrats have used the economy to create their vision of the good life and provide for the welfare of the country's citizens. Sweden's social welfare system has been built through political and economic legislation and reform. Economic planning is one way that the Social Democrats help Swedes find enjoyment and comfort in life.

CASE STUDY:

CHILD CARE

Sweden's economic policy stresses the need to provide for the people. As you read this Case Study, think about how this child care policy helps parents.

In many places in the world, having a child can be costly both in terms of medical expenses and lost wages. But, in other places, it actually pays to have a child. In Sweden, having a child does not hurt the family income. Swedish maternity or paternity leave allows parents up to 15 months (450 days) leave when having a child. Parents receive 90 per cent of their salary during the leave.

What makes Swedish and Canadian maternity leave different is how the Swedish families are treated. Some countries allow fathers to take time off, although few allow the mother and father to take the time off at the same time. Sweden's system permits this. Another feature of this system is that the parents do not have to take all the time at once. They can space out the leave and take it any time up to when the child is eight years old.

If a child is sick, parents are encouraged to stay home with the child. Nearly 80 per cent of Swedish mothers whose children are under the age of seven work. Parents can take off up to 60 days per year without a loss of pay. Who pays for all this? The Swedish people do! Taxes in Sweden are among the highest in the world.

QUESTIONS:

1. What do the benefits for parents tell you about Swedish ideology in regard to families? Write a generalization that expresses the ideas you think lie behind these benefits.

    Questions 2 to 6 ask you for your own opinion. Read these questions and think about them carefully. As you take a position on them, write down some of your reasoning.

    What do you think?

2. Is 15 months too long to stay home with a child?

3. Is it fair to the employer to have workers take such a long leave?

4. Are high taxes worth paying to have that much time off?

5. Should both mother and father be allowed time off to have a child?

6. Should Canada adopt a similar maternity/paternity leave system?

People shopping on this street in Old Stockholm participate in a mixed economy.

is responsible for making all policy decisions. Each cabinet minister appoints an undersecretary to plan and supervise the work of that ministry. The government employs a large number of civil servants who join with management, labour, and other experts to study economic problems. In Sweden, a policy is likely to be approved if it will advance the standard of living. After political decisions are made, central administrative agencies, like the National Board of Health and Welfare, make sure that government policies are carried out.

Many outsiders think that because Sweden is highly bureaucratized the economy is centrally planned. But Sweden, with its population of more than 8.5 million people, has never had a centrally planned economy. The high level of exports and imports (about 35 per cent of GNP) would make it difficult to implement a detailed plan of any sort. The Swedish government has, instead, practised **indicative planning**. Indicative planning means that the government *indicates* the general direction the economy should go by providing guidelines for economic activity.

Indicative planning has been very successful, and there has been little need for central government control. Thousands of organizations within the Swedish system all act like miniature governments. Each organization promotes many different objectives, including some that are economic. Swedes tend to work closely with economic organizations. By working cooperatively with labour and business, the Swedish government finds it easier to reach decisions that meet its economic objectives.

How Does the Government Make Decisions?

As in Canada, the Swedish prime minister selects the cabinet from the Riksdag (parliament). The cabinet

Cooperation

Canadians might wonder how such groups, each working for what seem to be conflicting interests—like labour and management—could do their jobs without grinding the economy to a halt. Here's where the Swedish government does take a central role. Although

In Sweden, government has encouraged business owners and workers to cooperate. What might be some of the benefits of a system that encourages cooperation between government, workers, and business?

it seems like a simple answer to a big problem, the Swedish government encourages business and trade unions to work together. The pattern of thinking in Sweden stresses cooperation, and the Swedish system works on the ideological principle that humans will work together. The government often gets involved in discussions and negotiations with business groups. Communication, rather than power, is the organizing principle of the Swedish system.

The Employee Participation in Decision-Making Act, for example, says that unions should be consulted when changes are made in a company. Mandatory legislation gives labour organizations a seat on the board of directors of any company with more than 100 employees. In this way, workers help their employers answer the three basic economic questions. The Employees Unions and the Employer's Confederations meet together at regular intervals to negotiate agreements for entire industries. For example, salaries for all Swedish shipbuilders are settled by bargaining and negotiations at these meetings.

While this system of bargaining has worked well for many years, the future is hard to predict. It appeared that this uniquely Swedish system was breaking down in 1988 when SAF (Swedish Employers' Federation) reached a contract agreement with a single group—the metal workers. In any system, decisions have an impact. How this decision will affect years of traditional decision-making in the Swedish economy is not yet clear.

The Balance between Public and Private Enterprise

There are three main types of ownership in Sweden. As in Canada, most Swedish businesses are private enterprises. The other two forms of ownership are examples of public ownership. Within the business sector, 85 per cent of the companies are privately owned and sell products on the open market. Of the remaining 15 per cent, 10 per cent are owned by the state and 5 per cent are owned by cooperatives. In retailing, the cooperatives receive 20 per cent of domestic sales.

As a society, Swedes believe that industries are run more efficiently by private owners than by the government. However, the Swedish government also believes there are times when industries should be nationalized, or purchased and run by the state. But, the Swedish government views nationalization as only one way to achieve economic goals, especially the goal of full employment. Nationalizing makes sense if an industry is in financial trouble and jobs are in danger.

Employment

The Swedish government judges the effectiveness of its economy by its unemployment rate and is proud that most people have jobs. For 1989, Sweden's unemployment rate stood at about 1.8 per cent, compared to Canada's unemployment rate of 7.5 per cent.

The difference in unemployment rates between Canada and Sweden could reflect different beliefs about why there is unemployment. The Swedish economy is based on the belief that people want to work, and will, if they have the chance. Some people believe that the economies of Canada and the US are based on a belief that people would rather receive government assistance if they can, and that they only work because they have to. In the United States, the belief that humans are basically lazy has been a strong argument against a highly systematized social welfare structure. The old Puritan ethic that stated "If they won't work, they shouldn't eat!" still expresses the beliefs of some people in Canada and the United States. What do you think about that idea?

In Sweden, nationalizing an industry may help keep people employed. There is another reason for nationalization: to preserve the supply of a vital product or service even if it is not making money. The Swedish government may decide that the country's best interest is served by keeping the industry alive. But, for the most part, Swedes have allowed the market to decide which companies survive. In the minds of many who study economics, this makes Sweden more capitalistic than socialistic.

Business

Although the Swedish government allows the free market to determine whether a Swedish business survives or dies, another area of the economy is completely under governmental control. A Swedish government agency sets the prices of all goods and services. In the Swedish system, products of governmental businesses usually compete directly with those of private businesses. With this government agency, goods or services provided by private industry would have a comparable price to similar goods or services provided by the government.

Swedish businesses may be privately owned or owned by the Swedish government. A Swedish company may also be jointly owned by the government

In Sweden, a government agency sets the prices for many goods and services. How does this differ from the other systems you have studied? How is it the same?

Government Intervention in the Swedish Economy

The Bank of Sweden controls monetary and fiscal policy to regulate the business cycle. Monetary policy helps control other aspects of economic growth because it controls the supply of money and interest rates. Two specific monetary policies the Swedish government uses are:

1. manipulating discount rates and
2. manipulating interest rates.

Discount rates are notes or other bills of exchange, minus a deduction to cover the interest rate of a purchaser. When people sell these notes, they sell them for *face value*, and if interest rates have increased, will not make as much money as they might if interest rates had fallen.

By manipulating interest rates, the government can influence the number of loans consumers take. If interest rates go down, loans are cheaper and easier to obtain. People are more likely to purchase homes or cars. The government can decrease spending by increasing interest rates and making it more expensive to pay back loans.

Fiscal policy controls tax rates and government spending. When the government raises or lowers taxes, it affects consumer spending. If people pay more tax, they have less money to spend. If they pay less tax, they have more money to spend. The human tendency is to spend rather than save. Governments know this tendency and use it to advance economic goals they believe are best for the country.

Like all governments, the Swedish government encourages the expansion of profitable business enterprises. The Swedish government provides incentives

and a private owner. If the government owns a minority share (less than 50 per cent), the private owner manages the business like any other private business. If the government owns a majority share (50 per cent or more), the government chooses how the company is managed. It may appoint public servants to run the company or it may leave management in the hands of the private owner.

The goals of public ownership are to safeguard employment, to expand profits, and to develop jobs in economically depressed areas. Public ownership is primarily limited to the mining, steel manufacturing, shipbuilding, public utility, and transportation industries. The Swedish government will prop up these businesses to keep them operating. On occasion, the government may even start a business in these areas if private companies feel they cannot make a profit. More than half the goods and services produced in the areas of mining, steel manufacturing, shipbuilding, utilities, and transportation come from state owned firms.

to both enterprises and consumers through subsidies, grants, loans, and tax breaks. These incentives might be used to encourage businesses to start production in economically depressed areas. Controls help guide the economy toward government objectives. Some controls are more direct than others. Direct controls include price-fixing for agricultural products, setting levels for the amount of rent that landlords can collect, and providing loans and interest subsidies for housing.

Direct taxes include a national income tax, a local income tax, a national wealth tax levied on high incomes, and a combined inheritance and gift tax. The Swedish government has recently replaced indirect sales taxes with a value-added tax. This tax, in many ways, is like the Goods and Services Tax (GST) in Canada. In Sweden this tax is paid on almost all goods and services.

In Sweden, direct taxes average about 40 per cent of a worker's total wages. To keep its system of social assistance operating, Sweden has one of the highest income tax rates in the world. But under tax reform scheduled for 1991, tax rates will decrease from 72 per cent to 50 per cent in the high income bracket.

By world standards, Swedish incomes are high. Swedish employers not only pay workers' salaries, they also must provide pensions and other social benefits. The level of these payments is negotiated as a part of labour-management agreements. Employers also finance a government-run supplementary pension system, health care, sick pay, and a number of other social insurance programs.

Government grants are used to encourage cooperatives, especially if the cooperative will provide goods or services in an area where private businesses and the government are unwilling to become involved. Cooperatives own and operate about 24 per cent of the retail stores in Sweden. More than 80 per cent of Swedish farm produce is handled by agricultural cooperatives.

Many Swedes complain that their taxes are too high. What are some of the potential problems in a society where people feel they are too heavily taxed?

Economic Equality in Sweden

Because of its all-encompassing social welfare legislation, Sweden has often been called *the welfare state.* The Swedish system of social welfare is based on the fundamental principle that every Swedish resident should be guaranteed a minimum standard of living in terms of food, housing, and health care. Because Swedes believe all people should be economically equal, they attempt to narrow the gap between different income groups and provide economic security to all residents of the country. For example, the explicit goal of Swedish health care is to provide health care for the entire population. The Swedish health care system is, indeed, one of the most extensive in the world.

Health

Health care is especially important to Swedes. Because Sweden places such a priority on health, the Ministry of Health and Social Welfare has the largest budget of any ministry. In 1986-87, this budget was 26 per cent of the entire fiscal budget. Education followed with 13 per cent.

Social insurance is offered to all residents of Sweden. The National Insurance Act covers everyone living in Sweden. It includes medical and hospital care, dental care, old age pensions, and parental insurance. Each individual pays a small amount for visits to the doctor or for hospitalization. If Swedes miss work due to illness, they receive a taxable allowance. In most cases, this allowance covers 90 per cent of regular pay. The rest of the costs of illness are covered by the National Health Insurance Plan (NHIP). The NHIP pays for ambulances, physiotherapy, and the cost of prescription drugs. Dental care is free to all people under 19.

Forty per cent of the cost of dental care is paid for those over 19. How does this compare with the Canadian medicare system?

Not only are doctors' visits paid for by the health plans, travel to and from the doctor's or dentist's is also covered. Prescriptions are subsidized by health care plans. No matter how much prescription medicine is needed, the total cost to the individual will be very small. In total, patients pay only four per cent of all medical fees. This extensive coverage means that all Swedes, rich and poor, have equal opportunity for a healthy life. This coverage helps Sweden work towards socioeconomic equality, one of the basic goals of the Swedish system.

Education

Government allowances help Swedes provide better care for their children. These allowances are tax-free and provided for all children under the age of 16. Education is free as are school lunches, text books, and instruction. Children must attend school between the ages of 7 and 16 years. Grants, interest-free loans, government allowances, and stipends are provided for full-time university students.

Citizens in Sweden are protected by government programs from birth through old age.

Pensions and Housing

A pension is paid to people who are 65. Pension supplements are given to people with no other source of income. At age 65, an individual is provided with an indexed pension (pension that rises in response to inflation). These pensions are equal to about 65 per cent of the average of the 15 years of their highest incomes. Some pensions include disability payments and housing allowances if a person's income was very low.

Families with children may apply for a housing subsidy. New construction is regulated by the government to be sure that the same high standards are met in both public and private construction. The average Swedish family pays approximately 22 per cent of its income for housing. Unlike the situation in Canada, interest from mortgages is tax deductible. In Sweden, however, profits from real estate transactions are heavily taxed.

Unions

Unions operate most of the unemployment insurance plans. Plans for both employers and employees are funded from payroll deductions. These plans include job retraining for those who want it, scholarships for those who desire further education, and public work projects for those who want jobs but cannot find them in the private sector. The government relocates workers and pays expenses for those who are unemployed, or soon will be. Paying expenses allows people to travel and look for job prospects. But, workers must be willing to move in order to find work. One reason the Swedish government supports these different programs is because there has been a shortage of skilled workers in Sweden. In recent years, this shortage has been especially acute and has caused a decline in national productivity.

Ideology

The Swedish government believes that work, basic services, and a healthy and positive social environment should be accessible to everyone who lives in Sweden.

For this reason, government spending exceeds 60 per cent of the Gross Domestic Product in Sweden. The Gross Domestic Product is a measure of the country's economic output or income. Canada's spending is 40 per cent of GDP. Sweden's rate of public spending in relationship to the GDP is one of the highest in the world for its population. By spending money, the government can control the economy. The greater the amount of the GDP any government spends, the more control that government can have over its economy. The Swedish government has a great deal of control over the domestic economy.

Social Democrats have argued that high standards of government services and social welfare benefits promote economic growth. During the 1950s and 1960s Sweden's economy grew quickly. While the national debt of most industrialized countries has continued to grow and has become an increasing problem, Sweden's national debt is shrinking. Quite simply, Sweden pays its bills. As the national debt goes down, things look up in the Swedish economy.

However, some Swedish budget items must be increased. The movement of workers from rural jobs in forestry, agriculture, mining, and fishing to higher paying jobs in cities has increased government costs. As people move to cities, the government must provide new schools, hospitals, transportation systems, and subsidies for urban housing. The Swedish government hopes that by fighting inflation and keeping unemployment down, the economy will stay up. So far, it has. Sweden's national debt is being eliminated faster than most people in Sweden expected.

Many workers in Sweden are moving away from traditionally rural industries like copper mining, to urban jobs in the cities.

Other Aspects of the Swedish Economy

In Sweden, radio, television, and newspapers may freely inform the electorate about government activity. Like the Canadian government, the Swedish government licenses radio stations. The largest radio station in Sweden, *Sveriges Radio* (the Swedish Broadcasting Corporation), is privately owned. However, the

PEEK	
AT SWEDEN	
Politics	**Economics**
- Social Democrats - prime minister, cabinet, and Riksdag (parliament) - extensive social welfare system	- indicative planning by the government - cooperation between businesses and trade unions
Environment	**Knowledge**
- growth of transnational corporations and globalization of economy means Swedish companies must become more competitive	- social welfare and equality are dominant attitudes - recognition of need for cooperation between workers and business
Field of Action	
- ongoing experimentation to achieve social policy that reflects the needs of all sectors of the economy and society	

Swedish government appoints the chairman of the board and half the board of directors. Although Swedish television and radio are much like Canadian stations, there is one big difference. Commercial advertising is not allowed on radio or television in Sweden.

The Swedish government controls the economy by setting standards for what is produced. For example, if the government wants to encourage production of a particular item, it may relax standards to encourage private owners to get into business. If too many businesses are after a share of the market, high standards can be set. Higher standards usually mean higher production costs. They also use standards to provide for the safety of citizens. An example of this is setting standards to provide seat belts for children.

SUMMARY

In Sweden, the three basic economic questions are answered as follows:

1. What goods and services will be produced?

    In Sweden, businesses decide what goods and services are produced, based on consumer demand. The government also practises indicative planning.

2. How should goods and services be produced?

    In Sweden, businesses decide how goods and services will be produced. Business works to produce goods efficiently and cheaply. Lower production costs mean higher profits. In Sweden, profits are heavily taxed. The government may also make production decisions, based on what resources are available, and if it owns more than 50 per cent of the company.

3. How should goods and services be distributed?

    In Sweden, goods and services go to those who can pay for them. However, the Swedish government manipulates the taxation system and provides subsidies so all residents of Sweden have equal access to those goods and services that the government believes are basic.

GETTING ORGANIZED

1. What principles does the Swedish government use to make economic decisions? In what ways is this like our own government? In what ways is this different?

2. Why do you think the Swedish government is called socialist when the vast majority of its businesses are privately owned?

3. In any democratic government, providing economic equality is a high priority. Make a chart to show the ways in which the Swedish government attempts to provide economic equality.

4. In Sweden, political and economic decisions are often made in response to concerns for people who don't do well in the market system. Think about the Canadian system. Make a list of the workers who seem to do poorly in the market system. If Canada worked on the same principle as Sweden, what changes could it make to help the people you have listed? Name two changes.

5. One unique structure of the Swedish system is that the government tends to settle contracts with entire industries. The result is that carpenters, steel workers, and teachers are paid using the same pay scale. What changes would occur in Canada if we adopted this system? How might it affect your choices about your future? Could it work here?

6. In Chapter 11, you worked together to brainstorm a definition of the concept "common good." Now you are better prepared to answer the important economic question: To what extent should governments pursue the common good? Prepare a two-minute radio editorial that answers this question. Tape the editorial and present it in class. (You may even want to tape a five-minute radio spot, including music of your choice, and the editorial. Play it in class.)

REACHING OUT

1. It is difficult to be rich in Sweden. Rock performers have discovered this. In the 1970s, groups like ABBA faced huge tax bills on their royalties. Roxette, the Per Gessle and Marie Fredriksson duo, and Joey Tempest are stars of the 1990s. Working in an industry that draws much of your income away leads to the temptation to move to a freer, less intrusive market economy like the US. Yet the highly regulated Swedish rock industry has its advantages. Air play is loaded with Swedish groups and Swedish song writers and composers are guarded by a host of protectionist legislation.

   (a) Study the life of an Swedish rock performer to determine how elements of his or her career were influenced by Swedish political and economic systems.

2. Sweden has had a reputation of leadership on environmental issues. After substantial pollution was discovered in the Baltic Sea, steps were taken to eliminate pollutants such as dioxin, which is the by-product of bleaching pulp with chlorine. By 1995, chloride waste will be limited to 1.5 kilos per metric tonne of pulp produced.

   In Canada, dioxin pollutants are an important subject. Both the Swedish and the Canadian economies rely heavily on the pulp industry, and both economies have regulations governing the industry.

   (a) Interview representatives from the pulp and paper industry as well as from environmental lobby groups. Ask them: To what extent should the pulp and paper industry be controlled?

   Do you agree with the points made in the presentation? What information would you need to fully assess the comments made by the presenter?

3. Think about crime in Canada. What are the different points of view on the question of rehabilitation? What costs and benefits are included?

   Your class might invite a probation officer or social worker to respond to this question. You might explore the issue of rehabilitation in further detail. Is this a political or an economic issue, or is it both?

Chapter Fourteen:

CANADA

GETTING IT STRAIGHT

1. What is the structure of the Canadian economy?
2. Why did Canada start social security programs?
3. How is the government's role in the economy changing?
4. How is income earned in Canada?
5. How does the Canadian government attempt to fine-tune the economy?
6. What is the difference between direct and indirect foreign investment?
7. How is the Free Trade Agreement affecting Canada?
8. How does Canada answer the three economic questions?

Canada is the world's second largest country; only the USSR is larger. Canada occupies the northern half of the continent of North America, stretching east to the Atlantic Ocean, west to the Pacific Ocean, and north to the Arctic Ocean. Canada contains 10 provinces and 2 territories, a variety of natural geographical beauty, and a diverse, though small, population.

Canada is rich in agriculture and minerals. Growing out of the land are numerous forests, making Canada's pulp and paper industry one of the largest in the world. Underneath Canadian soil lie treasure stores of mineral resources, making Canada one of the leading mining countries in the world.

THUMBNAIL FACTS

Area: 9 976 185 sq. km

Population: 25 693 000

Density: 2.6 people per sq. km

Chief Cities: Ottawa (capital), Montreal, Toronto, Vancouver, Edmonton, Calgary.

Type of Government: Constitutional Monarchy

Per Capita Income: $12 280

Most Important Industries: pulp and paper, agriculture, petroleum products, iron and steel, motor vehicles, aircraft, machinery, chemicals, aluminum, fishing.

Agriculture: wheat, barley, oats, rye, potatoes, cattle.

Minerals: oil, iron ore, gold, silver, platinum, copper, nickel, cobalt, zinc.

Most Important Trading Partners: United States, Japan, United Kingdom.

GNP: $245 billion

Canadian wheat is a particularly important export crop.

What Is Canada's Economy Like?

Canada is highly industrialized. Mechanization has improved production of consumer goods and increased agricultural efficiency. Almost half of Canadian agricultural and forestry products are exported. Wheat is a particularly important export crop. Oceans provide an abundance of fish. Seventy-five per cent of the fish are exported to other countries.

Canada's abundance of natural resources has made it attractive to Europeans and has provided great wealth to the country. But Canadians have become dependent on foreign investment to build the Canadian economy. The international environment is very important to understanding how Canada's economy has evolved.

Canadians use the theory of the market system to run their businesses. The Canadian government also intervenes in several ways. When possible, the government attempts to balance the needs of producers and consumers. The Canadian government believes that all people should be guaranteed a basic standard of living. At the same time, it tries not to restrict freedom of opportunity. The role of the government is large. In 1990, all government spending in Canada was close to half of the GNP of Canada.

In principle, the Canadian government supports private ownership of property, individual competition among businesses, the profit motive, and the workings of a free market based on supply and demand. The government also believes that consumers and producers should be free to make their own economic choices. Yet, the government is not afraid to become an active player in the economy, at times competing with private business.

FREE TO BUY AND FREE TO SELL: *COOPERATIVES*

Cooperatives are quite visible in western Canada. A cooperatively-run store involves a group of people joining together to save money by purchasing goods in large quantities. "The Co-op" store is in most communities. These stores carry groceries, hardware, and lumber for members.

Customers (members) pay a small membership fee to join. Each time they make a purchase, the total is recorded.

At the end of the fiscal year the store calculates its profit. The store will either invest the profit in more capital, or pay dividends to its members.

CASE STUDY:

TO BE FUN, PRETTY, HANDSOME, WONDERFUL— DO I REALLY HAVE TO BUY THAT?

Are you a smart consumer? Thoughtful, aware, careful to consider the difference between advertising hype and the truth? As you read the following Case Study, ask yourself if you are aware of how advertising affects your purchases.

The first purpose of advertising is to sell products. The primary techniques used by advertisers are colourful packaging to catch the eye, and promises of a better life to catch the dreams. Packaging is one part of advertising. Promises are another.

In almost every case, advertising adds to the expense of a product. Do Ninja Turtles *really* need a large colourful backing on them? Catchy lyrics are also used by advertisers. Is this *really* the Pepsi generation? Stars are used to advertise. Does Michael Jackson *really* drink Pepsi? Does Wayne Gretzky *really* eat Pro Stars cereal? Image is used to advertise. Do you *really* get the girl when you buy the car? Can you *only* have fun by drinking beer?

Advertising is very powerful. It can create a demand for a product, like cigarettes, that nobody needs. It encourages consumers to feel incomplete and out-of-date. However, in an economic sense, advertising supports the market economy. It creates greater competition. Advertising offers alternatives to the public.

QUESTIONS:
1. Next time you watch television, notice the ads. What is the advertisement really selling?
2. What does the ad promise?
3. Besides the product, what does the ad imply the consumer will get?
4. Choose a favourite ad on television. Answer questions 1-3 focusing on this ad.

Canada is a vast land with a relatively small population. Its size has been both a blessing and a problem. The Canadian government recognizes that individual entrepreneurs cannot create profitable businesses where there is a small population. The remote areas of Canada represent a particularly difficult market because people are scattered, transportation costs are high, and distribution is difficult. Yet, Canadians living in the remote regions of Canada still require links and services with the rest of the country. Therefore, the Canadian government provides services by publicly owning corporations like the Canadian Broadcasting Corporation (CBC) and the Canadian National Railways (CNR).

In Canada's vast landscape, the village of Rae in the Northwest Territories needs many of the same services as Toronto.

The Start of Social Security

Throughout Canadian history, during times of economic difficulty, new federal and provincial political parties have often gained power. The Great Depression proved to be one of the most important events in Canadian history. Government responses to the depression changed the whole fabric of the Canadian economy. The Canadian government came to realize that many ordinary Canadians needed help.

Today, Canada has a comprehensive social security system designed to provide a reasonable standard of living, and economic security to those who cannot provide that for themselves. Social insurance programs include unemployment insurance (UIC), medical care, welfare, family allowances, veterans' allowances, and workers' compensation. These social insurance programs were originally designed to protect people against a total loss of income during tough economic times.

In 1937, the Rowell-Sirois Royal Commission on Dominion-Provincial Relations paved the way for much of Canada's social welfare legislation. When the Commission's report came out in 1940, it proposed changes in federal-provincial relations. These changes included a federal unemployment insurance program and a system of equalization payments to help equalize incomes in poorer provinces. In return, it was suggested that the provinces leave the responsibility for unemployment insurance (UIC) with the federal government.

In 1940 the UIC Act was passed. This was later complemented by other federal social welfare legislation, such as the Family Allowance Act and the Old Age Security Act. Pensions were paid to people 65 and over, with higher amounts going to those with greater needs. Today, Canadian pensions are indexed to inflation after the first 3 per cent. In other words, if inflation is 5 per cent, pensions go up by 2 per cent.

In 1966 the Canada Pension Plan (CPP) came into being. Unlike pensions in Sweden, this plan is paid for by individuals. A certain amount of money, based on a percentage of income, is deducted from an individual's pay cheque. Employers also pay a matching amount. The plan supplements the Old Age Pension. Canadians can start collecting a small pension

CASE STUDY:

TOMMY DOUGLAS AND THE MEDICAL CARE SYSTEM

This Case Study tells how how medicare was first envisioned in Canada. As you read, think about your own medical coverage today.

The following excerpt was taken from an article by Tommy Douglas which appeared in the Toronto Star Weekly, in 1960.

When I was a boy in Scotland before World War I, I fell and hurt my knee. A bone disease called osteomyelites set in and for three or more years I was in and out of hospital.

My father was an iron moulder and we had no money for doctors, let alone specialists. After we immigrated to Canada the pain in my knee came back. Mother took me to the outdoor clinic of a Winnipeg hospital. They put me in the public ward as a charity patient and I still remember the young house doctor saying that my leg must be cut off.

But I was lucky. A brilliant orthopaedic surgeon, whose name was Smith, came through the wards looking for patients he could use in teaching demonstrations. He examined my swollen knee and then went to see my parents. "If you'll let me use your boy to help teach medical students," he said, "I think I can save his leg. His knee may never be strong again but it can be saved."

I shall always be grateful to the medical profession for the skill that kept me from becoming a cripple, but the experience of being a charity patient remains with me.

Had I been a rich man's son the services of the finest surgeons would have been available. As an iron moulder's boy, I almost had my leg amputated before chance intervened and a specialist cured me without thought of a fee.

All my adult life I have dreamed of the day when an experience like mine would be impossible and we would have in Canada a program of complete medical care without a price tag. And that is what we aim to achieve in Saskatchewan by 1961—the finest health service available to everyone in the province, regardless of ability to pay. This is our goal of a compulsory prepaid medical care insurance.

QUESTIONS:

1. Who was Tommy Douglas?
2. What memories about this one incident were most important to Tommy Douglas? Have you had a similar experience that has helped to shape your vision or ideology in a particular way? What was it? How has it helped to shape your ideology?
3. What does "universal medical coverage" mean? Which social groups would probably support it? Which groups might not support it?
4. In a short paragraph, list ways that rich and poor people might see this article differently.
5. Make a list of occupations you do not believe should be allowed to go on strike. Beside each occupation, give a reason for your answer.

at age 60. At age 65, they can collect pensions at the normal rate. All provinces and territories except Quebec take part in the plan. Quebec has created its own pension plan and opted out of the federally-run plan.

The Family Allowance Act pays a monthly allowance to the parents of each child in Canada until their child reaches the age of 18. Each province or territory may supplement the family allowance if it wishes. As a result, the amount of family allowance differs from place to place. Quebec, for example, gives every parent a one-time grant of $500 for each of the first two children. Parents who have more than two children receive a $3000 grant for each additional child, as well as the regular monthly allowance.

By providing special grants, the government of Quebec intervenes into the lives of its citizens. These grants show how governments can work to reach particular political goals. The Quebec government wants to increase child births. Quebec's birth rate of 1.4 children per female of child-bearing age is very low. A birth rate of 2.1 children per female of child-bearing age is needed to replace the current population. Unless its government can

Why might the government of Quebec want to encourage a higher birth rate?

successfully intervene, Quebec may actually lose population over the next several years. In Quebec, the government intervenes in an attempt to influence not only the structure of the economy but the environment as well.

The Changing Role of Government in the Economy

Canadians have strong universal social programs. Anyone who needs assistance, regardless of social status, sex, or race, receives social benefits. However, the universality of social programs may end in Canada. Two questions remain to be answered. One is an ethical question: How would the end of universal social programs affect the disadvantaged in Canada? The other question is political: How would the end of universal social programs affect voters' opinions during the next election?

In late 1989, Brian Mulroney's Progressive Conservative government announced that it would begin taxing back universal old age security payments of people whose family income (combined income of all members of the household) was $50 000 or more. This tax is known as a **claw back**. Technically, benefits remain universal. The elderly will still receive security cheques. However, when a family's income is over the magic figure, then the government will get back the benefit in taxes. Since the average 1990 Old Age Security cheque was $340 per month, some people may owe the government more than $4000 at the end of the year. Families with two pensions may owe the government $8000.

The Progressive Conservative government has hinted that it may end universality in the Family Allowance program. Again, when a family's income reaches $50 000, there may be a claw back of the family allowance benefits. Since their inception, the universality of Canada's social programs has been considered a sacred trust. Prime Minister Mulroney guaranteed the continuation of these programs on several occasions during his 1988 election campaign. Technically, the claw backs do not end universality. All Canadians will receive the benefits of social programs. However, fewer Canadians will be allowed to keep them.

Part of the reason that the government might be looking into claw backs is that pressure to maintain government programs at current levels has played a role in increasing Canada's national debt. At the beginning of the 1990s, Canada's total debt amounted to approximately $390 billion. That's over $12 000 for every man, woman, and child in Canada. Canada's yearly debt in 1990 was expected to be approximately $28.5 billion, but it was much larger (approximately $30.5 billion). Interest payments alone amounted to about $34 billion a year.

What Affects Income Levels?

The Economic Council of Canada defines any family which spends more than 70 per cent of its income on food, clothing, and housing as poor. By this formula, one-third of all Canadians live below the poverty line.

Many factors determine a person's income, besides winning the 6/49 lottery or inheriting daddy's or mommy's fortune. Education may be the most important. Even when income loss and expenses are calculated for the years students attend a post-secondary institution, statistics show that the lifetime earnings of a university graduate are higher than those who did not attend.

More educated people are able to earn higher incomes longer than less educated people because mental abilities last longer than physical abilities. Education is needed in more highly skilled jobs, but strength and experience are more valuable in a physical job. An oil rig worker may make "big bucks" early in his working career, but by the age of 55 may find the physical labour too strenuous and be forced to quit. Although manual labourers earn high hourly wages, the work

Many women in Canada work in clerical jobs, in what some researchers call "pink collar ghettos."

is usually seasonal. An office manager does not find the daily routine as physically strenuous. She can more easily work past the age of 55.

Discrimination by sex, religion, or ethnic origin keeps the earnings of some Canadians low. Despite recent improvements in their economic status, women and non-whites still make less money than white males. Discrimination based on age or physical disability also affects Canadians. Although Canada has set up human rights boards to counteract these inequities, changes come slowly.

Geographic location also determines income level. The Atlantic provinces continually have a high unemployment rate and low wages. A large part of the maritime economy is the fishing industry, which is seasonal and very sensitive to supply and demand. The Atlantic provinces have fewer natural resources than the rest of Canada. Natural resource-based industries generally pay higher wages than agriculture and fishing.

Occupation also determines income. Those who work for others generally make less money than those who run their own businesses. Exceptions are farmers, fishers, and artists who traditionally make less money than other self-employed Canadians.

CASE STUDY:
INCOME LEVELS OF WOMEN

As you read the following Case Study, think about the idea of equal pay for equal work. Do you agree with it? Why or why not?

In 1990 women still earned about 65 per cent of what men earned. This figure had remained relatively unchanged for a decade, although some advances were made. In 1989, more women and non-whites were hired by the federal government than in 1987. Over 55 per cent of women received promotions, a jump of 4 per cent in 2 years. However, two-thirds of women with full-time jobs held clerical positions in 1989.

Under the Employment Equity Law (1986), federally regulated employers with more than 100 employees must file reports detailing how they are progressing in hiring women and non-whites. Firms can be fined up to $50 000 for not filing such a report. Women make up 42 per cent of the federally regulated work force, and 44 per cent of the total workforce.

QUESTIONS:
Consider all the reasons you could give to support your answers. For each question, choose only the best reason you have thought of.

1. Why do you think women earn less than men?
2. Should we have legislation to force the hiring of more women or non-white males?

HOW DOES CANADA ATTEMPT TO REDUCE ECONOMIC INEQUALITY?

Economic inequality has two basic sources—unequal earnings and inheritance. All income taxes are paid to the federal government. The federal government then sends the provinces and territories their share. Each province and territory sets its own tax rate.

The Canadian government uses a number of **indirect taxes** like sales tax, the Goods and Services Tax, the excise tax, and tariffs (a tax on imported goods). These taxes may be "hidden" in the price of goods or service and individuals seldom know how much extra they pay for a product as a result. Taxes which are not hidden in the price of a product, such as income tax, are called direct taxes.

Tax experts argue about whether or not taxes actually lessen the inequality of income in Canada. Because so many taxes are included in the consumption of goods, everyone pays them.

WHAT ARE SOME CRITICISMS OF THE CANADIAN ECONOMY?

Poverty is, and will always be, a problem in free market systems. The Canadian government intervenes to redistribute wealth and ensure that all Canadians enjoy the basic necessities of life. Experiments in other countries have attempted to introduce a guaranteed income. Still, the poor remain poor.

Guaranteed incomes have moved the poverty line up but have not ended poverty. Guaranteed incomes have even made the rich richer. The inflation that results from higher prices and higher wage demands is never felt equally by the rich and the poor.

It appears that no matter what governments or people do, there will always be poverty, even in a land of plenty. But, poverty is relative. Those who are considered poor in Canada may be considered rich in other countries. Canadians expect certain services and a certain standard of living. Should a family with only one car be considered poor? In some market economies, like Japan, a car is a luxury only the very wealthy can afford. Most families in Canada have a car, a television set, a video cassette recorder, and a microwave oven. Are these people poor?

Attempts at Fine-Tuning the Economy

The Canadian government can influence the economy by using its monetary and fiscal policies. By controlling legislation and cutting back some services the economy can be fine-tuned.

Monetary policy can either stimulate or slow the economy. In 1991 the policy was to provide more money to consumers. This decision increased economic growth because manufacturers sold more, produced more, and needed more workers. By adjusting monetary and fiscal policy, the government can affect the unemployment rate.

Monetary Policy

Monetary policy is set by the Bank of Canada which reviews interest rates every Thursday. In Canada's recent past, interest rates have been kept higher than the business community feels they should be. The current Governor of the Bank of Canada, John Crow, indicates that interest rates will remain high until inflation has ended. Inflation was approximately 5.5 per cent in 1989-1990 when Crow made his high interest rate policy. In early 1991, interest rates fell in order to encourage people to borrow more money. Canada was in a recession when unemployment was high and growth was declining.

Which question do you think best describes the cartoonists' point:
1. *Why does the Canadian government deport some people and not others?*
2. *What are some ways the Canadian government combats its deficit?*
3. *How does monetary policy work in Canada?*

CASE STUDY:
POLITICAL INTERVENTION IN THE ECONOMY

As you read the following Case Study, think about the importance of Canadian ownership.

The 1990s will see the continued growth of corporations, especially transnationals. The concentration of corporate ownership is growing in Canada. Big corporations are becoming ever larger and more powerful. In 1976, 500 corporations made 53 per cent of all sales in Canada.

These same 500 companies received 64 per cent of all corporate profits and held 65 per cent of all assets. Yet, these companies represented fewer than 0.25 per cent of all companies operating in Canada. This means that 99.75 per cent of all companies in Canada shared only 47 per cent of sales, 46 per cent of profits, and 35 per cent of assets. The end result of corporation concentration may be the reduction of competition for Canadian business and a movement away from the principles of the free market.

QUESTIONS:

1. Should the Canadian government pass a law to stop corporate concentration? Why or why not?
2. Should the Canadian government ensure that more corporations are owned by Canadians? Why or why not?

Fiscal Policy

Fiscal policy affects the tax rate. By raising or lowering taxes, the government can stimulate or slow the economy. The Canadian government is concerned about its high deficit. Canada's finance minister must carefully balance an increase of personal income tax with the slow-down in the economy because raising taxes could send the country into a recession. If taxes are not raised, how will the government continue to supply needed social services to Canadians? And, how can Canada decrease the national debt (deficit) without raising taxes? These are difficult questions.

The Competition Act

The Competition Act legislation in Canada is aimed at preserving the free market system by preventing large corporations from cornering markets. It outlaws price-fixing arrangements among producers. Canada allows monopolies in utilities like natural gas and telephone companies, but the government regulates price increases.

To be convicted under the Competition Act, it must be proven that the corporation has created a monopoly that results in public harm. In 1977, the federal government took Canadian millionaire K.C. Irving to court when he gained control of all five of New Brunswick's daily newspapers. The Supreme Court ruled that the Crown had not proved ill effects. It was able to prove a monopoly was created, but not that the public would suffer as a result.

Staying in Touch

Transportation and communication have always been important to Canadians. The Canadian Pacific Railway was built in the nineteenth century to provide a transportation route across Canada. Private transportation companies would not offer the services because routes were not profitable. The Canadian Broadcasting Corporation was built with the best interests of all Canadians at heart. Due to high operation costs, the government recently cut back both services. The government claims that the high cost of subsidizing the services was too great, and the cost of operating expenses was too high to be paid by the customers.

In all of the above ways, the government attempts to control the economy. However, there are some things the government cannot control, for example, the international environment.

Foreign investment — is it good or bad? This is a hotly debated question in Canada. What are some arguments for or against foreign investment?

The International Environment and Canada's Economy

Throughout history, Canada has been a source of raw materials for other nations. But Canada is trying to regain control over its own resources. The petroleum industry reflects the present attitude of the Canadian society. After World War II, Canada was flooded by **direct investment**, mainly from the USA, to develop its oil industry.

Direct investment by foreigners means that non-Canadians set up their own companies in Canada, and take home the after-tax profits. Direct investment creates jobs, but has drawbacks. Specifically, direct foreign investment results in foreign ownership of Canada's resources. Indirect investment means that others lend money to a Canadian whom they may use to set up Canadian owned companies. The money that was borrowed from the non-Canadian is then paid back with interest.

In 1982 almost 70 per cent of Canada's oil industry was owned by foreigners, mainly Americans. Almost half of Canada's economy was controlled by foreigners. Those who favoured this investment believed that foreign capital was essential for the development of natural resources and that the development of natural resources was, in turn, essential to Canada's development. Without outside capital Canada could not have developed to the point it did. Foreign ownership also helped to create a large number of jobs for Canadians.

Those who do not favour foreign investment say that capital could have been acquired through **indirect investment**. Canada would have retained ownership and control over its economy. They state that economic control is followed by political control. Opponents of foreign investment fear Canada's loss of ownership and control of its own economy.

Petro-Canada was created as a Crown Corporation designed to wrestle control of Canada's oil industry away from foreign ownership.

Foreign ownership means that eventually Canadians have nothing to show for the time and effort they put into their country. The foreign investor ends up with the ownership, paid for by Canadian effort and money. In addition, when foreign corporations decide what goods and services will be produced in Canada, Canadians are left with less decision-making power in their own society.

Free Trade

Beginning January 1, 1989, Canada entered into a free trade agreement with the United States. The agreement opened larger markets in the United States for Canadian companies. Trade barriers began coming down in 1989. By 1999 barriers will be erased on most goods and services.

At the time of the agreement, approximately 75 per cent of all of Canadian trade with the United States was already free (not subject to tariffs). Critics see the Free Trade Agreement as a sell-out of Canadian

CASE STUDY:

THE GOVERNMENT IN BUSINESS

As you read the following Case Study, think about the competitive nature of Crown Corporations.

One of the most controversial companies in Canada is Petro-Canada. The federal government created Petro-Canada in 1975 in an attempt to wrestle control of Canada's oil industry away from foreign ownership. This action was one of the few times the Canadian government has nationalized part of an industry to gain more control over resources. Today, Petro-Canada's assets are second only to the huge Exxon Corporation from the United States, called Imperial Oil (Esso) in Canada.

The goals of the Canadian government were to make Canada self-sufficient in oil production by 1990 and to reach 50 per cent ownership of the domestic petroleum industry. These goals were never reached; however, gains were made. In 1977, Canada owned 10 per cent of the petroleum industry. By 1980, Canada owned 28 per cent. And, by purchasing other companies, Canada's assets were close to 50 per cent by 1984. In 1990, Canada owned about 40 per cent of its own resources. The decrease occurred when Amoco, a large US company, purchased Dome Petroleum in 1988 when Dome was in financial difficulty.

Petro-Canada is an active publicly owned company. It works with Panarctic Ltd to explore the North for oil. It has a 15 per cent share in the Syncrude project in the Alberta tar sands, a 25 per cent share in the Hibernia oil project off the coast of Newfoundland, and 37 per cent of Westcoast Transmission—which will help build the upgrader project in Lloydminster—and is involved in joint ventures with private companies looking for oil throughout the world. These include projects in the North Sea, Spain, and China. In addition, it is researching ways to develop new and more efficient ways of bringing conventional oil reserves and heavy tar sands oil to the surface.

Petro-Canada is a big business, and a controversial one. Should the federal government run such a large business? Can a publicly owned business make a profit? The Mulroney government is selling shares in Petro-Canada, mainly to Canadians, while retaining control of the company. Other Canadian publicly owned businesses have already been sold, since the Mulroney government first came to office in 1984. One of the larger sales was Air Canada. The government sold one round of shares to the public in 1988 and plans to sell more. Other publicly owned enterprises, including de Havilland Aircraft of Canada, have also been sold.

QUESTIONS:

Read each question. Choose a position on each question and defend that position.

1. Why was Petro-Canada formed?
2. Should the Canadian government enter into direct competition with private enterprise?
3. Should the government sell Petro-Canada?
4. Should Petro-Canada have been involved in sponsoring the Olympics and the Olympic Torch Run?
5. When should government be involved in private industry?

resources to the USA and the beginning of the end of Canadian sovereignty.

Supporters insist that free trade will create larger markets for Canadian goods and services, and will result in lower prices and more jobs. By 1990, one year after the agreement came into effect, Canada had

suffered a net loss of jobs because companies moved to the US to be closer to the bigger markets. Campbell's Soups is one example of the many companies that moved. Critics also wonder whether economic control will be followed by political control. In February 1991 the Canadian government began free trade negotiations with Mexico in collaboration with the United States.

How has the Free Trade Agreement affected your province or territory? Your community? Have any companies opened or closed as a result of the agreement?

PEEK
AT CANADA

Politics	Economics
- federal union with provincial and territorial governments - growing tensions from territories and provinces to gain control of social and economic policies	- private ownership combined with government ventures - regulation of private sector (e.g. pollution control)

Environment	Knowledge
- growing globalization of world economy makes trade important - "resource economy" vulnerable to swings in world prices (e.g. oil, pulp and paper)	- faces the dilemma of believing in national goals (e.g. to protect economic security of citizens) while lowering federal debt

Field of Action
- a democracy that struggles to meet diverse regional needs through a variety of government interventions in economic and social life

SUMMARY

How does Canada answer the three basic economic questions?

Canada operates as a mixed economy with a tendency toward free enterprise. However, the Canadian government regulates the economy when it thinks intervention will help Canadian consumers. The three economic questions for the Canadian economy are answered as follows:

1. What goods and services are produced?

   In Canada, it is generally true that any goods and services demanded by consumers are produced. However, the government may influence the production of certain goods and services. Advertising plays a role as well. Marketing is an important fact of life in the structure of Canada's economy.

2. How are goods and services produced?

   In Canada, goods and services are produced in the least expensive and most efficient way. Businesses attempt to maintain high standards in an attempt to sell more products than competitors. The government may influence production through regulations that help to ensure safety and quality standards. In Canada, two changes are expected. One is the growth of corporations because of freer trade among nations. The second is the growing concentration of corporate wealth.

3. How should goods and services be distributed?

In Canada, goods and services are distributed to those who can and will pay. The Canadian government provides universal social services to Canadians because some people cannot provide for their basic needs on their own. Distribution of goods and services is a joint effort of both the private and public sectors in Canada.

GETTING ORGANIZED

1. Phone the local agency responsible to determine the level of benefits for unemployment insurance, welfare benefits, and workers' compensation. Do you think these agencies provide enough money for most people to live respectably? Do Canadian tax payers pay too much and discourage people from looking for work?
2. List all the gas station chains in your community. From which does your family buy gas? Find out which ones are owned by Canadians, and which are owned by foreigners.
3. Canada has relied heavily on both direct and indirect foreign investment in Canadian business. List the companies in your area. Which are Canadian, and which are owned by foreigners? Organize a debate on the following question: Should Canada encourage foreign ownership of Canadian resources?
4. Find out the income tax rate for where you live. How much would a single person earning $50 000 pay? How much would a one-income family of two adults and two children pay? Do Canadians pay too much tax?
5. How has the Free Trade Agreement affected Canada? Find out the number of companies that have increased production and that have moved out of Canada since the agreement took effect. Have more jobs been created, or have more jobs been lost since

it took effect? What would happen if all trade between Canada and all other countries was free? What would the political and economic systems be like? What affect would it have on you? Would this help or hurt Canadian business?

6. Review the chapter. As you do, list any situation you see where an individual (or group of individuals) exerts influence over their political and economic system. When you have finished, make a chart that answers the question: How do individuals exert influence within each of the major political and economic systems? List at least two ways for each system.
7. Your definition of democracy and how you act upon it may be the most important thing you learn in this study of political and economic systems. Look back at question 1 on pages 38–39. Answer part (b) of the question. Consider the implications of your answer carefully.

REACHING OUT

1. In groups of four, review the chart, *PEEK At Canada* on page 187. Each member of the group should research one of the elements of Politics, Economics, Environment, or Knowledge. Make a collage of magazine photos that display the four elements of the PEEK box.
2. Taxes are a fact of life in Canada. The most recent major tax reform of the 1990s was the GST. Collect all the receipts and store tapes from purchases your family makes in a week. Add up the total tax paid by your family in the week. Compare your GST with others in the class.
3. Obtain a Revenue Canada tax form and guide. Your teacher might be able to provide assistance. In class, complete the tax form for a single individual with no children and an income of $40 000. Any other information you require can be based on your own personal situation. Having completed the form, what are your impressions of the role of the government in your life?

Epilogue–Drawing It All Together

In this textbook, you have learned that there are important differences in the ways people and societies make decisions to satisfy their needs and wants. Human needs are basically the same everywhere. In their attempts to survive from one day to the next, humans have created political and economic systems to help them.

If you want to understand how individuals and societies make decisions, you must study them carefully. Any human decision must be understood within its context. As the PEEK boxes have shown, this context includes knowledge, economics, environment, and politics. Differences between societies reflect the values placed on individual and collective goals within the political and economic systems in those societies.

How To Understand Political Organizations

In order to make decisions, all societies form political organizations. Decision-making may be democratic or dictatorial, but all forms have rules to provide order and security.

Citizens may or may not support the political organization within their society. If a large number of citizens choose to accept the political organization of their society (as in Canada), their actions tend to support the structure. If a large number of citizens do not support the political organization (as in Romania), they work to overthrow that political organization. Sometimes citizens have little choice, or political power, either to support or to reject the political organization that governs them.

Power is divided differently in different societies. In some societies, like the fascist regime of Nazi Germany and the Soviet Union in the years just after the Communist Revolution, an elite minority assumes great political power. These regimes work hard to make sure citizens cannot have a powerful say in the government. In other societies, like Canada, the USA, and Sweden, power is divided among a greater number of citizens who assume greater decision-making responsibility.

The world changes and the environment in which political systems exist changes with it. Sometimes resources, like oil, become scarce. Changes, such as the rapid increase in nuclear capabilities, threaten the security of a society. It is not, and never has been, enough to make one good decision and have that decision last for eternity. To understand political systems it is important to understand how political systems change.

Let us quickly review the range of political relationships discussed in this textbook. The following scale will help you understand the nature of political systems in any further reading or research you do. You might want to review the chapter summaries to check on the listings provided.

Structure of Political Relations

How do democratic and dictatorial governments compare? It is useful to think of this question in terms of the degree to which different governments protect the security of the regime (those who govern) or of individuals (those governed). Consider a vertical line from 1 to 10. Whose security and interests are protected by the structure of political relationships?

Respect for Human Rights

Low

Totalitarian Dictatorship	1	Rights are ill defined.
	2	
	3	
Military Dictatorship	4	Rights are protected
One Party	5	for selected groups
Dictatorships		or elites.
	6	
Limited or Majoritarian Democracy	7	
	8	
	9	Rights are protected
Participatory		(in constitutions, in
Democracy	10	separations of powers)

High

How To Understand Economic Organizations

Humans organize politically to meet their needs for security, and they organize economically to meet their needs to grow and develop. As you have learned in this text, one of the most basic economic understandings is that resources are limited, and need to be distributed and used carefully. This is why economic decisions must be made.

Within different societies, different economic systems have developed. Like political systems within these same societies, economic systems are based partly on history and partly on ideology. Some societies believe more strongly in individualism. Some believe

more strongly in collectivism. Yet, all economic systems are organized to deal with the problem of scarcity.

Different economic systems are based on different theoretical models. Some, like the United States, are based on the private enterprise model. Others, like the Soviet Union, are based on the public enterprise model. Still others, like Canada and Sweden, have chosen a mix of both private and public enterprise.

Like in politics, every economic system grows and develops by making a series of day-to-day decisions. Some of these economic decisions work well, others do not. To evaluate an economic system, it is important to understand the basic resources that system has. It is also important to understand the historical and day-to-day economic decisions a society makes.

Governments constantly intervene within their economic systems to influence economic decision-making. Historically, governments have provided economic incentives, like subsidies, to encourage economic growth in certain sectors of the economy and to discourage growth in others. Governments may also manipulate interest rates and money supplies to accelerate or slow economic growth. Taxation is both a way to raise money for the government and a way to redistribute income within a society. In a variety of ways that are unique from society to society, economic systems are undergoing constant change as they attempt to meet the challenges of rapidly-changing, global circumstances.

Now it is time to review the range of economic relations that countries have developed. As with the previous political scales, this one will help you compare the relative nature of economic systems you may explore in further research. You might quickly check the chapter summaries to review the terms listed.

Structure of Economic Relations

Economic systems exist on a scale from highly decentralized or market structures to highly centralized or planned economies. Consider a horizontal line from A to J.

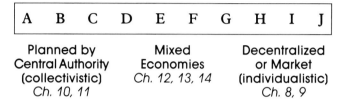

| A | B | C | D | E | F | G | H | I | J |

Planned by Central Authority (collectivistic) Ch. 10, 11   Mixed Economies Ch. 12, 13, 14   Decentralized or Market (individualistic) Ch. 8, 9

Drawing Together Political and Economic Relationships

ORGANIZING WHAT YOU KNOW

Simply taking these two scales we can see the total range or combinations of political and economic fields of action possible for modern governments.

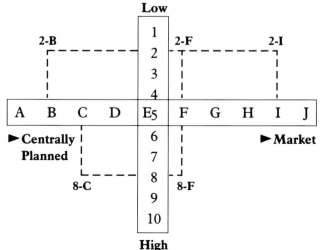

Respect for Human Rights

Low

2-B ... 2-F ... 2-I

| A | B | C | D | E5 | F | G | H | I | J |

► Centrally Planned   ► Market

8-C   8-F

High

Political Relations Scale: 1-10
Economic Relations Scale: A-J

QUESTIONS

Identify the correct placement of the countries listed below on the combined political and economic scales.

1. An extreme form of dictatorship and central planning (Soviet communism under Stalin). (Answer: 2-B)

2. An extreme form of dictatorship and market economy (few real examples, some Latin American regimes such as Chile under Pinochet). (Answer: 2-I)

3. Dictatorship combined with a combination of market and central planning structures (Nazi Germany under Hitler). (Answer: 2-F)

4. Democracy combined with central planning (Sweden). (Answer: 8-C)

5. Democracy combined with a market-central planning (mixed) combination of economic structures (Canada). (Answer: 8-F)

APPLYING WHAT YOU KNOW: STUDENT PROJECT

PROJECT ISSUE: What steps should a nation take to deal with the political and economic challenges it faces?

YOUR OWN CASE STUDY

Select a country undergoing major political or economic challenges today. Prepare an essay that presents the factors at work in that country in terms of each of the four elements of the PEEK box. Answer the project question using the PEEK approach.

Using the guide questions in the PEEK box on the next page will help you organize a lot of information during the research phase of your project.

P E E K

AT INQUIRY
INTO POLITICAL AND
ECONOMIC SYSTEMS

Politics	Economics
- Whose security is protected? - Who makes the rules? - How strictly are rules enforced?	- What is the level of technology? - What economic factors are available to the society (in terms of land, labour, and capital)? - How are the three basic economic questions answered?

Environment	Knowledge
- What are the outside physical influences on the society? - What international factors are having an impact on the society?	- What are the dominant or important understandings of the society? - How does the society interpret and evaluate problems in terms of beliefs and attitudes?

Finally—

What have you learned in this text? You have learned more about how political and economic systems work. You have learned that all people have the same needs, but in each society, their needs are met in different ways. You have learned that political and economic decisions are based on different circumstances, different ideologies, and different histories.

Finally, you have learned that the study of political and economic systems is based on a few very simple questions which have extremely complex answers. Understanding the politics and economics of your country and other countries is a lifelong, exciting task. We hope this book has given you a basic understanding of the systems at work in your world.

Appendix

Cooperate or Defect?

A Variation of the Prisoner's Dilemma

In chapter 1, the concept of reciprocity was explained. This game will stretch your imagination and help you better understand this important idea.

Two people play this game. Each player has two pieces of paper, one that reads Cooperate, and one that reads Defect. Each player also has a piece of paper and a pencil for keeping score.

The object of the game is to score points by guessing what the opposing player will do, cooperate with you, or defect. **There can be no communication between the players before or during the game, other than to show the piece of paper reading COOPERATE or DEFECT**. No agreements, no threats.

Winning or losing, you must stick to the agreed number of rounds of the game. The players do not take turns. They turn over their pieces of paper at the same moment.

In any one turn, there are three possible combinations:

1. Both players cooperate. In this case, each players scores $3.
2. Both players defect. In this case, each player scores $1.
3. One player cooperates, and one player defects. In this case, the defector scores $5, and the cooperator scores zero.

Remember to record your score after each turn. Keep a running tally of your winnings.

Each pair of players should play 10 times, then move on to other players. Your class might want to set up a tournament and have each student play 10 or more different players. Play the game to see which strategy wins out!

Why?

This is just a game, right? It doesn't really mean much, right? Maybe. Robert Axelrod, the American political scientist, played this game with many different groups of people, hundreds of thousands of times. He invited leading scientists, computer specialists, mathematicians, students, teachers, and others to play. Axelrod made a contest out of the game. He challenged people to find the most successful way to play and win.

Axelrod took the entries as he received them. He then played these against each other in a round robin tournament. A computer program that made random choices was also part of the tournament.

What does all this mean for social organization and the way people make political decisions? Axelrod's work shows that defections may seem to get people ahead, but are usually not the best strategies. His work also suggests that cooperation is not only ethical, but practical, too.

So What?

While Axelrod's work can be dismissed as just a game, the ramifications are important to the human race. What if people knew there would be no second round, as in the case of a full-scale nuclear exchange?

Sometimes it would seem sensible to defect, to make sure you would win. But Axelrod's work suggests some of the practical problems of betrayal. Cooperating on the first round, by disarming your missiles, might be very dangerous. Cooperating with Hitler in the first round, for example, proved to be too forgiving. The world discovered this in 1939 when he invaded Poland, despite Britain and France agreeing to his earlier demands. Axelrod is not saying that cooperating all the time is a good idea, nor is he saying defecting all the time is a wise route. Both these actions are absolutes, which may not hold in real life situations.

The Prisoner's Dilemma shows that in situations of public and private life, the action that yields the greatest long-term benefit is reciprocity. Axelrod offers a number of examples of how reciprocity has worked in real life:

1. Soldiers on both sides of the trenches in World War I developed informal and unspoken agreements. One French soldier explained that if the Germans shot once, the French returned two shots. The French would never fire first, but always responded in a tit-for-tat manner. Eventually, the Germans stopped firing, and all fighting stopped.

When the commanders learned of this agreement, they were not impressed. Fighting men were supposed to fight. The soldiers were more interested in surviving than they were in shooting. The soldiers had more in common with each other than with their own commanders.

2. A different example of cooperation also comes from the World War I trenches. It was tempting to shell behind the enemy's trenches and cut off roads and supply lines. But since both sides had shells, and both were capable of the same thing, neither side actually did it. They both adopted a live-and-let-live attitude.

Men on both sides climbed out of the trenches at night to repair barbed wire. It was not considered fair to shoot during such repairs. Also, both sides feared rifle grenades. One grenade could kill a dozen people if it landed in a trench. One side would not use them unless the other side used them first.

3. The British high command estimated that the live-and-let-live system emerged in about one-third of the trenches during World War I. Eventually, soldiers were ordered out of the trenches to attack the enemy line. These orders were given in an effort to boost the morale of the soldiers who had grown weary of the war. Suddenly, because neither side could anticipate their enemy's next move, the live-and-let-live system broke down. Escalation of the conflict followed.

Glossary

Accountability is the idea that those with power are responsible to others and must show that they have exercised their powers properly. In Canada, elected officials are responsible to, or accountable to, the electorate.

Anarchists are people who do not believe that governments are good. Although anarchists are often thought of as only those people who recklessly cause lawless confusion and political disorder, this definition is too narrow.

Anti-politics is a name for actions and beliefs that do not fit into the system of politics. They are often undertaken by those who are either disenchanted with the system or who feel their power is so small they have few other choices.

Apartheid is a system of racial separation which restricts the freedom of some people based on their skin colour.

The word **Aryans**, for our purposes, was used by the Nazis to mean Caucasians of non-Jewish origin.

An **authoritarian** system is one which concentrates power in the hands of one person or a very small group. A dictatorship is an authoritarian system.

Bureaucracy is the group of officials that administer the government.

A **cabinet** is a body of official advisors and executive officers that work for the head of a country, as heads of departments. In the United States, the president's cabinet members cannot hold another legislative office. In Canada, the prime minister appoints a cabinet from elected members of parliament.

Capital is the economic term used to describe all the buildings, money, equipment, and inventory used in the production of goods or services.

Charisma means extraordinary personal charm or power. Pierre Trudeau was said to have been a very charismatic prime minister, particularly during the early 1970s when thousands lined the streets to see him.

A system of **checks and balances** is a system that monitors the government in order to keep the balance of power equal and appropriate within the different branches of the government. Governments provide for ways that the different branches of government can assure that another branch cannot abuse its power.

Class conflict was the term that Karl Marx used to describe the series of conflicts between workers and owners in society. Marx suggested that there would be an eventual revolution by the workers against those of the higher classes who oppressed them.

A government **claw back** occurs when the funds for a social program are paid to citizens but then the funds are reclaimed from some citizens in taxes which vary according to income.

Collective farms are those Soviet farms run by groups of people. The workers' salaries are based on the farm profit.

Collectivized land is land worked collectively and cooperatively by a group of people, rather than one farmer.

Competition is the process of striving for the same objective. In the economic sense, competition means two or more products striving for a greater share of the market.

A **compromise** is a settlement made when both sides of a disagreement make concessions. Unless one country has been totally defeated in war, most international treaties involve both sides compromising something important to them.

Conscription means the compulsory enrollment of a person into a job or assignment. During war, most countries conscript young people into the armed forces.

A **consensus** means that there is general agreement within a specific group of people. Although there were dissidents, there was a general consensus that the world should use force to constrain the political aspirations of Saddam Hussein in early 1991.

When someone **consents**, it means he or she gives approval of what is done or proposed by another. Consent can be both assumed and granted. For example, a school works under assumed parental consent, but parents need to sign consent forms for individual field trips.

A **constitutional monarchy** is a system of government where the powers of the monarch have been defined, and usually restricted, by a written constitution. Great Britain is a constitutional monarchy.

Constitutionalism is the theory that people should have their rights protected and their responsibilities laid out in a written document, or constitution. The founding fathers of confederation believed that the government should express in writing the contract between the people and the government.

Constraint is the use or threat of force to prevent an action. In the past, the use of the strap was seen as a way to constrain behaviour in schools.

Consumer goods are those items, such as radios and televisions, produced for the general population.

Consumer sovereignty means that the consumer determines the types and quantities of goods produced in an economic system based on what they purchase.

Consumption means using goods to satisfy needs or wants. Consumption includes activities as diverse as collecting hockey cards to using a mouthwash.

A **corporation** is a legal body formed and allowed to conduct a business enterprise. Although a corporation is composed of a group of people and may sell shares, it does business as though it were an individual.

Coup d'état is a quick, forceful blow. Usually it means an attempt to overthrow a government.

A **democracy** is a form of government controlled by a group which represents all the people in the society. In democratic countries, the population elects representatives who are responsible to their constituents.

Democratic systems are those in which the process of majority rule is practised. Democratic systems may be organizations as large as countries and as small as group projects for school.

In a **dictatorship**, leaders take political power and authority, and the people submit to the leaders' power.

A **direct democracy** is a system in which all citizens can vote on all issues.

Direct investment means that a group from one country sets up or invests in a company in another country and takes home the after-tax profits. Direct investment creates jobs, but results in foreign ownership of the resources.

Direct taxes are those paid directly by citizens, and are not hidden in the cost of a product. One example is income tax.

Dissidents are people who disagree with a doctrine or belief set down by an established authority. For example, when a country has voted to go to war, anti-war protesters are dissidents.

Economic stagnation means that the economy slows down almost to a standstill. Economic stagnation occurs when consumers cannot or will not purchase goods or when businesses are not capable of producing goods.

Economic systems are organized ways communities attempt to control the production and distribution of wealth and materials. An international example is oil-producing Arab nations attempting to work together to control the price and sale of oil to other countries.

When rules are **enforced**, someone makes sure they are carried out.

Entrepreneurs are businesspeople who have ideas for businesses and often start up, organize, and manage businesses.

Environmental factors include anything that may be happening in the world that will affect political action. For example, advances in technology and stories about the mysteries of the eastern world influenced explorers who first travelled to North America.

The **executive branch** of government is that group responsible for enforcing, or executing, laws. In the United States, the president is called the chief executive officer of the country. In Canada, the executive branch consists of the prime minister and his cabinet.

Fascism is a dictatorial form of government which advocates the building of a highly nationalistic state. It usually encourages private ownership.

The **field of action** is an expression that is used to show the stage on which a particular political action is played out. Actors in the field of action include any participant who has any impact, even a minor one, on the political drama that is unfolding.

Fiscal policy is the range of government spending and revenue-generating programs (example: social programs, taxation).

Free trade means that trade between people or countries has no restrictions. Specifically, the Free Trade Agreement between Canada and the United States works gradually to remove tariffs and duties placed on goods being shipped from one country to the other.

Translated from Russian, **glasnost** means a spirit of political openness.

In economic terms, **goods** are any valuable possessions or pieces of property.

A **government** is the group of people who direct the affairs of a country.

A **governor general** is a substitute for the monarchy when the monarch cannot be present. In Canada, the role has become mostly symbolic.

In the United States, the **House of Representatives** is an elected body of legislators from each state. States have different numbers of legislators, depending on their population.

Ideology means a way of thinking influenced by one's values, morals, and beliefs. Ideology includes choices that are consciously made and those ideas that are so much a part of one's lifestyle that they are taken for granted, and are unconscious.

Imperialism means the spirit of the empire. Historically, it is used to describe one nation's attempts to dominate other nations, both politically and economically.

A government uses **indicative planning** to direct business, without forcing companies to follow its plan.

Indirect investment is when investors lend money to be used for setting up companies in other countries. The money is then paid back with interest to the investors.

Indirect taxes are those hidden in the price of goods or services. They include manufacturers' tax, excise tax, and tariffs. Buyers seldom know how much tax has been added to the cost of manufacturing, transportation, and store mark-up.

Inflation means a sharp and sudden rise in prices of consumer goods in an economy.

Institutions are organized bodies of people formed to serve a particular function. Institutions may include governmental agencies, but they could also be charities, sports conferences, or schools.

An **invisible hand**, in a market or a mixed economy, is the self-regulating mechanism that sees individuals pursuing their own self-interest but benefiting society in general. Producers make high quality products at competitive prices in order to stay in business. Students work hard for high marks in order to get a good job.

The **judicial branch** of a government is the group of people responsible for interpreting the laws. In both the United States and in Canada, if there is some dispute about a law, the Supreme Courts interpret the law.

Kinship means a family relationship. Early humans built communities of families.

Labour is the economic term given to all work done by humans.

In an economic sense, **laissez-faire** means that the government will not intervene into the workings of the economy.

Land is the economic term given to all natural resources used in the production of goods and services.

The **left-wing** is the most radical political group, interested in change toward more equality and away from tradition.

The **legislative branch** of the government is the group of people who are responsible for making laws. In Canada, the elected members of parliament make up the legislative branch of the federal government.

Liberals are people who believe in progress and democracy. Liberals believe that the individual is the most important unit in society.

Limited liability in business means that a person's risk is limited to the amount of money he or she has invested directly into a business.

A **majority government** is formed when a political party wins over 50 per cent of the seats in the legislature. In Canada, it is very difficult for the opposition to defeat a majority government.

A **market economy** is an open economy. It refers to any economy where consumers can buy or sell anything of their choice, and producers can determine what to make and when.

A **marketplace** is any location where business or trade takes place, like the local grocery store or the farmers' market. Marketplace also refers to the world of business.

Marxists are those who believe in the political ideas of Karl Marx. These ideas include working for the good of all, government control of the economy, and workers' control of their work.

The **means of production** include all the things that allow industry to take place, such as land, labour, and capital.

A **minority government** is formed when a political party wins less than 50 per cent of the seats in the legislature, but still more than any of the opposition parties. In Canada in 1979, Joe Clark's Conservatives formed a minority government. It was quickly defeated.

Monetary policy refers to a government's control of the supply of money by adjustment of interest rates.

A **monopoly** is a circumstance where one business or company controls a very large share of the market, with almost no competition.

When countries have a **mutuality of interests**, they share or agree on the same ideas or goals. For example, during the Gulf War in 1991, Saudi Arabia, Kuwait, and the United States formed a coalition that attempted to drive Saddam Hussein from Kuwait because they shared a mutuality of interests.

Nationalism is the belief in the strength and uniqueness of one's own nation.

When a business is **nationalized**, all its properties are given over to the control of the state.

Natural rights are basic freedoms that human beings should have naturally. For example, according to John Locke humans should have the right to live and to have property.

An **oligopoly** is a circumstance in which a small number of businesses or companies controls a very large share of the market.

An **organizing principle** is an important belief that a group holds. These principles form the basis for thought and action within that group. For example, the organizing principle for a democracy is that the people have both the right and responsibility to govern themselves.

A **parliament** is an assembly of elected national legislators. In Canada, members of the parliament form the legislative branch of the Canadian government.

A **parliamentary democracy** is a system of government in which the executive is reponsible to an assembly or parliament, and carries out the wishes of the legislature.

Perestroika is a Russian word which describes the Soviet attempt to encourage reform in its economic sector.

In a **planned economy**, all or some of the economic decisions are made by a central government agency.

Political relations include the interactions between humans as they attempt to secure their goals and aspirations. Political relationships include both interactions within a society, for example, between unions and the government, and interactions between nation states.

A **political system** is the organization which enables members of society to protect their way of life. It is the management of government.

Politics is the attempt by individuals and groups to protect and promote their security. By definition, political action involves trying to further one's interests. Politics can involve a range of activities from the decision to boycott meat products because of a concern for animal rights, to contributing to a candidate's election campaign fund.

Power in its simplest sense means the ability to get something done. In a political and economic sense, it also means the right or capacity to exercise control and to act.

Precivilized refers to a state in which aspects of civilized society, such as intellectual, social, and cultural organization, are not in place.

In a **presidential system**, a president leads the government with the help of a group of executives.

In a **private enterprise** system, there is an economic emphasis on individual ownership and control, rather than government control.

Production is the creation of goods and services that can be used, bought, or sold. Production can describe the creation of any goods, from automobiles to poetry.

The **proletariat** are the working classes.

Public ownership of property means that the government, rather than individuals, owns property and businesses.

Racism is any belief that is used to justify treating people differently because of their ethnic or cultural backgrounds.

Reactionaries are people who resist change. The groups who hold power are likely to be reactionary to those who wish to gain power.

Reciprocity is a mutual exchange, or equal giving and taking.

Regimes are orderly systems of management. In this text, the word regime is used to mean any orderly government in which decisions are made and citizens' lives are regulated. A regime can be either dictatorial or democratic.

In a democratic system, a **representative** is a person elected from a constituency to represent his or her constituents. Both Canada and the United States have representative governments.

Political **repression** means the act of holding other ideas or people in check. A powerful elite will try to repress anyone who seeks to overthrow it.

Revolutionaries are those who seek to violently or totally change or overthrow the person or group holding power. Revolutionaries may use either legal or violent tactics to wrestle power away from those who hold it.

The **right-wing** is the most conservative political group. A right-wing group is usually more opposed to change than other political groups.

Scarcity simply means that there is not enough of something, or that it is unavailable.

To have **security** is to have protection from danger. For citizens of modern states, security includes protection from threats to their traditions, to the human rights their society holds dear, and to the quality of their lifestyle. For example, in 1991, Iraq threatened the American lifestyle by jeopardizing cheap fossil fuel supplies in the Persian Gulf.

A **senate** is part of the legislative branch of a government. In Canada, the Senate is an appointed body. In the United States, senators are elected.

Separation of powers means that the total power and authority of government is spread among the government's different branches so that the danger of political power overcoming public interest will be minimized. In Canada, separation of power means that the different branches of the government work independently of each other.

In economic terms, **services** are any valuable activities done by one person or group for another.

Social Darwinism is the belief that only the strongest people survive and that only the strongest society will survive and prosper. It is a belief often used to justify the use of power against weaker opponents.

To be **specialized** is to be skilled in a specific area. For example, a baker specializes in baking.

State farms are those managed by Soviet government boards. All produce and profits go to the state. Some state farms do research and develop better farming techniques.

Structures of knowledge are the bases of experience we consider when we act. They include history, philosophy, religion, and other factors.

Subsidies are sums of money granted for a particular purpose. Subsidies are often given by governments to help businesses meet their expenses. The Canadian government pays subsidies to farmers to help them stay in business.

Tax incentives are tax breaks given by the government so that beginning or continuing business is more likely to be profitable.

A government uses a **tight money policy** by adjusting monetary or fiscal policy to relieve the pressure of inflation brought about by excess demand.

In a **totalitarian** government, a small elite controls every aspect of the country and suppresses any group attempting to oppose it. Most totalitarian elites use force ruthlessly to retain their power.

Transnational literally means across nations. A transnational company is one which conducts business in a number of different countries.

Universal social programs are those which are available to all citizens or residents.

Universal suffrage means that all citizens of voting age can participate in elections. Canada denies people in prison or in mental institutions the right to suffrage.

Utopian Socialists are people who advocate the building of an ideal state. Because Utopianism is a reaction to social needs, many of its principles are socialistic.

A **value-added tax** is a tax added at each stage of production of a product.

Bibliography

Avineri, Shlom. *The Social and Political Thought of Karl Marx*. Cambridge University Press, 1968.

Axelrod, Robert. *The Evolution of Cooperation*. New York: Basic Books, 1984.

Badgley and Wolfe. *Doctor's Strike*. Toronto: Macmillan, 1967.

Bell, Daniel. *The Coming of Postindustrial Society*. New York: Basic Books, 1973.

Bell, David and Lorne Tepperman. *The Roots of Disunity*. Toronto: McClelland and Stewart, 1979.

Best, Judith. *The Mainstream of Western Political Thought*. New York: Human Sciences Press, 1980.

Billingsley, Lloyd. *The Absence of Tyranny*. Portland: Multnomah Press, 1986.

Buchheim. *Totalitarian Rule*. Middletown, Conn.: Wesleyan University Press, 1968.

Butler, Egmon. *Hayek*. New York: University Books, 1983.

Christenson et al. *Ideologies and Modern Politics*. Third edition. New York: Harper and Row, 1981.

Coes, Robert. *The Political Life of Children*. Boston: Atlantic Monthly Press, 1986.

Deutscher, Isaac. *Stalin*. Oxford: Penguin, 1974.

Echikson, William. *Lighting the Night*. New York: William Morrow and Company, 1990

Francis, Diane. *Controlling Interest*. Toronto: Macmillan, 1986.

Fried and Sanders, (ed.). *Socialist Thought: A Documentary History*. Chicago: Aldine, 1964.

Gairdner, William D. *The Trouble With Canada*. Toronto: Stoddart, 1990.

Gorbachev, Mikhail. *Perestroika*. New York: Harper and Row, 1988.

Heilbroner, Robert L. *Marxism, For and Against*. New York: W.W. Norton, 1980.

Hitler, Adolf. *Mein Kampf*. Boston: Houghton-Mifflin, 1971.

Hurtig, Mel (ed.). *If I Were Prime Minister*. Edmonton: Hurtig Publishers, 1987.

Kennedy, Paul. *The Rise and Fall of the Great Powers: Economic Change and Military Conflict from 1500 to 2000*. New York: Random House, 1988.

Keohane, Roberta O. *After Hegemony, Cooperation and Discord in the World Economy*. Princeton: Princeton University Press, 1984.

Kome, Penny. *Women of Influence: Canadian Women and Politics*. Toronto: Doubleday, 1985.

Kuper, Adam and J. Kuper. *The Social Science Encyclopedia*. London: Routledge, 1985.

Locke, John. *Two Treatises of Government*. New York: New American Library, 1985.

Macpherson, C.B. *The Rise and Fall of Economic Justice and Other Essays*. Toronto: Oxford University Press, 1987.

McCan, Robert. *An Outline of American Economics*. United States Information Agency, 1987.

Miller, David et al. *The Blackwell Encyclopaedia of Political Thought*. Oxford: Basil Backwell Ltd., 1987.

Neatby, Blair. *The Politics of Chaos*. Toronto: Macmillan, 1972.

Nimmo, Dan and J.E. Combs. *Mediated Political Realities*. New York: Longman, 1983.

Novak, Michael. *The Spirit of Democratic Capitalism*. New York: Simon and Schuster, 1982.

Nyberg, David. *Power Over Power*. London: Cornell University Press, 1981.

Papadakis, Etim. *The Green Movement In West Germany*. New York: St. Martin's Press, 1984.

Payne - O'Conner, Josephine. *Women In Politics—Vancouver Island Profiles*. Victoria: Kaching Press, 1986.

Peeler, John A. *Latin American Democracies*. London: University of North Carolina Press, 1985.

Power, Jonathan. *Amnesty International—The Human Rights Story*. New York: McGraw-Hill, 1981.

Rourke, John T. *International Politics on the World Stage*. Guilford, Conn.: Sluice Dock, 1989.

Rubin, Barry. *Modern Dictators*. Scarborough: New American Library, 1987.

Samuelson and Scott. *Economics*. Toronto: McGraw-Hill, 1968.

Shub, David. *Lenin*. Massachusetts: Penguin, 1966.

Stern, S. and T. Schoenhaus. *Toyland*. Chicago: Contemporary Books, 1990.

Strange, Susan. *States and Markets*. London: Pinter Publishers, 1988.

Talman, J.L. *The Origins of Totalitarian Democracy*. New York: Norton, 1970.

Tinder, Glenn. *Political Thinking*. Toronto: Little, Brown and Company, 1986.

Tyre, Robert. *Douglas in Saskatchewan: The Story of a Socialist Experiment*. Vancouver: Mitchell Press, 1962.

Watson, Patrick. *The Struggle for Democracy*. Toronto: Lester and Orpen Dennys, 1988.

Wearing, Joseph. *Strained Relations—Canadian Parties and Votes*. Toronto: McClelland and Stewart, 1988.

Young, Walter D. *Democracy and Discontent*. Toronto: McGraw-Hill Ryerson, 1969.

PERIODICALS

Douglas, Tommy. *Star Weekly*, Toronto Daily Star, June 4, 1960.

Fact Sheets on Sweden, the Swedish Institute, 1988.

Hossie, Linda. *Globe and Mail*, Women in Politics, November 3, 1989.

Maclean's, Toronto: Maclean-Hunter, November, 1989 – May, 1990.

New Internationalist, May 1986.

Pakula, Hannah. *Vanity Fair*, Elena Ceausescu—The Shaping of an Ogress, August 1990.

Pakula, Hannah. *Mirabella*, Royals in Waiting, April 1990.

Soviet News and Views from USSR, Embassy Press office, September—December 1987.

This is America, US Information Agency, 1987.

Index